Praise for Yes We Did?

"In this thoughtful and thought-provoking study, Cynthia Fleming deftly weaves interviews and her own deep understanding of history to provide context for how black leadership has developed and shaped American life. A fascinating read."
> —Guy and Candie Carawan, editors of *Sing for Freedom:*
> *The Story of the Civil Rights Movements through its Songs*

"This study of African American leadership is unlike others of this genre. Grounded in extensive interviews with a broad range of male and female leaders on the national and local levels in a variety of venues, the author provides a needed context for understanding the emergence of Barack Obama. How President Obama's historic election relates to recent developments in African American leadership is exhaustively and imaginatively explored in this exciting new study."
> —Dennis C. Dickerson, author of *Militant Mediator:*
> *Whitney M. Young Jr.*

"Fills an important void in post-1960s analyses . . . links us to the legacy of the King era but challenges us to confront the contradictions of what has transpired, and what has not transpired, since King's death."
> —Barbara Ransby, author of *Ella Baker and the Black*
> *Freedom Movement: A Radical Democratic Vision*

Yes We Did?

YES WE DID?

FROM

King's Dream
TO
Obama's Promise

Cynthia Griggs Fleming

The University Press of Kentucky

Copyright © 2009 by The University Press of Kentucky

Scholarly publisher for the Commonwealth,
serving Bellarmine University, Berea College, Centre College of Kentucky,
Eastern Kentucky University, The Filson Historical Society, Georgetown College,
Kentucky Historical Society, Kentucky State University, Morehead State University,
Murray State University, Northern Kentucky University, Transylvania University,
University of Kentucky, University of Louisville, and Western Kentucky University.
All rights reserved.

Editorial and Sales Offices: The University Press of Kentucky
663 South Limestone Street, Lexington, Kentucky 40508-4008
www.kentuckypress.com

13 12 11 10 09   5 4 3 2 1

Library of Congress Cataloging-in-Publication Data

Fleming, Cynthia Griggs, 1949–
     Yes we did! : from King's dream to Obama's promise / Cynthia G. Fleming.
        p. cm.
     Includes bibliographical references and index.
     ISBN 978-0-8131-2560-2 (hardcover : alk. paper)
     1. African American leadership. 2. African Americans—Politics and government.
3. Civil rights movements—United States. 4. United States—Politics and
government—1945-1989. 5. United States—Politics and government—1989-
I. Title.
     E185.615.F56 2009
     323.1196'0732—dc22   2009022456

This book is printed on acid-free recycled paper meeting the requirements of the
American National Standard for Permanence in Paper for Printed Library Materials.

Manufactured in the United States of America.

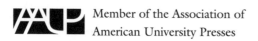 Member of the Association of
American University Presses

To three African American leaders who remained committed to the struggle for equality all their lives, who were kind enough to share their wisdom with me for this book, and who have all recently passed away:

Attorney J. L. Chestnut Jr.
Dr. John Hope Franklin
Rev. Abraham Woods

Contents

Photographs follow page 122

Participants

JAMES ARMSTRONG, an Alabama native and a longtime Birmingham resident, participated in the historic Selma-to-Montgomery march, and for most of the march, he was the designated bearer of the American flag.

FRANK BALLANCE, a North Carolina native, was elected to the House of Representatives from North Carolina's First District.

JAMES BEVEL, a native Mississippian, was a member of the Nashville student movement, the Student Nonviolent Coordinating Committee, and the Southern Christian Leadership Conference.

TIMUEL BLACK, a native Mississippian and a longtime resident of Chicago, is a community activist and a member of the Congress of Racial Equality.

UNITA BLACKWELL, a native Mississippian, was a member of the Student Nonviolent Coordinating Committee during the civil rights movement. Blackwell was also a member of the Mississippi Freedom Democratic Party during Mississippi Freedom Summer in 1964 and was the first black mayor of Mayersville, Mississippi.

JOANNE BLAND, a native of Selma, Alabama, is a community activist and the cofounder of the Voting Rights Museum in Selma. She was on the Edmund Pettus Bridge on March 7, 1965 (Bloody Sunday), when voting rights demonstrators were beaten and teargassed.

JULIAN BOND, a native of Atlanta, Georgia, was the communications director for the Student Nonviolent Coordinating Committee during the civil rights movement. He was also one of the youngest people ever elected to the Georgia state legislature.

ROBERT BOOKER, a native of Knoxville, Tennessee, and a community activist, was a leader of the Knoxville sit-in movement and was the first black candidate from East Tennessee to be elected to the Tennessee State Senate since Reconstruction.

CAROL MOSELEY BRAUN, a native of Chicago, Illinois, has been a key participant in Chicago politics for some time, and she is the only African American woman in American history to be elected to the U.S. Senate.

KWAME BROWN, a native of Washington, D.C., and the son of a Student Nonviolent Coordinating Committee member, serves on the District of Columbia City Council.

J. L. CHESTNUT, a native of Selma, Alabama, was a civil rights lawyer who did a great deal of the legal work for Alabama civil rights activists during the civil rights movement.

DOROTHY COTTON, a native of South Carolina, worked in the civil rights movement in Richmond, Virginia, with Southern Christian Leadership Conference insider Wyatt T. Walker. Later, Cotton served as the SCLC director of education.

COURTLAND COX, a native of New York and a longtime resident of Washington, D.C., was a member of the Student Nonviolent Coordinating Committee's executive staff during the civil rights movement. Later, he occupied several positions in the District of Columbia city government.

GEORGE CURRY, a native of Tuscaloosa, Alabama, is a well-known black journalist. He is a former editor of *Emerge* magazine and was the first black reporter on the staff of *Sports Illustrated*.

ARTUR DAVIS, a native of Montgomery, Alabama, is a congressman representing Alabama's Seventh Congressional District.

JOHNNY FORD, a native of Tuskegee, Alabama, became the first black mayor of Tuskegee. He was also elected to the Alabama State Legislature. He later changed his party affiliation from the Democratic to the Republican Party.

JOHN HOPE FRANKLIN, a native of Tulsa, Oklahoma, became the first black professor to head an all-white college history department. He was a prolific writer and one of the foremost experts on the history of African Americans.

LAWRENCE GUYOT, a native of Mississippi and a longtime resident of Washington, D.C., was a member of the Student Nonviolent Coordinating Committee during the civil rights movement. He served as the head of the Mississippi Freedom Democratic Party during Mississippi Freedom Summer in 1964.

RICHARD HATCHER, an Indiana native, became the first black mayor of Gary, Indiana.

BENJAMIN HOOKS, a native of Memphis, Tennessee, has been active in local politics for years. He served for a time as the national head of the NAACP.

ALEXANDER JEFFERSON, a native of Detroit, Michigan, served as a member of the famed Tuskegee Airmen during World War II. His plane was shot down and he was held as a German prisoner of war. He later returned to Detroit, where he taught school and eventually became a principal.

EDDIE BERNICE JOHNSON, a native of Texas, has served in the U.S. House of Representatives for several terms, representing a district in Dallas.

COLONEL STONE JOHNSON, a native of Alabama, was a member of Rev. Fred Shuttlesworth's church during the civil rights movement. When the fiery minister began receiving death threats, Johnson was one of the church men who served as Shuttlesworth's bodyguards.

CHARLES JONES was a member of the Charlotte, North Carolina, student movement and the Student Nonviolent Coordinating Committee. He helped inaugurate SNCC's Jail No Bail policy.

SAMUEL BILLY KYLES, a native of Mississippi, a longtime resident of Memphis, Tennessee, and pastor of Monumental Baptist Church, was an activist during the civil rights movement. He was the only other person standing on the balcony of the Lorraine Motel on April 4, 1968, when Dr. Martin Luther King Jr. was assassinated.

BERNARD LAFAYETTE, a native of Florida, was a member of the Student Nonviolent Coordinating Committee during the civil rights movement. He participated in the Freedom Rides and was SNCC's project director in Selma, Alabama. He was working on the Poor People's Campaign with Dr. King when King was slain.

JAMES LAWSON, who was a divinity student at Vanderbilt University during the movement in Nashville, Tennessee, conducted nonviolent workshops for students who later participated in lunch counter sit-ins in downtown Nashville. Lawson later became a very close confidant of Dr. King in the Southern Christian Leadership Conference.

JOE LEONARD, a native of Texas, is a recent Ph.D. in history from Howard University. He was a member of Jesse Jackson Sr.'s Rainbow/Push Coalition.

JOHN LEWIS, a native of Troy, Alabama, served as the head of the Student Nonviolent Coordinating Committee during the civil rights movement. He is a member of the House of Representatives from Atlanta's Fifth Congressional District.

CYNTHIA MCKINNEY, a native of Atlanta, Georgia, has served two terms as a congresswoman from Atlanta. She was the Green Party's nominee for the 2008 presidential race.

HAROLD MIDDLEBROOK, a native of Memphis, Tennessee, was an activist during the civil rights movement. He has served as pastor of Canaan Baptist Church in Knoxville, Tennessee, for many years.

ELEANOR HOLMES NORTON, a native of Washington, D.C., was a member of the Student Nonviolent Coordinating Committee during the civil rights movement. She has been a member of the House of Representatives, representing the District of Columbia, for several terms.

T. RANDEL OSBURN, a native of Alabama, worked in the Southern Christian Leadership Conference during the civil rights movement. He was a close confidant of Dr. King.

JAMES PERKINS, an Alabama native, was elected the first black mayor of Selma, Alabama.

AL SHARPTON, a longtime resident of New York City, is the leader of the organization he founded, the National Action Network.

FRED SHUTTLESWORTH, an Alabama native, was an activist during the civil rights movement. He was especially active in the Birmingham campaign.

MAUREEN TAYLOR, a native of Detroit, Michigan, was a member of the Detroit Chapter of the Black Panther Party for Self Defense and a community activist in Detroit, where she hosted her own weekly public affairs television show.

C. T. VIVIAN, a native of Missouri, was a leader in the Nashville civil rights movement and went on to become a member of SCLC's executive staff. He became a close confidant of Dr. King and was appointed the organization's director of affiliates.

EUGENE WALKER, a native of Thomaston, Georgia, was elected to the Georgia state legislature from Dekalb County and went on to serve five terms representing what was at the time a majority white county.

ABRAHAM WOODS, a native of Alabama, was a community activist and a Baptist minister during the civil rights movement. He was an important leader of the Birmingham campaign.

SAMUEL YETTE, a native of Harriman, Tennessee, was one of the first black reporters employed by *Life* magazine. Later he became one of the first black reporters for *Newsweek*.

ANDREW YOUNG, a native of New Orleans, became a member of SCLC's executive staff and was a close confidant of Dr. King during the civil rights movement. He went on to serve as mayor of Atlanta, a member of the House of Representatives, and U.S. ambassador to the United Nations.

Foreword

Cynthia Griggs Fleming's book responds to a need felt by many people today to understand how the previous half-century of civil rights activity transformed the status of African Americans and led to the election of the first African American president. The election of Barack Obama requires a reevaluation of racial progress—an understanding of how Obama's election fits a pattern of racial change. It is too early to evaluate Barack Obama's presidential achievements, but Fleming succeeds at identifying the antecedents to his place in history. In what she calls "history combined with social commentary," Fleming offers the voices of those who lived this history to show how our country has gone "from King to Obama." These contributions are valuable both to present and future scholars.

Fleming identifies Martin Luther King Jr.'s life as the watershed in African American advancement, which began with the protests by black people who survived the Middle Passage to become slaves in America. Before the Civil War, when the national economy was tethered to slavery, organized resistance to racial oppression was impossible. Even the tenets of Christianity were twisted by those who wished to condone slavery and discrimination on a national level.

No genuine progress occurred for African Americans until slavery ended. After the Civil War, W. E. B. Du Bois, Booker T. Washington, and other black leaders created the first coherent African American strategies for freedom, using long- and short-term relief in the courts, opportunities offered by black institutions of higher learning, and political pressure directed at the federal government to challenge state-sanctioned racial hostility and discrimination. They challenged Jim Crow laws, lynching, and other systemic violence and intimidation in the southern states and elsewhere. The NAACP, whose founding by black and white reformers at the turn of the twentieth century was a defining event in the history of the black struggle, led and often created the new strategies. NAACP chapters sprang up across the country, releasing the pent-up desire of African Americans to protest their condition.

Following the initiation of organized protest by the NAACP, grass-roots resistance to segregation took off with the Montgomery bus boycott led by Dr. Martin Luther King Jr. Thousands of black people boycotted segregated buses and organized alternative means of transportation. Their victory, the first major triumph of the "civil rights revolution," launched a national movement that subsequently transformed American institutions, culture, and attitudes, and gained enactment of the great civil rights trilogy of laws. Unlike revolutions born from violence, the nonviolent rebellion of African Americans did not repudiate but rather updated and adapted an extraordinary variety of strategies that penetrated every corner of society and made change irresistible.

Despite differences in approach, blacks who organized under different banners had energy and determination to topple the steel girders of legalized racism. King and members of the Southern Christian Leadership Conference were able to openly lead protests in hostile southern territory because black ministers, employed by black congregations, possessed freedoms most African Americans were denied at that time. Students without jobs or property at stake, such as members of the Student Nonviolent Coordinating Committee, were the first blacks in significant numbers to incur daily frontline risks for equality. The NAACP had led black people on matters of protest, policy, and law, such as the decades-long litigation strategy culminating in *Brown v. Board of Education*. The movement needed the NAACP's 1954 school desegregation victory to make "separate but equal" an oxymoron.

The National Urban League was created out of the struggles of African Americans who migrated from the South in search of employment during World War I. Over time, the League formed alliances with the progressive business sector, especially through its self-help programs in the in the rapidly changing 1960s.

As the civil rights movement reached a zenith, the efforts of these and many mainstream organizations together with a growing base of Americans of every background pulled off the largest protest march ever held in Washington, D.C. With nine other leaders, the labor icon A. Philip Randolph and his lieutenant, Bayard Rustin, organized and produced the first national protest for racial equality. Called the March on Washington, it was as openly debated in 1963 as the election of Barack Obama was in 2008; skeptics predicted that it would be neither peaceful nor successful. The March brought a quarter million blacks and whites to the capital demanding an end to discrimination. This evidence that change was underway without the "power structure" leading or controlling it shook the country and within a year brought about results such as passage of the 1964 Civil Rights Act and 1965 Voting Rights Act. The 1968 Fair Housing Act followed the assassination of Dr. Martin Luther King Jr., the man for whom the march is most remembered.

The magnificent interracial unity at the March embodied the success of a hundred-year struggle that began before the Civil War with white abolitionists and a few free blacks and continued after the Reconstruction. If any one day marked the high point of the civil rights movement and the death of the old American racial order, it was August 28, 1963. With the March began the transition "from King to Obama," from a country anchored in inequality to one in which many Americans continue to struggle today against the disadvantage of race, even in the era of Obama.

Using the insights of activists who helped initiate and continue racial transformation, Fleming analyzes both the idea and reality of an African American president in 2009. She understands the contrast between dramatic high points in history, such as the March on Washington and the 2009 inauguration, and the everyday reality that millions of African Americans face after the marches and the election jubilation fade from memory. In spite of ongoing racial disparities in every layer of American life, the concept of a post-racial society has been debated since the first successes of the civil rights movement and the legislation it produced in employment, voting, housing, and income. Fleming is not confused about the significance of the progress for African Americans that began in the last century, and she appreciates milestones such as the March on Washington and the election of Barack Obama. But she does not flinch from examining the difference between visible progress at the top echelons of government and the racial reality that continues to define our country at the grass roots.

—*U.S. Congresswoman Eleanor Holmes Norton*

Acknowledgments

As I worked on this study, there were many people who helped me a great deal, but I would like to begin by thanking all the African American leaders who took time from their busy schedules to grant me an interview. Without their unique perspectives, the book could not have been written. One of those leaders, Lawrence Guyot, was especially helpful in facilitating contacts with other leaders.

I would also like to thank Congresswoman Eleanor Holmes Norton, who took time from her busy schedule to write the foreword for this book.

Here at the University of Tennessee, I would like to offer special thanks to Sharonne L. Winston, whose technical expertise has been a lifesaver on many occasions. The same goes for Felicia Felder-Hoehne, a member of the UTK library staff, who always finds the information I need in record time. Other individuals whose assistance made this project possible by their valuable assistance in making contacts and finding information are Anthony Smith of the University of Miami, Howard Lindsey of DePaul University, Toni Caron of John King Books, and Allison Bechman.

I would also like to thank the Howard Baker Center for Public Policy; the Exhibit, Performance, and Publication Expenses Fund; and the Department of History of the University of Tennessee for their generous support.

Finally, I offer special thanks to the hardworking editorial staff at the University Press of Kentucky, in particular the director of the Press, Stephen Wrinn, and his assistant, Candace Chaney. Steve has believed in this project since I first proposed it. He has been a tireless cheerleader and a steady source of support as I agonized over the difficulties of trying to write this blend of history and social criticism.

Prologue

August 28, 1963, Washington, D.C.

Nearly 250,000 people are gathered on the mall in front of the Lincoln Memorial. The mood of the crowd is buoyant. Even the blazing sun beating down on the tops of their heads cannot dampen their high spirits. They have come from everywhere; they represent labor unions and churches, schools and community groups. They are black and white, young and old, Christian and Jew. But despite their differences, they are united by an infectious excitement born of their conviction that they are about to witness history. All afternoon they listen politely and enthusiastically to an impressive array of powerful speakers.

One of the speakers is to be the very young John Lewis. Lewis is the head of the Student Nonviolent Coordinating Committee, and unbeknownst to the eager audience, he is at the center of a generational conflict among the black leaders who are present that day. The basis of the conflict is the speech that Lewis is getting ready to deliver. When older civil rights leaders read the prepared text of his speech just before Lewis steps up to the podium, they are horrified. They fear that the revolutionary tone of the speech will derail the civil rights bill pending in Congress, and they insist that Lewis soften the tone. But Lewis, along with the other young leaders in SNCC, is adamant: the speech will not be changed because its assertive tone is both appropriate and necessary. The prepared text of Lewis's speech declares, "The revolution is at hand" and goes on to offer details of the impending revolution in terms that engender consternation in some and enthusiasm in others: "We will march through the South, through the Heart of Dixie, the way Sherman did. We shall pursue our own 'scorched earth' policy and burn Jim Crow to the ground—nonviolently. We shall crack the South into a thousand pieces and put them back together in the image of democracy."[1]

1

The huge crowd attending the March on Washington never hears that version of Lewis's speech because, just moments before he is scheduled to speak, Lewis and his SNCC colleagues defuse the controversy by finally agreeing to change the speech in the interest of unity and out of respect for A. Phillip Randolph, the primary architect of the March. Unaware of all the behind-the-scenes drama, the crowd receives Lewis's revised speech warmly. Soon afterward, excitement ripples through the crowd as word spreads that Dr. Martin Luther King Jr. is making his way to the podium. Nearly everyone standing on the mall has read quotations from King's speeches in the newspapers. Many others have seen film clips on the evening news of the civil rights leader's impassioned speeches. So when the young Baptist preacher approaches the podium, expectations are high, and a hush falls over the scene. In his musical southern black Baptist preacher's voice, King invites the crowd to come with him on his journey of hope: "I say to you today, my friends, so even though we face the difficulties of today and tomorrow, I still have a dream." The crowd's enthusiasm builds as King continues, "It is a dream deeply rooted in the American dream. I have a dream that one day this nation will rise up and live out the true meaning of its creed—we hold these truths to be self-evident, that all men are created equal."[2] Black and white throats alike erupt in roars of approval.

The Americans of various creeds and colors on the mall in Washington are transformed by the power of the young preacher's words. "This is our hope. This is the faith that I go back to the South with. With this faith, we will be able to hew out of the mountain of despair a stone of hope. With this faith we will be able to transform the jangling discords of our nation into a beautiful symphony of brotherhood."[3] The cheers from the crowd are deafening. It is apparent that Martin Luther King Jr.'s powerful words convince many people on the mall in Washington that day, along with many more who watch his speech on television in their homes, that America can and will live up to her creed of equality for all citizens.

August 28, 2008, Denver, Colorado

An interracial crowd numbering 84,000 is gathered in Denver's Invesco Field to hear a young black man speak. Millions of others at home are watching on their television sets. All evening, the excitement builds as the crowd waits for Barack Obama to step up to the podium and make history by accepting the Democratic Party's nomination for the presidency of the United States of America. Like Martin Luther King Jr. before him, Barack Obama is an eloquent and talented orator. Finally, when it seems that the stadium is about to explode from all the excitement, Obama appears from behind the stage and takes his place at the podium. The crowd erupts in enthusiastic cheers and chants of "Yes we can, Yes We Can, YES WE CAN." Obama holds his arms out to the crowd, signaling them to quiet down so that he can begin his address. Finally, they comply, and the young candidate begins. He speaks of an American Promise "that binds us together in spite of our differences. That makes us fix our eye not on what is seen, but what is unseen. That better place around the bend." The crowd roars its approval, and Obama declares, "That promise is our greatest inheritance." "Yes we can, Yes We Can, YES WE CAN," the crowd thunders back.

Although Barack Obama is speaking in 2008, he clearly feels the weight of history and connects the American Promise that endures into this new millennium to the American Dream that Dr. King spoke of. The candidate's rich baritone voice rises to a crescendo. "It is that promise that forty-five years ago today brought Americans from every corner of this land to stand together on the mall in Washington before Lincoln's memorial to hear a young preacher from Georgia speak of his dream." A thunderous roar from the crowd greets Obama's reminder of Dr. King's "I Have a Dream" speech. Finally, the roar subsides and Obama continues. "The men and women who gathered there could have heard many things. They could have heard words of anger and discord. They could have been told to succumb to the fear and frustrations of so many dreams deferred. . . . But what the people heard instead; people of every creed and color; from every walk of life; is that in America our destiny is inextricably linked. That together, our dreams can be one." Chants of "Yes we can, Yes We Can" begin building slowly. The young candidate exhorts his audience, "America, we cannot turn back. Not with so much work to be done. . . . America, we cannot turn back. We cannot walk alone; at this moment; in this election. We must pledge once more to march into the future. Let us keep that promise; that American Promise." Many people in Invesco Field that magical night weep, and as Obama reminds the crowd of America's Promise and of their responsibility to see that the promise is fulfilled, the chants of "Yes we can, Yes We Can, YES WE CAN," are deafening.

In many ways, the crowd's affirmation of Obama's message on August 28, 2008, is also an affirmation of the call issued by Dr. Martin Luther King Jr. at the March on Washington exactly forty-five years earlier when he preached, "When we allow freedom to ring, when we let it ring from every village and every hamlet, from every state and every city, we will be able to speed up that day when all God's children—black men and white men, Jews and Gentiles, Protestants and Catholics—will be able to join hands and sing in the words of that old Negro spiritual, 'Free at last, free at last; thank God Almighty, we are free at last.'"⁴ "Yes we can, Yes We Can, YES WE CAN," the large enthusiastic crowd in Denver chants, affirming both King's dream articulated in 1963 and Obama's promise articulated in 2008.

In the forty-five years between the two remarkable events, Dr. King's "I Have a Dream" speech and Barack Obama's acceptance of the Democratic Party's nomination for president, the development of black leadership in this country underwent seismic changes. Back in 1963, Martin Luther King's emergence on the national scene in the wake of the March on Washington put a very public face on black leadership, because for the first time in this nation's history, a black leader's words were brought right into America's living rooms through the fledgling medium of television. King's fire, his eloquence, and the chemistry he had with his audience were conveyed to millions of Americans who had never had such an intimate view of a black leader before. And so, to countless Americans, Martin Luther King Jr. came to represent black leadership in America. Thus, when the young civil rights leader was slain just five years after his famous speech, the inspiring image of him speaking of his dream in the shadow of the Lincoln Memorial remained fixed in the minds of Americans. After all, that view of King had been their first real introduction to black leadership, and by remembering King this way they could rise above the ugliness of the assassination to the heights of hope that had inspired them in the first place. Thus, for years, the image of King the dreamer has been such a comfortable one for generations of Americans that for a long time, it was the standard against which all black leadership was measured—until now with the emergence of Barack Obama.

The way the American public became acquainted with the young black preacher from Georgia over forty-five years ago is not very different from the way Americans of today have become acquainted with the young black politician from Illinois. Barack Obama burst on the scene when he addressed the Democratic National Convention in 2004, and his speech was televised to a national audience. Once again, Americans from all walks of life were moved by a black leader's vision. As people listened to the political neophyte from Illinois, his eloquence was obvious and his confidence was infectious. Soon Democratic circles began buzzing with excitement. Before long, when the Obama presidential candidacy became a reality, twenty-first-century mass communication—television and the Internet—not only spread the candidate's message but also conveyed his eloquence and charisma. Like Dr. King before him, Barack Obama possesses a charisma that excites and energizes his supporters. In fact, charisma and eloquence have always been a critical ingredient of successful black leadership, and African Americans expect them from their leaders. But as Democratic presidential nominee Obama reached out to supporters beyond the black community, his campaign strategists were faced with the unique challenge of fusing this charismatic black leadership tradition that is part of the African American heritage with a national political campaign.

With all the publicity generated by these two crucial black leadership milestones—King's dream and Obama's promise—it is easy to lose sight of the continuing importance of a variety of black leaders who struggle to embrace new opportunities even as they face new obstacles. From community activists to educational leaders, and from elected representatives to religious leaders, black leaders continue their efforts, often quietly and out of the limelight, to help black people reach the American dream King talked about forty-five years ago and realize the promise Obama talks about today. The efforts of these black leaders in post-civil-rights-era America fascinate scholars and social critics alike, and as a result countless books and articles on black leadership have been published. Most of these works are built around analytical frameworks that help readers understand the unique challenges facing African American leaders who are themselves members of an unequal minority. However, there is still a need for black leaders to speak for themselves, and in the following pages forty-two black leaders do just that. They are old and young, northern and southern, male and female. Some have national name recognition; others are local leaders virtually unknown outside their own communities. Some are historical figures in the twilight of their careers, and others are young people still formulating their leadership strategies. They represent politics, education, religion, and community activism. They comment on everything from the generational divide between black leaders and their constituents to the social, economic, political, cultural, and educational issues that shape their leadership agendas and define the lives of their constituents in the new millennium.

In order to highlight the leaders' voices, this book includes many direct quotations accompanied by just enough analytical framework to organize them. Thus, the black leaders' voices are not circumscribed by the analysis; instead, their voices shape the analysis. This study is history combined with social commentary. It explores the idealism and the pragmatism that are often at war in the psyches of black leaders as they seek solutions to the twenty-first-century problems facing African Americans. Many recent scholarly works on modern black leadership have been sharply critical of black leaders. Although this study does not seek to answer any of those criticisms directly, it does allow black leaders to articulate their own visions. As they do so, their voices are steeped in the history and tradition of the difficult struggle that has always faced black leaders in what many still regard as a white man's country. In the pages that follow, African American leaders speak passionately about the problems they have experienced, the prospects they see, and the perils that remain, even in an America where a young black politician can convince millions of Americans of all colors that the greatness of the nation is still contained in the promise that ordinary Americans of all colors have the power to make a difference. "YES WE CAN."

1. Yes We Can

In late summer 2004, Barack Obama was a young black Illinois politician and the Democratic standard-bearer for a seat in the U.S. Senate. After a sordid scandal forced his Republican opponent to drop out of the race, Obama's victory in November seemed all but certain, and he was poised to make history by becoming only the third African American since Reconstruction to be elected to the Senate. As the Democrats prepared to hold their convention in Boston that summer, the young black soon-to-be senator came to the attention of the Democratic National Committee, and they decided to ask him to deliver the keynote address to the convention on Tuesday evening. America was about to be introduced to the charismatic politician from Illinois.

From the moment Obama arrived in Boston for the convention in August 2004, there was a buzz of excitement surrounding the candidate, and he was subjected to intense media scrutiny. By the time he stepped onto the CBS set of *Face the Nation* in advance of his convention address, the buzz had reached fever pitch, prompting *Face the Nation* host Bob Schieffer to exclaim, "You're the rock star now."[1] However, Obama already fully appreciated what a unique opportunity the DNC's invitation presented. But if he was nervous about it, he did not show it. As he prepared his speech, the words came easily. "This was not laborious," he said, "writing this speech. . . . It came out fairly easily. I had been thinking about these things for two years at that point. I had the opportunity to reflect on what had moved me the most during the course of the campaign and to distill those things. . . . It was more a distillation process than it was a composition process."[2]

Finally, the big night came, and Obama stepped out onto the national stage. He began his keynote address with a self-deprecating characterization, calling himself "a skinny kid with a funny name" in whom this country had inspired hope.[3] He quickly moved on, his voice gathering strength, and when he reached his stride, his tone and cadence made one think of a southern black preacher. He reached the crescendo as he exclaimed, "There's not a liberal America and a conservative America— there's a United States of America." In response, a deep roar of approval began to build among members of the audience. "There's not a black America and a white America and Latino America and Asian America." After the briefest of pauses for dramatic effect, he hammered his message home: "There's the United States of America. . . . We are one people."[4] The audience in the convention hall went wild. Delegates were cheering and weeping at the same time. Americans sitting in their homes watching this previously unknown young black man from Illinois on television were also deeply moved. It seemed that he had a magical charisma that catapulted him right into their living rooms. The stage was set for Barack Obama to make history.

After his grand debut on the national stage that summer, Obama went on to win his senate seat in the fall by the largest margin in Illinois history: he received a whopping 70 percent of the vote. His attention turned from the national scene back to his constituents in Illinois; but there were influential people on the national scene who did not forget about Barack Obama. The convention speech had left such a lasting impression that journalists continued to write excitedly about the previously unknown black politician from Illinois. And in the afterglow of his electrifying speech, other Americans from all over the country also continued to be intrigued by the young black senator-elect from Illinois. Some of those who paid close attention to Obama after he took his senate seat and began to learn his way around Washington were members of the Democratic Party establishment. When his party recaptured control of Congress in the midterm elections of 2006, the buzz surrounding the freshman senator from Illinois became more intense. Among those buzzing the loudest were the senator's closest friends and advisers; they began to think the unthinkable and quietly began discussing the prospect of a run for the presidency. Undoubtedly, Obama's advisers understood what a long shot it was: not only was Barack Obama a black man in a country that had never elected a black president, but he was a freshman senator who had barely begun to learn his way around the corridors of power in the nation's capital.

Regardless of how improbable it was, however, months before the others around the young senator began to speak of the possibility of an Obama presidential candidacy, Barack and Michelle Obama's oldest daughter, Malia, had no trouble envisioning it. The subject came up on the day Obama took his oath of office for the Senate. Right after the solemn ceremony, he and his family were strolling around the capitol grounds savoring the moment. At one point on that magical afternoon, Malia paused and earnestly looked up at her father, asking, "Daddy, are you going to be president?"[5] Anyone who overheard the innocent question six-year-old Malia asked her father that afternoon would have simply smiled politely at the child's obvious faith in her father. But from her vantage point as a twenty-first-century black child who had never had her vision of prospects and possibilities circumscribed by the ugly reality of legal segregation or the frightening brutality of racial violence, the question was a perfectly logical one.

Some months later, Barack Obama was part of a crowded field of Democratic hopefuls in the race for the party's nomination. Then in January 2008, when he went to the snowy white state of Iowa, Obama emerged from the pack to make history again. January 3, 2008, was a cold, snowy night in Des Moines, Iowa. But inside the hall where presidential candidate Barack Obama, the forty-six-year-old junior senator from Illinois, was delivering his victory speech after winning the Iowa Caucus, the air was warm and the atmosphere crackled with excitement. The hall was jam-packed, and the nearly all-white crowd roared its approval when Obama said, "Hope—hope is what led me here today— with a father from Kenya; a mother from Kansas; and a story that could only happen in the United States of America. Hope is the bedrock of this nation; the belief that our destiny will not be written for us, but by us; by all those men and women who are not content to settle for the world as it is; who have the courage to remake the world as it should be." Obama's victory as a black candidate in one of the whitest states in the country was remarkable. Some even said it was a miracle.

Col. Alexander Jefferson is also black. That January evening, Colonel Jefferson was sitting in his living room in Detroit, Michigan, the blackest city in America, and he was thrilled by Obama's victory. Jefferson is a retired army officer, and even in his eighties his military bearing is still obvious: his body is slender and straight, and his gaze is just as sharp as it was over fifty years ago when he was flying a plane as one of the famed Tuskegee Airmen searching the skies for German aircraft. A native Detroiter, he is acutely aware that his city has an astronomical budget deficit, an unemployment rate that is out of control, and a public school system in crisis. But despite the problems all around him, Jefferson was heartened by Obama's victory. When he reflects on Obama's Iowa victory and his ultimate success in the national election, he shakes his head in amazement. "I never thought I'd see it happen in my lifetime," the old man says in a voice tinged with wonder.[6] Regardless of whether Obama's success will have any impact on his city's crisis, Colonel Jefferson, like African Americans everywhere, basks in the symbolism of this black electoral victory. However, it is not only Obama's color that strikes a chord with African Americans, but also his words. That night in Iowa when the he clearly associated his quest for the presidency with the black freedom struggle of the 1960s, African Americans smiled. Obama said, "Hope is what led a band of colonists to rise up against an empire; what led the greatest of generations to free a continent and heal a nation; what led young women and young men to sit at lunch counters and brave fire hoses and march through Selma and Montgomery for freedom's cause." Obama was making a clear connection between the civil rights movement of the 1960s and his historic candidacy, and black people, especially those from the civil rights generation, said "Amen."

Barack Obama's unprecedented electoral success came exactly forty years after Dr. Martin Luther King Jr., the most potent black leadership symbol of the twentieth century, was assassinated. Thus, even as African Americans look forward to the tantalizing possibilities for African American progress that an Obama presidency holds, many find themselves looking backward, reflecting on the impact on black progress of King's death forty years ago. Just as Barack Obama has become the most famous black leader in the twenty-first century, Martin Luther King had become the most famous black leader of the twentieth century by the time of his death. King never ran for political office, never held any government post at all. Nevertheless, he was widely admired because of his unshakable commitment to the cause of social justice, his ability to empathize with the disparate elements of his broad constituency, and his remarkable oratorical skills.

It was his empathy with one group of his constituents, striking sanitation workers in Memphis, Tennessee, that prompted one of the most masterful speeches of his career: it was the last speech he ever gave. King delivered that speech on the evening of April 3, 1968, in Memphis. It was a stormy night, and as he spoke, brilliant flashes of lightning and loud claps of thunder eerily punctuated his powerful words: "I've been to the mountaintop. . . . I've looked over and I've seen the Promised Land. I may not get there with you. But I want you to know tonight that we as a people will get to the Promised Land."[7] The audience was swept up in the confidence of King's prediction, and their applause was deafening. After it was over, King was so drained that two of his close associates, Rev. Ralph Abernathy and Rev. Samuel Billy Kyles, had to help him to his seat. Even those closest to King, who had heard him speak countless times before, realized that they had just witnessed a remarkable performance, even for King.[8]

The next day, King spent hours with close advisers planning the Poor People's Campaign. They met in room 306 of the Lorraine Motel in the heart of Memphis's black community. By that evening, the mood of the group turned lighthearted, and as they engaged in good-natured banter, a pillow fight broke out. It was a remarkable sight: Dr. Martin Luther King Jr. and some of the best-known leaders in the Southern Christian Leadership Conference pummeling one another with pillows as they laughed, teased, and joked. Local Baptist minister and activist Samuel Billy Kyles turned into the parking lot of the Lorraine Motel at five o'clock that afternoon. After parking his car, he walked up the stairs closest to room 306; he had come to pick the group up and take them to his house for dinner. Although Kyles had told King he would be there by five, he was not surprised that King was not ready. As he recalls, "Doc was always late, so I told him I'd be there by 5:00, and I knew that he would probably be ready by 6:00." Kyles's strategy worked: as six o'clock approached, the pillow fight broke up, and the others drifted off to their rooms to freshen up for dinner. Only King, Abernathy, and Kyles were left in room 306. All the motel rooms opened out onto a balcony overlooking the parking lot and a swimming pool below, and just then King and Kyles walked out of room 306 together onto the balcony. They paused, and then Kyles turned and began walking toward the stairway to his right. King was left standing alone on the balcony, gazing off into the distance. Abernathy was still in room 306, putting the finishing touches on his appearance. By this time, other members of SCLC's inner circle had already descended the stairs to the parking lot.[9]

Kyles was halfway between the stairs and the lone figure of King lost in thought on the balcony when he heard the loud report of a gunshot. He froze. It took his mind a few seconds to process what had just happened behind him. When he whirled around, he saw King lying on his back with a gaping wound to his jaw. In the parking lot below, James Bevel, a young Southern Christian Leadership Conference (SCLC) strategist, was actually looking up at the balcony at the precise moment when the shot rang out. In that awful instant, Bevel was smiling, still buoyed by the playful mood left over from the pillow fight. And besides, Bevel recalls, "I thought Bernard [Lafayette] was playing a firecracker trick on us." Bevel explains, "Bernard used to do this kind of stuff. He'd light a firecracker and then fall out." But as the sight of King's fallen body finally registered on Bevel's consciousness, the young activist's smile disappeared, replaced by a look of shock, horror, and profound disbelief. With tears in his eyes, the young activist mumbled to nobody in particular, "No. That's King. He don't play like that."[10]

Kyles closed the distance between himself and the fallen King in three giant steps just as Bevel and the others in the parking lot below came charging up the stairs. With barely a pause, Kyles quickly ran into room 306 to call for an ambulance. In those days, many motel phones did not have dials; the only way to make a call was to pick up the receiver and wait for the hotel operator to answer. Kyles lunged at the phone and grabbed the receiver almost before his whole body was in the room, but the operator did not come on the line. The frantic minister waited for some seconds and then rushed back out on the balcony and asked one of the many Memphis police officers hovering around the scene to use his radio to call for an ambulance. It was only later, after the chaos had subsided, that Kyles discovered that the motel operator, who happened to be the motel owner's wife, had left the switchboard and run out into the parking lot when she heard the shot, leaving the untended switchboard buzzing. When she looked up at the balcony and realized the enormity of the tragedy unfolding there, she collapsed from a massive heart attack right on the spot. She later died without ever regaining consciousness.[11]

In a matter of minutes the ambulance arrived, and Memphis police officers helped the attendants carry the wounded King down the stairs and into the ambulance. As it took off, tires screeching and siren wailing, many of those left behind who had just been laughing and talking and throwing pillows at King and at each other looked on in silence, tears coursing down their cheeks. For all of these men, the loss they suffered that day as a result of the events on the balcony of the Lorraine Motel was a very personal one. They had prayed with Martin Luther King, they had marched with him, they had plotted strategy with him, they had celebrated with him, and they had cried with him. Now they were crying *for* him and for themselves. How could they continue the struggle without him?

All over the country, African Americans recoiled in shock and horror and reacted with rage when they heard the awful news. Even those who had disagreed with parts of King's philosophy were deeply affected. That moment on April 4, 1968, was a defining moment for the African American freedom struggle and for the future direction of African American leadership. During his brief thirteen-year career as an activist, King had achieved a visibility and renown unparalleled by any other African American leader in the history of America. By this time, King's name had become synonymous with the civil rights movement in the minds of most Americans, black and white, and he seemed equally comfortable meeting with President Lyndon Baines Johnson in the White House or with black sharecroppers in the Black Belt in Alabama. King's message of nonviolence and Christian love gained the attention of many Americans during the turbulent decade of the 1960s. The learned phrases that were so characteristic of King's speeches were a consequence of his eastern education, and they mixed easily with his soft southern accent and the simple homilies from his African American culture. These elements, combined, enabled him to craft eloquent orations that appealed to his varied countrymen.

But the Martin Luther King this country has mourned and eulogized ever since that fateful day in Memphis is not the man who died April 4, 1968. Instead, in the days and weeks following the traumatic assassination, many Americans reached back into the past and resurrected a younger version of King to mourn. Substituting their idealized version of King absolved them of the responsibility to face the stubborn and continuing problems that the mature King recognized before his death. The younger, more popular version of Martin Luther King Jr. is still alive and well in the new millennium, and he seems to be caught in some sort of cosmic loop, forever standing on the steps of the Lincoln Memorial in Washington, D.C., delivering his "I Have A Dream" speech over and over again. Many Americans who were alive at the time nostalgically remember the sight of the young preacher standing in the hot sun while the musical phrases of the masterful speech rolled off his tongue: "Now is the time to rise from the dark and desolate valley of segregation to the sunlit path of racial justice. . . . Now is the time to make justice a reality for all of God's children." King admonished his audience, "In the process of gaining our rightful place, we must not be guilty of wrongful deeds. Let us not seek to satisfy our thirst for freedom by drinking from the cup of bitterness and hatred. . . . Again and again we must rise to the majestic heights of meeting physical force with soul force." King's voice soared in mighty triumph as he ended his speech: "Free at last! Free at last! Thank God Almighty, we are free at last!" It was a message that made Americans feel good about themselves and optimistic about the future of their country.[12]

By the time Martin Luther King Jr., the mature activist, came to Memphis in the last hours of his life, he had changed. Standing on the balcony of the Lorraine Motel on April 4, 1968, and gazing off into the distance, he was able to see far beyond the colored and white signs, the separate drinking fountains, the separate bathrooms, and his "I Have a Dream" speech. This more mature King had advanced to a point in his thinking where he focused on basic issues of economic justice that reached far outside the South. He had come to believe that African Americans suffered because of a systemic inequality in American society. "Depressed living standards for Negroes are not simply the consequence of neglect," King insisted. "Nor can they be explained by the myth of the Negro's innate incapacities, or by the more sophisticated rationalization of his acquired infirmities (family disorganization, poor education, etc.). They are a structural part of the economic system in the United States. Certain industries and enterprises are based upon a supply of low-paid, under-skilled and immobile nonwhite labor."[13] King was by this time secure enough in his leadership stature to challenge America to live up to its creed for all its citizens, irrespective of race, even secure enough to denounce the nation's participation in the Vietnam war.

King's growth as a leader during his thirteen years of civil rights activism expanded the definition of black leadership far beyond the bounds that had previously circumscribed it. In this way King achieved a victory like no previous civil rights victory. But the success of King's leadership did not happen in a vacuum. It was part of a mix that included the hard work and dedication of many others as well; and as a result, some very public and very dramatic civil rights movement victories occurred. With each succeeding victory, black hopes for real substantive change soared. However, because American society continued to demonstrate reluctance to change, a serious crisis loomed. Thus, in post-King America, as black hopes for greater progress have been dashed, many African Americans have lost confidence in their country's commitment to the racial justice that was at the core of the civil rights movement, prompting individuals to become cynical and bitter.

Now, in the wake of Barack Obama's election, black hopes for change have soared once more. At the same time, the focus of both African Americans and Americans in general has clearly shifted from the civil rights leaders of the 1960s to a new generation of African American leadership. Although these new leaders share many values with earlier black leaders, there are important differences that constitute potentially fertile ground for generational conflict. Before the 2008 election, Rev. Jesse Jackson made a comment that was critical of Obama's views on a particularly sensitive issue, illustrating well how generational differences can blossom into conflict. Jackson is one of the most public and enduring symbols of the civil rights movement of the 1960s, and he is also a past black presidential candidate. Both Obama and Jackson call Chicago home. Yet, reports of strained relations between the young candidate and the seasoned civil rights leader were circulating. Things came to a head when Jackson made a crude comment attacking Obama with reference to his view of parental responsibility in the black community. During his campaign, Obama had been clearly and unequivocally warning black audiences about the decline of parental responsibility, particularly paternal responsibility, in the black community. In most cases, his message was warmly received by the enthusiastic black crowds that turned out to see him. However, Jackson took issue with Obama's position on this sensitive issue, and he expressed his disapproval in personal terms. When Jackson's statement became public, it took many by surprise—including Jackson himself: the reverend had spoken while he was seated next to a microphone he thought was turned off. In no time, the older black civil rights leader's ugly words were all over the news and all over the Web. Jackson had said he wanted to "cut [Obama's] nuts off" for "talking down to black people."[14]

Predictably, reactions to Jackson's comments were swift and sure. But one reaction in particular demonstrates how complicated the generational context surrounding the troubling comment is: Jackson's own son, Congressman Jesse Jackson Jr., said he was "deeply outraged and disappointed by Reverend Jackson's reckless statement." Although the younger Jackson went on to say that he loved his father, he refused to retreat from his denunciation, concluding, "So I thoroughly reject and repudiate his ugly rhetoric." This incident reveals the very real potential for generational conflict that can further complicate African American leadership.[15]

Black leaders, whatever their generational perspective, are faced with a broad range of difficult problems in the new millennium. Some of the problems have plagued African Americans for generations, while others are of much more recent origin. Of course, at the top of the list is economics. African Americans are still the poorest group in America. At the end of the twentieth century, 10.2 million African Americans, nearly one-third of this country's total black population, lived below the poverty line. What makes this grim statistic worse is the chronic nature of black poverty.[16]

Of course, a host of other problems are closely related to the continuing poverty and joblessness that affect such a large portion of the African American population. Black public health is one of those issues. African Americans have always been sicker than the rest of the American population, and in the years since the civil rights movement, problems with black health continue. Compared to statistics for white people, black infant mortality rates are still higher, black life expectancy is still lower, and there are new complications like the AIDS epidemic that is afflicting huge numbers of African Americans. Obviously, the black health crisis is worsened by the serious problem of inadequate access to health care that plagues most poor Americans, irrespective of color. But in the end, many people argue that regardless of the other issues involved, any evaluation of the black health crisis in this country must recognize that race still matters. It is a lingering legacy from the past.

Because nineteenth-century white physicians commonly believed African Americans were inferior, they concluded that poor health was an expected consequence of innate black inferiority. According to this line of reasoning, "there were . . . anatomical and physiological differences between [the African American] and the Caucasian—differences which made him not only inferior to the white man but which predisposed him to disease, high mortality, and race deterioration."[17] Thus, in the years before the civil rights movement this country's medical establishment was not looking for ways to improve black health; they were simply making excuses for their inaction. The problem was so severe that it prompted nineteenth-century black leader Booker T. Washington to propose that the country should recognize the problem by observing National Negro Health Week every year. Some current black scholars go a step further and charge that the suffering of African Americans at the hands of America's medical establishment exceeded simple neglect and entered the realm of callous disregard and deliberate exploitation. For example, Harriet Washington, in her recent study of unauthorized medical experimentation on black patients, charges that there is a "history of ethically flawed medical experimentation with African Americans. Such research has played a pivotal role in forging the fear of medicine that helps perpetuate our nation's racial health gulf. Historically, African Americans have been subjected to exploitative, abusive involuntary experimentation at a rate far higher than other ethnic groups."[18]

One of the other crises for African Americans and their leaders in the post-King era is the epidemic of black incarceration. According to one particularly telling statistic, by the last decade of the twentieth century, there were 609,690 black men between the ages of twenty and twenty-nine in prison or jail, on probation, or on parole. During the same period, only 436,000 black men in this age group were in college.[19] The unprecedented number of young African Americans who are caught up in the criminal justice system is having a profound effect on black communities all over the country. In particular, the absence of so many young men has upset the male-female ratio in many black communities and has had a devastating impact on the structure of the black family. Furthermore, an especially troubling attitude accompanies the high incarceration rate: in recent years, some young African Americans have begun to consider a prison record as a badge of honor.

Some social critics even go so far as to charge that the creation and popularity of rap music and the hip-hop culture it spawned in recent years has promoted this attitude. This new culture associated with post-civil-rights-era black youth has turned many of the black community's traditional values upside down and left older African Americans, especially those from the civil rights generation, shaking their heads in consternation. As far as many older African Americans are concerned, these young people do not talk right, dress right, or act right. Many members of the younger generation, for their part, are convinced that older black folks "just don't get it." In the words of self-appointed hip-hop historian Todd Boyd, "Hip hop has rejected and now replaced the pious, sanctimonious nature of civil rights as the defining moment of Blackness. In turn, it offers new ways of seeing and understanding what it means to be black at this pivotal time in history."[20]

It is ironic, however, that as these young people try to proclaim their independence from the recent past by self-consciously breaking all of polite black society's old rules, many of them fail to realize that the roots of their challenge to traditional African American behavioral norms are located squarely within the civil rights movement of the past century. During the height of the movement, when young activists went south to organize African Americans, particularly in rural areas, one of the biggest obstacles to their success was the long-standing black deference to authority that was part of the culture. They had to work hard to persuade African Americans in this setting to defy authority in order to fight for their rights. Often that authority was the local white power structure; but just as often the authority was found in the local black middle class, which did not always support demonstrations in their community. For example, one black public school teacher in a rural Alabama county disapproved of the challenge to authority sparked by civil rights workers in her county. She accused the civil rights workers of systematically teaching disrespect to her county's young people: "They would teach the children don't [say] miss [to] anybody. Don't even say Mississippi."[21] That same teacher is still dismayed as she views today's black youth culture. Yet, despite any connections between the movement of the past and the existence of African Americans in the present, some in the hip-hop community see only an obstacle when they look back on the civil rights movement. Todd Boyd explains, "Again, this is why hip hop is so important: it forces us to move on by knocking down these obstacles from the past, by breaking all those rules, in order to get past this novocaine-like relationship that so many have to civil rights and recognize the more nuanced forms of racism that continue to dominate our society. To me this transition from civil rights to hip hop is akin to a line from an old Bohannon cut, 'Wide Receiver': the first time we knocked on the door, this time we gonna kick the muth-afucka in!"[22] This kind of sentiment frustrates some older African Americans, angers many others, and has engendered a widespread fear among members of the civil rights generation that black progress is in jeopardy.

The picture is further complicated by the views of many white Americans who are just plain tired of hearing about black problems. Most are convinced that this country has far more serious problems to deal with, such as a broken economy, wildly fluctuating energy costs, inadequate health care, and a social security system on the verge of collapse. Above all, many Americans do not feel safe in their own country anymore since the catastrophic events of September 11, 2001. In the midst of these critical issues, many white Americans find it comforting to believe that the serious black problems that were exposed by the civil rights movement of the last century are problems their country has already solved. They can accept the movement mythology that black people had a great leader (King) and a victorious movement, and the country responded by righting all the past wrongs. The election of the first black president only forty years after King's ascendancy has put the exclamation point on the narrative of black progress in the twenty-first century. The logical conclusion is that if the masses of African Americans are still lagging behind, plagued by all these problems, they and their leaders must not be trying hard enough.

In the context of such attitudes on the part of white people and the daunting problems facing American society, the discourse in the African American community has become sharp, emotional, and exhausting. On any given day, a black leader might be called upon to face young African Americans with their rap music, "fashionably" baggy clothes, and apparent disdain for authority. The leaders must also consider the views of black superstars and super-rich entertainers and sports figures, who are often labeled as examples of black success in post-civil-rights-movement America. (Of course, the question on the minds of many Americans is, "They made it, why can't the rest of you do better?") Black leaders must also find a way to communicate with those upwardly mobile African Americans whose blackness is only incidental to their identity because they see themselves as just Americans. Isn't that what the civil rights movement was all about? many ask themselves. Of course, one of the loudest collective black voices directed at African American leaders comes from the millions of African Americans who are striving to achieve the classic vision of the American dream, complete with a two-parent family, home ownership, two cars, well-adjusted and well-educated children, and a comfortable financial cushion in the bank, goals that match those of their white neighbors.

But alongside these black middle-class Americans, there are large numbers of African Americans who have fallen far short of the American Dream. Many of them are poor black urban residents who are still trapped in big-city ghettoes where there are virtually no prospects for gainful employment. In today's unprecedented economic emergency facing American society, they are left to try to navigate an increasingly complex welfare system, avoid drive-by shootings, and find a way to ensure that their children will get at least some kind of education. Even though they call out in despair, their voices are often disregarded by legislators as close as city hall and as far away as Washington, D.C. Another segment of the black poor whose voices are routinely ignored is those who live in rural areas. In many ways, these people are the nation's forgotten black poor. They live in some of the most remote areas of the Deep South, and many of them can trace their ancestry in an unbroken line back to slavery. Even though they do not live in slavery in the twenty-first century, they live in desperate poverty, very much as their ancestors did. While some of them cry out, all too often their concerns are ignored, too.

Among all these different African American voices, harmony is unlikely and unity is virtually impossible. In the case of older African Americans, one of the few things they seem to agree on is their own version of movement mythology. At any given time, older African Americans from all walks of life nostalgically remember the good old days. They fondly recall the glorious victories of the civil rights movement of the previous century, how proud they were to be black, and how hopeful they were for the future. But then they look around them and scratch their heads and wonder what happened. Have things really changed that much? Many doubt it. Where did all the time go? It wasn't that long ago, was it? Then they sigh and take refuge in the sounds of the sixties that articulated their hopes, their optimism, and their determination. They play their old albums and listen to Curtis Mayfield singing in his distinctive falsetto voice, "Keep On Pushin'," or they choose something lively and upbeat from the Motown sound, something like Martha and the Vandellas singing "Dancing in the Streets"; and then they listen to Gil Scott Heron rap (a generation before the birth of present-day rap music) "The Revolution Will Not Be Televised."

As black leaders view each other across a generational divide, they must try to break out of the long shadow of the recent past and give their attention to a competing cacophony of black voices in the present. They must work to inspire confidence in their leadership as they try to fashion new definitions of black leadership for a new millennium. Yet, regardless of their generational orientation, most recognize that the ascendancy of Barack Obama is a potent symbol of national black leadership success and a real point of pride for the broadest constituency of African Americans since King's death. They understand, though, that neither King's death nor Obama's success will change the difficult issues they face in their daily struggles to help their black constituents. In the following pages, a variety of black leaders talk about their hopes and fears, their triumphs and disappointments, and their attempts to persuade their constituents that although the victories of the recent past are powerful symbols, serious black problems persist that must be addressed, because as remarkable as those victories are, they have not gone far enough.

2. Black Leadership in Historical Perspective

In 1895, when Booker T. Washington delivered his famous Atlanta Compromise address at the Atlanta Cotton States Exposition, he was a young black educator from Alabama, not very well known. But Washington's speech contained a poignant plea that gained the attention of his largely white and southern audience. Speaking of black people, he declared: "As we have proved our loyalty to you in the past, in nursing your children, watching by the sickbed of your mothers and fathers, and often following them with tear-dimmed eyes to their graves, so in the future in our humble way, we shall stand by you with a devotion that no foreigner can approach, ready to lay down our lives, if need be, in defense of yours, interlacing our industrial, commercial, civil, and religious life with yours in a way that shall make the interests of both races one."[1] With that emotional appeal, Booker T. Washington catapulted himself onto the national stage and laid the groundwork for a national debate on the character of black leadership that has continued to rage until the present. That day in Atlanta in 1895, Booker's southern white audience smiled broadly and clapped enthusiastically. They could almost hear the Negro spirituals in the background as young Washington promised a continuation of the black loyalty and trustworthiness that was such an integral part of their romanticized image of the region's past.

African Americans were not nearly as happy with Washington's message, and the young educator candidly admitted that black reaction to his speech was mixed: "The coloured people and the coloured newspapers at first seemed to be greatly pleased with the character of my Atlanta address, as well as with its reception. But after the first burst of enthusiasm began to die away, and the coloured people began reading the speech in cold type, some of them seemed to feel that they had been hypnotized.

They seemed to feel that I had been too liberal in my remarks toward Southern whites, and that I had not spoken out strongly enough for what they termed the 'rights' of the race."[2] By the time Washington delivered his address, African Americans had been through a series of wrenching experiences that had brought them from the dizzying heights of savoring the day of Jubilee to the lows of Klan violence and federal desertion. Moreover, the very next year after Washington's speech, the Supreme Court decision in the landmark case *Plessy v. Ferguson* sealed the fate of African Americans all over the country: segregation based on race became the law of the land and continued as such for the next fifty-eight years. In this restrictive atmosphere, the options available to succeeding generations of black leaders were severely limited.

The consequences of *Plessy* in the ensuing decades confronted African Americans in ways that stretched far beyond the legal system. Historian Leon Litwack summarized the effects of the court decision: "What came to be impressed on several generations of black southerners . . . was the material, political, and military superiority of white people, the extraordinary power white men and women wielded over black lives and prospects in virtually all phases of daily life."[3] The reality of black powerlessness warped countless young lives as African Americans tried to figure out how to make their way in the world. Novelist Richard Wright explained the emotional trauma in personal terms: "Nothing challenged the totality of my personality so much as this pressure of hate and threat that stemmed from the invisible whites. I would stand for hours on the doorsteps of neighbors' houses listening to their talk, learning how a white woman had slapped a black woman, how a white man had killed a black man. It filled me with awe, wonder, and fear."[4]

The young white children who were Wright's contemporaries might have feared ghosts, goblins, or monsters from the pages of Grimm's fairy tales, but the only monsters that Wright feared as a youth were white people. They did not come out of young Richard's imagination to hide under his bed or wait in his closet to jump out after the lights were turned off. Instead, they were all around him every day in broad daylight in his Mississippi home. He never knew when one of them would pounce. He recalled, "It was as though I was continuously reacting to the threat of some natural force whose hostile behavior could not be predicted."[5] Pres-

byterian minister and educator Clinton Marsh experienced a similar fear
when he was a youngster growing up in Wilcox County, in the Alabama
Black Belt in the 1920s. As he put it, "You lived in a subliminal state
of fear. Not that every moment you were afraid, but if my mother sent
me . . . to the store, I could never be sure that no racial incident would
occur."[6]

That dark, formless fear was the constant companion of generations
of African Americans. All it took to make it blossom into full-blown ter-
ror was any one of the countless incidents that occurred with frightening regularity. For example, in Cordele, Georgia, in the early years of the
twentieth century, little Elijah Poole, an olive-skinned black boy who was
the apple of his father's eye, was in town with his sharecropping parents.
The family was dirt poor, and Elijah and his brothers and sisters had been
eagerly anticipating this trip into town. Elijah was excited by the country
stores that lined the main street, and he and his siblings excitedly peered
into the dim interiors of the establishments, trying to catch a glimpse of
what was inside. Like all black children growing up in the South, Elijah
knew to beware of white people, but in the midst of all these strange sights
and sounds, he was slow to react when a white man approached him. The
white man was well dressed, and he was smiling. Even though he feared
white people, Elijah's childish curiosity got the best of him that day, and
he could not help but look intently at the man as the man extended his
hand. With a shock, Elijah realized that the man was holding the severed
ear of a black person. Even though he desperately wanted to shut out the
bloody image, he was transfixed by the awful sight. It was almost as if
he was paralyzed for a few seconds. A short time later, just after Elijah's
sixth birthday, a man was lynched in Cordele's downtown business district. The trauma was so great that Elijah became a bed wetter, and the
problem continued for several years. His father was furious with him, but
no matter how hard the little boy tried, it seemed that he was powerless
to stop until after his twelfth birthday. When he was all grown up, Elijah Poole migrated north, changed his name to Elijah Muhammad, and
became the leader of the Nation of Islam.[7]

In the neighboring state of Alabama, Edna Bonner Rhodes observed
an incident during her childhood that completely convinced her that
she could not trust any white person. A local black man, Jonah Martin,

robbed a white-owned store in Camden, Alabama. It happened during the depths of the Great Depression, and Martin was desperate. Earlier that day, he had gone to the white store owner and requested a loan. The store owner refused. That night Martin robbed the store, and then he boarded a Trailways Bus, hoping to get out of town before the white store owner discovered the theft. But the store owner had already alerted the Wilcox County sheriff, and the sheriff had formed a posse to capture the fugitive. The posse managed to stop the bus, but before they could subdue Martin, Martin shot and killed one of the deputies and escaped into the surrounding woods. At that point, the sheriff put out a call for volunteers to help capture Martin. While little Edna was not surprised at the large size of the posse, she could not believe her eyes when they rode past her house: she recognized more than a few local white preachers in their midst. When they finally captured Jonah Martin, they shot him so many times that the flesh all over his body was ragged and bleeding. Then they proceeded to drag him back into town and lay his body out on the courthouse lawn, where it remained for days, decomposing in the southern Alabama heat.[8]

Dr. Benjamin Mays, a prominent black educator and the president of Morehouse College in Atlanta (Martin Luther King Jr.'s alma mater), described an incident that revealed how traumatic the reality of black powerlessness was for so many black youngsters. The incident happened to a Morehouse graduate, Arthur L. Johnson. When he was thirteen years old, Johnson was in downtown Birmingham, Alabama, one day with one of his uncles. The black teenager accidentally touched the shoulder of a little white girl who was about five or six years old. White reaction was swift, sure, and brutal. Johnson recalled: "This [white] man attacked me so violently on the street that I . . . didn't really know what happened until it was over." The pain that the badly beaten Johnson felt was compounded by the inaction of his uncle. He explained, "The thing . . . which stands out in my mind as a definite indicator of what that experience involved from the race viewpoint is that my uncle stood frozen in fear in the face of that attack." Johnson had a very difficult time dealing with the attack, but it was even harder to deal with his disappointment. He sadly insisted, "You know, it was natural for a boy to assume that an older adult in his family would come to his defense in a situation like that, but he didn't do it."[9] That day young Arthur Johnson learned a lesson in black powerlessness that he never forgot.

John Hope Franklin, who became one of this country's most influential black intellectuals, also learned an early lesson about African Americans' low position in society. One day when he was six years old, he, his mother, and his brother boarded a passenger train in rural Oklahoma for a shopping trip to a nearby town. People who lived in the rural areas far away from the nearest train station routinely flagged down the train when it approached their town. On this day, Franklin's mother stood next to the track and waved at the engineer, as she had done many times before. The train slowed to a stop, and Franklin describes what happened next:

> We just jumped on the train and sat down. The train by that time was already moving. Well, the coach we sat in was a white coach. The conductor came by and said that you can't sit there. You've got to move. My mother told him, "I can't move with the train moving, I've got two small children. I can't go from one coach to another." He said, "Well, I'll stop the train." He stopped the train and put us off in the woods. . . . So we had to trudge back through the woods, and I'm crying, of course. . . . And she said, "What are you crying about?" [Franklin answered,] "Well, you know, the man put us off the train." She said, "Well that? you don't cry about that. That's not worth crying about."[10]

Young John Hope Franklin's mother went on to explain that they lived in a segregated society, but she told him he should not let segregation get the best of him. He recalls her words clearly: "I don't ever want to see you wasting your tears and your crying and your getting upset about this." With a determined glint in her eye, she added pointedly, "Instead of you crying, you use your energy to prove to all of them that you're as good as they are."[11]

Over in Selma, Alabama, Joanne Bland was scarred by segregation as a young child. She was born in Selma in 1953 to a poor family. One day a box of clothes arrived from some of Joanne's relatives in faraway Detroit, Michigan. Joanne explains that "because we were poor, my relatives who lived in the North . . . Detroit . . . always sent us boxes three times a year of clothes they had collected for us. They were more often new clothing but, [regardless] they were new to us." It was near Easter, and the children were eager to see what kind of Easter outfits were in the box. Almost as soon as her grandmother opened the box, young Joanne squealed with delight, because "the first thing that came out was the prettiest blue dress I had ever seen in my entire life." Joanne's grandmother agreed that the dress was perfect for her excited granddaughter, but as Joanne looked through the accessories in the box, she soon realized that none of the shoes her relatives had sent fit her. Her grandmother quickly reassured Joanne that she would buy her a new pair of shoes. Joanne was ecstatic. "Not only did I have the best dress in the box . . . I get to get new shoes too."[12]

The next weekend, Joanne and her grandmother went downtown to shop for her new shoes. Because African American shoppers were not allowed to try on merchandise in department stores in the Jim Crow South, Joanne's grandmother went prepared. "That Saturday morning before we left, my grandmother took a ball of yarn, and she measured my foot, and put it in her pocket." Joanne could barely contain her excitement.

> I was holding her hand as we walked to town. Downtown was maybe three blocks away. There was a shoe store there—Meyer's Shoe Store, right on the corner, and you could see the shoes on the Broad Street side, and that's the side we came up. And I saw *my* shoes, you know, MY SHOES. I can't explain it any other way. . . . Well, I got excited, and I ran inside, and I put my foot in the shoe, and before I could put any weight on that foot, Grandmother had snatched me up out of that shoe, and she was shaking me, and she was going off, and I was so embarrassed.[13]

Looking back on that embarrassing moment, Joanne explains, "I knew that I had done something wrong, but I didn't understand what. It seemed like everybody in the store just stopped and was looking at me, and it was crowded in that store." Many years have passed, but Joanne has no trouble remembering her reaction: "I just wanted to die." However, as embarrassed as she felt at that moment, Joanne was even more mortified by what happened next. "The clerk picked up the shoe, and found the mate and put them in the box and she came over to my grandmother." The outraged clerk demanded that Joanne's grandmother purchase that pair of shoes, but the older woman protested that they were the wrong size. Then, she reached in her pocket for the piece of yarn that was the same length as Joanne's foot and insisted politely, "If you can get this size, I will gladly pay for them." The clerk rolled her eyes, and in a demanding voice, dripping with venom, she spat at the older black woman, "No one else will buy these shoes cause that little nigger put her foot in it." Joanne's grandmother ended up having to purchase the shoes that did not fit, and young Joanne had to wear her old scuffed-up shoes on Easter with her beautiful new dress.[14]

Several years later, when she was eleven years old, Joanne, still living in Selma, witnessed one of the most memorable events of the civil rights movement: March 7, 1965, christened Bloody Sunday, the day peaceful marchers at the foot of the Edmund Pettus Bridge were teargassed and beaten. A short time afterward, Congress passed the Voting Rights Act of 1965 and the president signed it.

Evidence of black powerlessness surrounded the generations of African Americans who came of age in the years between the Civil War and the civil rights movement. Along with these painful and constant reminders of their lack of power, black people were also plagued by vicious assaults on their self-esteem. African Americans in the late nineteenth and early twentieth centuries suffered continual demeaning of their intelligence, their morality, and their sexuality. The views out of which these assaults sprang are clearly articulated in the comments of a late-nineteenth-century white physician: "A native of Africa and a savage of a few generations ago, then a slave for several generations afterwards; this is the man and the race upon whom the high responsibilities of freedom have been thrust; a nation literally born in a day. The history of the world so far as I know, furnished no condition similar to that in which the Negroes of the South were placed in the first few years after the war."[15] As far as most white Americans of that era were concerned, African Americans were simply incapable of living up to the "high responsibilities of freedom" that they faced as freed people because of their innate inferiority. Some even argued that certain characteristics, especially sexual behavior, of the ex-slaves placed them closer to lower primates than to the human race. For example, another late-nineteenth-century physician insisted: "It is this sexual question that is the barrier which keeps the philanthropist and moralist from realizing the phylogenies of the Caucasian and African races are divergent, almost antithetical, and that it is gross folly to attempt to educate both on the same basis. When the education will reduce the large size of the Negro's penis . . . then will it also be able to prevent the African's birthright to sexual madness and excess—from the Caucasian's viewpoint."[16] Thus, at the beginning of the twentieth century, African Americans understood that no matter who they were or what they had accomplished, each one of them was vulnerable to vicious comments based on pseudoscience. African American leaders in the late nineteenth and early twentieth centuries spent much time and energy attempting to counter such notions.

Black female leaders were especially sensitive to the negative perceptions that targeted black women. The impact of the attacks on the black female character took on added significance because many people during this period eagerly embraced the Victorian-era tenets of the Cult of True Womanhood: piety, purity, submissiveness, and domesticity. Motivated by their conviction that those desirable traits were for white women only, both white men and white women maligned the character of black women as a group. For example, Eleanor Tayleur, a southern white woman of the Victorian era, insisted that black women were clearly inferior and said the only reason they had not sunk into total barbarity was their contact with white women during slavery. She explained, "Before the war the Negro woman was brought into intimate contact with the refined and educated women of the dominant race. . . . they copied the manners and morals of the mistress they served. Many a black woman was a grande dame who would have graced a court. . . . The modern Negro woman had no such object-lesson in morality or modesty, and she wants none."[17] Tayleur went on to argue that black women's depraved moral condition rendered them incapable of performing even the basic duties of womanhood. Thus, a black woman was inferior as a mother and ultimately as a woman:

For her children she has fierce passion of maternity that seems to be *purely animal,* and that seldom goes beyond their childhood. When they are little, she indulges them blindly when she is in good humor, and beats them cruelly when she is angry; and once past their childhood her affection for them appears to be exhausted. She exhibits none of the brooding mother-love and anxiety which the white woman sends after her children as long as they live. Infanticide is not regarded as a crime among Negroes, but it is so appallingly common that if the statistics could be obtained on this subject they would send a shudder through the world.[18]

Some other white people at the time were convinced that black women were not even able to take care of themselves. Tayleur, who endorsed this point of view, claimed that only white intervention could help black women improve themselves. She explained, "The mission of the white woman of this country is to the black woman. If ever there was a God given and appointed task set to the womanhood of *any* people, it is to the women of America to take these lowly sisters by the hand and lift them out of the pit into which they have fallen."[19] Late-nineteenth-century white women were joined in their attacks on black women by their white male contemporaries. Thomas Bailey, a dean at the University of Mississippi in this period, was convinced that black women were so depraved that they were less than human: "Southerners do not ordinarily have the biological and aesthetic repulsion that is usually felt by Northerners toward the Negro. . . . The memory of the ante-bellum concubinage and a tradition of animal satisfaction due to the average Negro woman's highly developed animalism are factors still in operation." He considered that "such Negroes [black women] are raving amazons . . . apparently growing madder and madder each moment, eyes rolling, lips protruding, feet stamping, pawing, gesticulating. . . . This frenzied madness seems beyond control."[20]

It was in this restrictive era, unfriendly to African Americans, that Booker T. Washington, whose leadership style and philosophy became the standard for national black leadership in the minds of many of his contemporaries, honed his skills. Washington's ascendancy during this low point in African American history, characterized as the nadir by historian Rayford Logan, exposes the fundamental conundrum that has plagued black leaders from that day to this: As powerless individuals attempting to facilitate the advancement of a powerless minority, how can black leaders gain and wield enough power to help their people without compromising their own integrity? Washington's answer was to base his strategies for black uplift on the doctrine of the accumulation of wealth, which was a defining characteristic of American society at that time. He routinely advised black people to concentrate their energies on accumulating property instead of on protesting against the oppression that scarred their lives. Once their economic status improved, Washington argued, white people would respect them, and then racial oppression would cease to exist. For much of the next century, these strategies were admired by some and vilified by others. And well into the twentieth century, the Wizard of Tuskegee's strategies were so well known that they were exported to other parts of the world: European powers searching for the most effective way to control the conquered populations in their new African colonies eagerly embraced Washington's methods. At home, the most influential white leaders in this country in business, industry, government, and education regularly consulted Washington on all matters pertaining to the "Negro Problem." Consequently, Booker T. Washington became the most influential black man in America, and through much of the twentieth century, the programs, progress, and effectiveness of succeeding generations of black leaders were compared to the leadership model he established.

Of course, any evaluation of the Washington leadership model must include at least a brief discussion of W. E. B. Du Bois. Unlike Washington, Du Bois did not urge African Americans to pursue a course of accommodation to the racial status quo. While Washington dealt mainly with practical solutions, Du Bois tried to heal the wounds inflicted on the black psyche by a hostile American society. He was persuaded that African Americans had to come to terms with their own identity before they could make any progress in combating the forces of racial oppression. In *The Souls of Black Folk,* his eloquent set of essays published in 1903, Du Bois enunciated the pain that African Americans felt because of their status as black outsiders in white America: "One ever feels his twoness,—an American, a Negro; two souls, two thoughts, two unreconciled strivings; two warring ideals in one dark body, whose dogged strength alone keeps it from being torn asunder."[21] Yet, by the early twentieth century,

Du Bois's eloquence notwithstanding, Booker T. Washington's philosophy was much more popular with the most powerful white men of the era. In the rarefied atmosphere of the boardrooms of major corporations, and in the conference rooms of the major education foundations, where Washington frequently met with the most influential white men of his day, his optimistic statements about black behavior and black prospects sounded quite reasonable. However, to black southerners who were ensnared by the neo-slave system of sharecropping, trapped by the restrictions of Jim Crow laws, and terrorized by the organized vigilantes and thugs in the Ku Klux Klan and other Klan-like groups, Washington's words rang hollow. But Du Bois's discussion of the pain of black identity in white America did not resonate with most African Americans either. The majority of black people did not need to read about their "twoness"; they understood it on the most fundamental level because they experienced it every day of their lives, and they were painfully aware that their experience did not suggest any practical solutions to their plight.

Despite the apparent disconnect between the reality of black lives and the pronouncements of either Washington or Du Bois, scholars and social critics alike have christened these two men as the most important black leaders of the early twentieth century. Furthermore, many have anointed Washington as *the* public face of black leadership during this time, particularly in view of his unique access to the most powerful white men of his day. Consequently, Washington's style influenced expectations of black leadership for generations to come. For much of the past century, though, many have pounced on the differences between Booker T. Washington and W. E. B. Du Bois and have refined their analysis of Washington's leadership model based on those differences. In some ways this is eerily similar to later comparisons of Dr. Martin Luther King Jr. and Malcolm X.

The inordinate amount of attention focused on the Washington–Du Bois dichotomy in discussions of twentieth-century black leadership served to masculinize popular notions of black leadership during this era and deflect attention from the emergence of a cadre of black female leaders on both the local and the national levels. In fact, during the late nineteenth century, black women organized numerous clubs designed to assist in racial uplift. In 1896 the clubs came together to form a national organization, the National Association of Colored Women, and they selected a very well-known and well-connected black female activist, Mary Church Terrell, to serve as their first president. By the time the NACW was established, several of the notable black women reformers had become convinced that they were the ones who had led and would continue to lead the fight for black uplift. One of the NACW's early presidents explained, "The Negro woman has been the motive power in whatever has been accomplished by the race."[22]

Other black women of this era were willing to express their disappointment in no uncertain terms over the inability of their men to make any real progress. An editorial in the group's organ, *Woman's Era*, charged that black men had failed "to strengthen the belittling weaknesses which so hinder and retract us in the fight for existence." In strong language the editorial demanded that "timid men and ignorant men" stand aside.[23] One of the most outspoken black female activists, Anna Julia Cooper, as she explained her view of black women's leadership, said that in the final analysis, it was the "colored woman's office to stamp weal or woe on the history of her people."[24] While some black men applauded the efforts of such strong black women leaders, others were extremely critical. The position of black intellectual leader John Hope, a college president and a close ally of Du Bois, was that black people "are in need of men," and "it [is] a great calamity for our women to act as substitutes." Hope argued that African Americans needed men to act like men, and in his view, "the surest way for our men to become more manly is for our women to become more womanly."[25]

Subsequent scholars and social critics have continued to view black leadership of this era through the masculinized prism of the Du Bois–Washington dichotomy. However, in recent years the scholarship on late-nineteenth-century black leadership has begun to explore additional complexities. For example, numerous recent works analyze the position of African American women in the black leadership equation of the time. The impact of much of this rich literature has been limited to scholarly circles, though, because in the popular consciousness, the acceptance of the Washington–Du Bois dichotomy as the basis for understanding late-nineteenth- and early-twentieth-century black leadership survives nearly unaltered and unquestioned. Likewise, the Martin Luther King Jr.–

Malcolm X comparison often influences analyses of modern black leadership, once again with the assumption that men rather than women will be the leaders. Moreover, this more recent connection between masculinity and black leadership was further reinforced because African American women leaders were obliged to develop their leadership capabilities and strategies in the hypermasculine atmosphere of the Black Power philosophy of the late 1960s and early 1970s.

Regardless of prevailing opinions on the subject of black leadership, generations of African Americans from the end of slavery to the beginning of the civil rights movement quietly kept their focus on the core values and beliefs that sustained them during slavery. According to historian V. P. Franklin, "Afro-Americans valued survival with dignity, resistance against oppression, religious self-determination, and freedom throughout the history of slavery in this country." The black commitment to literacy exemplifies African American interest in these core values in the years following slavery. Franklin explains that "there developed within the Afro-American nation a preoccupation with literacy, schooling, and education in general. For thousands of newly emancipated Afro-Americans the acquisition of knowledge became as important an objective as holding on to their freedom."[26] Both Booker T. Washington and W. E. B. Du Bois wholeheartedly embraced the necessity of education, but their emphases were quite different. Washington advised the black masses to pursue vocational training that would make them better manual laborers; Du Bois advocated classical liberal arts education for the "Talented Tenth" of the race. But the majority of their black contemporaries quietly continued to pursue their individual and collective educational goals based on their own ideas of what was appropriate and useful for them as free black people through the late nineteenth and into the early twentieth century.

Whether or not these African Americans agreed with the specific educational philosophy of either Washington or Du Bois, they could agree on one thing: education was necessary for black uplift in postslavery America. Solidarity on this basic premise ensured that, regardless of the specifics of their educational programs, both Washington and Du Bois operated within a broad context of black support of the need for formal education. However, a century later, as today's African American leaders fret about low test scores and high dropout rates among black inner-city youth, many of these leaders cannot rely on a broad black belief in the power of education to change black lives. So, black leaders in the new millennium shake their heads in dismay and wonder how to reach a black constituency whose faith in the power of education has been badly shaken.

Another core value that earlier generations of African Americans embraced was their sense of community. It was a source of comfort for countless African Americans: from Booker T. Washington to W. E. B. Du Bois, and from the poorest sharecroppers to the most comfortable middle-class black entrepreneurs. The inclusive nature of the community meant that African Americans all over the country were united by a set of shared experiences and assumptions based on their skin color. As early as the beginning of the twentieth century, W. E. B. Du Bois insisted that because of their shared experiences, black people had their own "Afro American cultural values," which included "the desire for freedom, the ideal of education and book-learning, as well as self-development and self-realization of black self-determination."[27] Nearly a half century later in 1946, anthropologist Melville Herskovits, in his seminal work *The Myth of the Negro Past,* theorized that certain African cultural traits had survived the Middle Passage between the west coast of Africa and the east coast of America and that they formed the basis of a distinctive African American worldview. Barely two decades later, James Forman, a civil rights activist and secretary of the Student Nonviolent Coordinating Committee, insisted that black people were united because of their shared experiences in the New World. Forman argued that African Americans "had been molded into a nation of people through the process of capitalist development inside the United States."[28] Many African Americans agreed. For example, a black urban contemporary of Forman's asserted bluntly, "I know that it will probably bother your white readers, but it is nonetheless true that black people think of themselves as an entity." She went on to conclude, "We don't really agree with white people about anything important. If we were in power, we would do almost everything differently than they have. We are a nation primarily because we think we are a nation. This ground we have buried our dead in for so long is the only ground most of us have ever stood upon."[29]

These days, as black people grope toward an understanding of what it means to be black in post-civil-rights America, many fear that the feeling of connection between African Americans from all walks of life that existed before the movement has been shattered because being black and being American in the new millennium mean different things to different black people. For some, the brave new world of legal desegregation provides opportunities and options that their parents could never have imagined. This new reality can fundamentally change the way they view their relationship to the nation. But members of America's black underclass, whether they live in isolated rural areas or dilapidated inner cities, have a vastly different view than their middle-class brothers and sisters of their relationship to the country of their birth.

Thus, shifting opportunities, options, and obstacles facing African Americans have disrupted the sense of connection that united previous generations of black people and has historically served as the bedrock on which the traditional black community rested. Many are therefore convinced that the sense of community among African Americans has been lost. Not everyone takes this position, though. For example, Congresswoman Eleanor Holmes Norton, expressing her belief in the continued existence of a "black community" in the new millennium, claims that, even now, "there is a common culture in the black community; that when you are in a black community of another state, and a very different community, you [a black person] are at home." Norton recognizes, however, that this sense of community is different from before: "There have been some changes that none of us embrace; some of the low levels of hip hop." But, she argues, "generally you go into [a black] community; the kind of food, the kind of way people talk, the ambience. You're right [at] home then, and that's in any northern city or any southern city."[30]

It is this fundamental notion of community that over the years has provided the context for the existence of black leadership. More than one hundred years ago, W. E. B. Du Bois argued that only the black community could claim authority to choose its own leadership, and on that basis he questioned the legitimacy of the designation of Booker T. Washington as a leader:

Among his own people . . . Mr. Washington has encountered the strongest and most lasting opposition, amounting at times to bitterness, and even to-day continuing strong and insistent even though largely silenced in outward expression by the public opinion of the nation. . . . If the best of the American Negroes receive by outer pressure a leader whom they had not recognized before, manifestly there is here a certain palpable gain. Yet, there is also irreparable loss,—a loss of that peculiarly valuable education which a group receives when by search and criticism it finds and commissions its own leaders.[31]

In the years after Du Bois articulated this idea, at least up to the era of the civil rights movement, African American communities continued to "find and commission" their own leaders. Regardless of which famous black person was recognized by social critics and scholars as *the* black leader, black people quietly looked to the natural leaders who emerged within their midst. What set the natural leaders apart was a deep understanding of the circumstances confronting their black brothers and sisters and the will and the skill to provide solutions to their problems. So, in the late nineteenth century, when southern white landowners cheated poor black sharecroppers out of their profit from the sale of their crop, or insisted that they send their children out to the fields to work instead of sending them to school, these poor African Americans looked to the black community leaders in their midst who could intercede with "the white man" for them. These community leaders understood the lives that the desperately poor black people around them were living. They were so close to the slave experience that had defined their lives before the Civil War that many of them imagined they could still hear the whistling sound the lash made when it flew through the air a split second before they felt the sting on their backs. They could hear the rumbling in their bellies that never seemed to go away because they did not have enough to eat. They could feel the cramps in their muscles from bending over in the fields day after day. They could almost taste the fear that was their constant companion whenever they had any dealings with white people. Black community leaders knew their poor constituents needed a leader who empathized with these feelings and fears.

From the end of the nineteenth century until well into the twentieth, African Americans all over the country looked to the local leaders within their midst who understood their plight and who were prepared to offer practical solutions. Many of today's African American leaders have vivid memories of local leaders who worked for community uplift. For example, in this new millennium, James Perkins, the first African American ever elected to serve as mayor of Selma, Alabama, sitting in his office in the Selma City Hall, speaks of the crucial impact that the black leaders in his community had on his early life: "The images of black leadership that I embraced during my childhood were local religious and business personalities. Some, in fact, were in my family." Frowning thoughtfully, Mayor Perkins insists that there is one quality in particular that all these leaders had in common: "COURAGE. These men and women, they stood up and stood out when their lives were on the line. They demonstrated courage."[32]

Civil rights attorney Charles Jones has his office in the same neighborhood in Charlotte, North Carolina, where he lived with his family as a youngster. After assuming a leadership role in Charlotte's sit-ins in 1960, Jones went on to become head of SNCC's voter registration wing. Gazing out the window at his old neighborhood from his vantage point in the new millennium, Jones speaks of the childhood years he spent in Chester, South Carolina, before his family moved to Charlotte so many years ago. His speech is passionate with a rhythm and cadence that is every bit as ministerial as it is lawyer-like—he is from a long line of ministers that includes his father. Jones's thick mane of hair is liberally sprinkled with gray now, but his voice has not lost any of its intensity as he describes an upbringing rich in leadership role models. There was a group of black leaders, Jones recalls, and "They were clearly male [and] out front, as much out front [as they] could be in Chester, South Carolina in 1937. But they were black men who were professional. My father was one . . . they were masons, and they worked together to provide what I now am amazed at . . . protection for us children. . . . So, they were working folks, professional people, men, all of whom would meet . . . and helped shape what was possible for black folks to get out of the system."[33]

Congressman John Lewis, in his district office in Atlanta, Georgia, comments on the many models of leadership that he observed when he was growing up in rural Alabama. As he speaks, there is still a hint of the rural Alabama accent of his youth. For many years, John Lewis's face has been recognizable to Americans, both black and white, who followed the progress of the civil rights movement of the 1960s. He was involved in sit-in demonstrations in Nashville, Tennessee, in 1960. From there he went on to become a Freedom Rider in the spring of 1961. Lewis's young battered and bloody face was one of those prominently featured in news coverage of the interracial groups of Freedom Riders who faced the dangers of mob violence in southern bus stations. Later, Lewis was there at the foot of the Edmund Pettus Bridge in Selma, Alabama, in 1965 when the infamous Sheriff Jim Clark of Dallas County, along with county lawmen and a contingent of Alabama state troopers, beat and teargassed unarmed demonstrators. Lewis is no longer that slender young student of over forty years ago, but his memory of the early black leaders in his community has not faded. He explains, "Teachers, ministers; these are the people that I came in contact with. During the week in school, then [on] the weekend; at church on Sunday. The religious leaders, the school teachers. These were the leaders. These were the pillars in the community." Lewis continues:

> These individuals were leaders because they stood out. . . . They got in the way. They were the movers, the shakers, the doers. They had influence in the community. But when I really think about it, it was not just the ministers, the religious leaders, the teachers. [Instead], there were people [who] because of age, or because of what their standing in the community [was]. It could have been a grandmother, or great grandmother. It could have been a deacon in the church, or a barber, or a beautician. . . . They could bring people together. If somebody in rural Alabama was building a barn, or somebody lost a house, [for example] there would be somebody who would go out and pull people together, collect money, rally people to help rebuild the barn, or help rebuild the house, and in my estimation, these people were leaders.[34]

Congresswoman Eddie Bernice Johnson, as a young person, also found that leaders arose from various occupations. Johnson grew up in Waco, Texas, "in a very diverse neighborhood. On the block where I lived was a college president, a bishop, teachers, beauticians, construction [workers]. . . . It was a variety. I guess to some degree there were different models of leadership."[35] Joanne Bland, who later became involved in her community's voting rights struggle, also saw diverse leaders in Selma, Alabama, when she was growing up there. People like "Mrs. Amelia Boynton, Ernest Doyle, and others," Bland recalls. When she thinks about what made these people leaders, she insists that it was their commitment to the black freedom struggle and their courage. "They talked about it all the time they were around; they talked about this thing called freedom. . . . You could tell they believed in what they were doing so passionately, and I [as a child] always thought they were never afraid."[36]

Rev. Harold Middlebrook, a Baptist minister in Knoxville, Tennessee, who was active in the civil rights movement in his native Memphis, is convinced that the indigenous black leadership in Memphis was exceedingly effective. "There was an innate kind of leadership," he explains. "People just rose to leadership positions. In every community in Memphis there was a person *not elected by anybody*. But this was the person that everybody looked up to, and this person organized the clean-up, paint-up fix-up campaign in our community. This was the person who, if somebody died, organized to get the food to the house and the flowers to the funeral . . . it was all over the city."[37] Rev. Samuel Billy Kyles has been the pastor of Monumental Baptist Church in Memphis for over forty years and has strong memories of the civil rights leadership in the city. However, Kyles also reports that long before the civil rights movement, there was a variety of leaders in the African American community. "You've always had those levels of leadership where people [would say] I need more than this. . . . It occurs to me that you reach people with different tools . . . and one person can't be everything to all people."[38] Richard Hatcher, the first black mayor of Gary, Indiana, and one of the first of the northern black mayors elected after the passage of the Voting Rights Act of 1965, did not have to look far to find leadership role models when he was growing up. In his estimation, the most important black leadership role models were in his own family. He feels that the attitude displayed by his family members made them leaders. "With my family, [it was] the idea of the fight and the struggle—that was just a part of our everyday life."[39]

Andrew Young, former ambassador to the United Nations, former congressman representing the Fifth Congressional District in Atlanta, Georgia, former mayor of Atlanta, and a member of King's inner circle in the Southern Christian Leadership Conference, also finds that the leadership examples that shaped his early life were in his own family. "I guess I had good models in my parents," he says, "my father and my grandfather. My mother was very active in everything. I mean, it was a socially responsible family." Young is also careful to point out that his father worked through existing black institutions: "Daddy was on the board of the YMCA and the Urban League, and the NAACP."[40] Black organizations routinely served as incubators for black leadership in the early twentieth century, and black educational institutions, in particular, supplied a large number of leaders for the black community in the decades approaching the civil rights movement. For example, Professor John Hope Franklin recalls that one of the most important black leaders in Tulsa, Oklahoma, where he was raised, was the principal of Booker T. Washington High School. Later, as a student at Fisk University, he quickly recognized the importance of the black scholars and intellectuals who visited Fisk's campus. "You see, when you don't have an unlimited number of leaders, the leaders become even more outstanding. . . . We knew what black leadership was in those days. And when Mordecai Johnson, or Benjamin Mays, or Howard Thurman came to Fisk, you could suspend the requirement of attendance because they'd be there. The kids would be there when the doors were opened, they'd be there. . . . So we just revered all these people. We thought they were wonderful." As he reminisces about these powerful speakers on Fisk University's campus, Franklin concludes, "Their leadership qualities were not separate from their intellectual and professional accomplishments."[41]

Julian Bond assesses the importance of the leadership roles of these early black scholars the same way. Bond, the son of a prominent black educator and college president, became the communications director for the Student Nonviolent Coordinating Committee during the civil rights movement. He has the look and the sound of a black patrician who was nurtured in the bosom of black academia, and as he recalls his early life in an academic atmosphere, the eloquence of his speech also identifies him as a scion of Du Bois's "Talented Tenth." Referring to black colleges, Bond says that "a steady stream of black leaders came to these places. These were the only places these people could go and speak and be heard or teach and work. So these campuses were a magnet for these kinds of people."[42]

According to Bond, knowledge was one of the most important tools in the arsenal of the early black leaders who sought to help their people combat the pernicious effects of racism. He argues that black scholars and leaders "tended to be people who used their academic training to disprove all of the stereotypes about black people, and who demonstrated, using their academic training, what the enormous disparities were between blacks and whites in education, in everything." Because of these early influences, Bond says, "I think I began to realize fairly early on that you could use knowledge to advance the race."[43] Even though Bond and many of his black contemporaries considered these black scholars to be leaders, they understood that the scholars did not necessarily have a local constituency. Thus, in some instances African Americans were drawn to leaders based solely on the message they articulated and the solutions they proposed.

This was definitely the case for former congressman Frank Ballance, who was born in rural North Carolina. He remembers being influenced by a black leader from far outside his community: "As a child, teenager, I was aware through radio primarily, and then later through television, that I had a representative in the United States Congress. He was from Harlem, New York, and his name was Adam Clayton Powell." It did not matter that the Ballance family lived far away from Powell's New York congressional district. What mattered was that the flamboyant congressman's vigorous and public defense of black rights resonated with young Ballance. He says, "Don't ask me who my legal representative was, cause I don't know. . . . The person who spoke my language and advocated the issues that I was concerned about was Adam [Clayton] Powell. . . . I just remember that he was my man."[44]

In the years before the civil rights movement, then, there were layers of leadership in the African American community. While there were recognizable national black leaders, much more of this early black leadership was local and pragmatic. African Americans responded to a variety of black leaders based on their own personal views and preferences. Most were looking for the leader or leaders who could most effectively articulate their hopes and fears and deal with their frustration and anger. But most importantly, they were looking for someone who could help them combat that suffocating sense of powerlessness they felt. These words of

Albon Holsey, a black teenager in early-twentieth-century America, speak for most African Americans at the time:

> At fifteen, I was fully conscious of the racial difference, and while I was sullen and resentful in my soul, I was beaten and knew it. I knew then that I could never aspire to be President of the United States, nor Governor of my State, nor mayor of my city; I knew that the front doors of white homes in my town were not for me to enter, except as a servant; I knew that I could only sit in the peanut gallery at our theatre, and could only ride on the back seat of the electric car and in the Jim Crow car on the train. I had bumped into the color line and knew that so far as white people were concerned, I was just another nigger.[45]

For black leaders who yearned to help such desperate black people, the challenge in the decades before the civil rights movement was that they were trapped in the same powerless status as their followers. Their options were therefore limited. In such an atmosphere, Selma, Alabama, civil rights attorney J. L. Chestnut says, some form of accommodation was the only workable option: "Any black leader at the time who was not an accommodationist was in deep trouble. He was either crazy, a lunatic, irresponsible, or something bad happened to him."[46] Given this reality, Chestnut reasons, African American leaders had to be careful in their dealings with white people, because "any black leader who started criticizing the status quo would find no more morsels of power thrown his way by white Selma. This was the awful dilemma of black leadership in Selma—and in America. . . . I saw and understood the nakedness of black leaders."[47] Of course, black leaders had to be especially careful about their image in the black community too. If they appeared to accommodate too much to the local white power structure, their constituency would become suspicious of their motives. Consequently, the leaders had to perform a delicate balancing act; to err too far in one direction or the other could mean the loss of their black constituents' support or the alienation of the white power structure. In either case, their effectiveness as a leader would be compromised.

Chestnut is quick to insist that being an accommodationist did not necessarily mean that a leader was a race traitor. In an effort to explain how it worked, Chestnut used the example of Rev. Claude Brown, a black Presbyterian minister in Selma on the eve of the civil rights movement. Brown was a tall, light-skinned man with curly hair and a dignified bearing. Before the movement, he was recognized as a man who could help local black people with many different problems. Chestnut explains, "Claude had relationships with the mayor, and with members of the city council. If a black person got in trouble with another black person and went to Brown for help, Brown would call the mayor who, in turn, would call the Chief of Police."[48] Within this system of accommodation, Brown worked tirelessly in an attempt to help local African Americans, but there was only so much he could do.

Then, the civil rights movement began. Chestnut shakes his head sadly as he remembers. "Brown wanted to be respected by blacks and whites as he had been up to that point. But now the civil rights movement imposed different standards, different values." Brown was unable to make the transition. He looked around him at the chaos that accompanied demonstrations in his city and was horrified. He pleaded with black Selma residents to stop their children from leaving school and participating in the demonstrations, because such actions would teach them to disrespect authority, all authority. Chestnut says that Reverend Brown, with his brow knitted in concentration and a sad faraway look in his eyes, quietly asked his friends and neighbors, "What's going to happen when the movement dies and we have to pick up the pieces, and you will have taught these children to disrespect all authority?" Chestnut recalls that the more Brown made that argument, "the more out of favor he was becoming in important parts of the black community; the more the white community lifted him up [and] the more the black community pushed him down."[49]

Reverend Brown was devoted to the service of his people, but when the civil rights movement ushered in new expectations and methods of operation for black leaders, Brown's followers turned their backs on him. Instead, many were irresistibly drawn to the bold and daring field secretaries and other activists sent out by the Student Nonviolent Coordinating Committee or the Southern Christian Leadership Conference. The case of Bernard Lafayette of the Student Nonviolent Coordinating

Committee is an example. In 1963, SNCC sent Lafayette to Selma to work with the voter registration drive in that area. Florida native Bernard Lafayette was a young ministerial student who had begun his activist career by participating in the Nashville sit-in movement in 1960, and by the time SNCC sent him to Selma, he had been involved in numerous movement campaigns, including the Freedom Rides.

When the slender young freedom fighter arrived in Selma, he exuded an intense commitment and a youthful enthusiasm that Selma's young people found irresistible. Chestnut recalls, "Being young himself, Bernard had a knack with young people. To them, he was a sort of hero, a celebrity—a Freedom Rider! He recruited them on the street and in their homes, and he slipped onto the campus at Selma University and Hudson High School. Joe Yelder, the principal at Hudson, threatened to call the police on Bernard, but that didn't stop the recruiting effort. Students he'd already recruited would recruit others."[50] Older African Americans were not quite sure what to think of the intense young outsider, but they came to respect him after the night that Medgar Evers was assassinated, June 12, 1963.

Evers had been the head of the Jackson, Mississippi, chapter of the National Association for the Advancement of Colored People (NAACP), and his death was front-page news. On the same night Evers was killed, Bernard Lafayette was savagely attacked and beaten in front of the house where he was living in Selma. Yet, despite the severity of the beating, Lafayette was back on the streets of Selma the very next day, recruiting for the movement. When Chestnut saw him, he could not believe his eyes. As the lawyer drew closer to the young man, he realized that the bruised and bloodied freedom fighter still wore the same T-shirt he had worn the night before when he was attacked. It was caked with dried blood. Chestnut advised, "you need to go clean yourself up." Lafayette replied, "No way. This is the symbol we need."[51] Word spread rapidly of the attack and Lafayette's surprising appearance the next day. In hushed tones black Selma residents asked each other "Have you seen him?" The answer was "Yes. And his head is wrapped in bandages and he has blood on his T-shirt." This clear demonstration of the young activist's resolve motivated more people than ever to come out to the mass meetings. Here was a new kind of leader.

In the black community's collective consciousness, there were many stories of black defiance. Anger and resentment at the injustice of segregation often bloomed into open rebellion as African Americans were brutalized, both physically and psychologically, in segregated America. There would have been more open defiance except that African Americans knew the terrible consequences awaiting anyone who challenged the racial status quo. At times, though, even realizing that they might be brutalized or killed could not stop them. When black defiance surfaced publicly, most African Americans admired the courage it took to stand up to segregation. In most cases, the black community would practically buzz with excited whispers about the fate of the person who had defied "the white man." (Of course they had to be careful to hide their admiration for such black bravery from white people.) The collective consciousness of countless black communities is full of accounts of black men being spirited out of town just barely ahead of a lynch mob, or black men who were unable to make it out of town before the lynch mob caught them. There was always a fear, a fascination, and an awe that swirled around these victims or all-but-victims, because they had had the audacity to stand up to segregation.

Bernard Lafayette excited that same kind of awe and fascination, and he not only lived to tell about it; he quickly did it again. Because his actions demonstrated that there were other ways of dealing with white authorities, black Selma residents became excited about their own prospects for defiance. It must be noted, however, that the context in which Bernard Lafayette moved had never existed before. When others before him had resisted, they had been all alone. But when Bernard Lafayette stood up to white authorities in Selma in 1963, his challenge was part of the program of a national civil rights organization. Furthermore, both the media and the federal government were watching these black challenges with a great deal of interest; this outside scrutiny and support changed everything.

Most practitioners of the old style of black leadership, symbolized by Claude Brown, were uncomfortable with the new methods of leadership symbolized by Bernard Lafayette. The inability of Brown himself to adjust to the new order left him a broken man. By the time of his death in 1975, Reverend Brown had become a serious drinker, and there was a profound sadness in his eyes that never quite seemed to go away. His longtime attorney friend J. L. Chestnut begged him to stop drinking, but Brown would not or could not. Chestnut recalls sadly, "He started serious drinking in 1965. He wanted to be a responsible man and do right in the eyes of God. He wanted to be respected by blacks and whites. Yet he was being called an Uncle Tom in the black community and ineffective in the white community."[52]

As the context for black leadership continued to shift in communities all across the country—particularly in the South—this leadership drama played out in myriad black communities through the latter part of the 1960s. At this pivotal point in history, nobody knew what impact the death of the old black leadership model would have on the racial situation in America. But everyone knew that, no matter what happened, things could never be quite the same again.

3. After King, Where Do We Go from Here?

By the end of the 1960s, new black leadership models had emerged, accompanied by broader options and soaring expectations. Of course, the African American leader whose life and work was the most potent symbol of this new black leadership era was murdered just as the new era was beginning. That awful event traumatized the nation in general and African Americans in particular. In the decades that have passed since then, Americans from all walks of life—scholars and journalists, teachers and preachers, politicians and activists—have tried to make sense of the remarkable black activism of the sixties, the new black leadership that emerged from it, and the man whose life and death became its most potent public symbol. The result of all that public scrutiny is a variety of competing analyses, all professing to reveal the truth. Consequently, there remains considerable confusion in the popular consciousness about the development of the civil rights movement that produced a new cadre of black leaders and about the progression of Martin Luther King Jr.'s ideas as he neared the end of his life.

One of the most outrageous and provocative of those analyses is contained in a book by Michele Wallace. Published ten years after Dr. King's assassination, Wallace's book, *Black Macho and the Myth of the Superwoman,* contains a pessimistic and sexualized analysis of the black freedom struggle. According to Wallace, the civil rights movement was a colossal failure: "The Civil Rights Movement was the great test of the theory that whites could be persuaded of the equality of blacks. The theory that self-improvement was the cure-all turned out to be only one step away from self-contempt."[1] Furthermore, according to Wallace, as the struggle unfolded, the sexual conquest of white women by black men became a prerequisite of black male freedom.

Under pressure the white man enacted meaningless legislation. He continued to debate the inferiority of the black race. He gave blacks the right to vote and nothing to vote for, the right to buy but no money to buy with, the right to go wherever they wanted, but no transportation to get there. And lastly he told the black man to keep his penis tucked between his legs or there would be nothing at all. With good reason, the black man grew blind with rage. He decided he would do exactly what the white man wanted him to do the least. *He would debase and defile the white woman.*[2]

Wallace's views generated a great deal of interest among her contemporaries; she held many book signings, she made the talk-show circuit, and she lectured on many college campuses. But her provocative interpretation of the movement is only one of many that have cropped up in the years since King's death; and anyone seeking a fair and balanced portrayal of the progression of the movement and the evolution of King's ideas during this critical time must sort through a morass of information, misinformation, and conflicting interpretations.

A logical place to start is with King's last book, *Where Do We Go from Here? Chaos or Community.* One of the issues King addressed in that book was his concern about the development of black leadership in the wake of the major civil rights campaigns of the 1960s. His leadership vision can be seen in his statement, "Ultimately, a genuine leader is not a searcher for consensus but a molder of consensus. . . . I would rather be a man of conviction than a man of conformity."[3] By the time King's words appeared in print in 1967, a critical discussion of black leadership was already under way. The bold and audacious actions of young leaders like Bernard Lafayette were helping to fuel the discussion. At the same time, however, the discussion was motivated by what many saw as a breakdown in the black unity that had assured the civil rights movement's success in the early sixties.

The black journalist Louis Lomax was one of many social critics during that period who contributed to the black leadership dialogue. In his critical examination of what he called the Negro Revolt, Lomax observed, "The crisis in Negro leadership is largely a matter of public confusion

brought on by overlapping programs and a lack of cooperative planning."[4] Many of Lomax's contemporaries readily agreed with his assessment. For example, in an article in *Life* magazine, John K. Jessup argued,
"There are almost as many opinions on where the Negro Revolution
should go next as there are articulate Negroes. They range from black
nationalists, who preach separation from the white man, to mavericks. . . .
who suggest reviving the word 'nigger' in order to shame their race into
a crusade for self-improvement." Jessup went on to insist that despite the
variety of competing philosophies expressed by contemporary black leaders, the "wider spectrum of leaders . . . still base their hopes and strategies
on King's dream."[5]

The examination of movement goals and leadership strategies was
prompted in large part by the growing anger and resentment swirling
beneath the surface in America's black inner-city neighborhoods. In
August 1965, just a few years after Lomax's *The Negro Revolt* was published, that turmoil erupted into a race riot in the Watts section of Los
Angeles, and as Americans watched TV news coverage of the riot night
after night, most of them searched in vain for some sign of the quiet,
resolute strength they had seen on the faces of black marchers in Selma,
Alabama, the previous spring. What they saw instead on the black faces
from Watts flickering across their television screens was a pure unadulterated rage that was frightening in its intensity. In the chaos of Watts,
the sweet strains of the civil rights anthem "We Shall Overcome" were
replaced by the chants of "Burn Baby Burn." The explosion of black rage
on the West Coast caught many Americans off guard, because only five
days before the riot started, President Lyndon Baines Johnson had signed
the Voting Rights Act of 1965. The unprecedented bipartisan support
for the passage of this landmark legislation revealed that many Americans
were sympathetic to the black plight. As a *Life* editorial said, "It has been
emphatically established that the right to vote is the one Negro rights
question very nearly beyond debate anywhere in the United States." The
same editorial predicted, "There may never be another rights issue so
neatly and easily settled, because we appear for now to have exhausted
the possibilities of legislated redress. From here on, progress will be difficult because the problems are more subtle."[6] However, black residents
of Watts did not think there was anything subtle about the problems

they faced: substandard housing, inferior education, police brutality, and a high unemployment rate.

It was against this background that President Johnson summoned black leaders to the White House in early June 1966 for a civil rights summit. With the specter of burning city skylines hovering in their consciousness, many of the nation's best-known black leaders agreed to meet with the president. All those who took a seat around the conference table that day were impeccably attired in conservative business suits, they were all clean-shaven with close-cropped hair, and they were all men. Despite the leadership displayed by numerous exceptional women in the civil rights movement up to that point, the Johnson White House did not invite any of them to the civil rights summit. Undoubtedly, the emphasis on male leadership in the popular press, in particular, combined with the limited notions of female capabilities in 1960s America in general were what ensured that black women activists of the time would receive little recognition for their leadership abilities and accomplishments. As the Black Power philosophy that was publicly introduced within days of this White House conference took root over the next few months, it only served to strengthen this preexisting male chauvinism. Consequently, black female leaders in the late 1960s and early 1970s had more difficulty than ever making their voices heard.

But back at the White House Civil Rights Summit in June 1966, the black men gathered around the conference table were not thinking about gender issues. They were consumed by worries about racial strife and continuing economic and educational inequities. Soon they were joined by the most famous Texan in the country, Lyndon Baines Johnson: a deal-making, back-slapping politician who had used the N word in the past. Nevertheless, by the time of this meeting, President Johnson had demonstrated the strongest commitment to black civil rights of any president in American history. The atmosphere at the historic meeting was somber, each man painfully aware of the potential racial calamity that could befall the nation if they did not find the right solution. A. Phillip Randolph, the architect of the 1963 March on Washington, was the most senior of all black leaders in attendance that day. As he sat looking at the faces of his colleagues, he put the fears of those gathered around the conference table into words. He warned that the civil rights struggle "is becoming increasingly explosive. . . . I believe this is perhaps the greatest crisis we have faced since the Civil War."[7]

Whitney Young, director of the National Urban League, was also seated at the conference table that day. He wore the mantle of leadership as comfortably as he wore the custom-tailored business suit that was part of his identity. In his estimation, the crisis brewing on the horizon could be averted with an economic solution that he summed up in three words: jobs, jobs, and jobs. He was persuaded that "the Negro in business, the Negro with cash in the bank is in a position to lead." Because of Young's aggressive pursuit of this strategy, he spent more time in corporate board-rooms with white heads of corporations than with the black people who were the backbone of his organization. As a result, Young was in an awkward position. He admitted, "It's getting to be embarrassing. . . . Every day when I come down on the train from Westchester, I think I should get off at 125th Street [Harlem], go to a pool hall, make a speech or something. This is what gets you the publicity—go on TV and denounce the white man. But I go on downtown and sit on another committee."[8]

Conspicuous by his absence was Stokely Carmichael, the charismatic young leader of the Student Nonviolent Coordinating Committee. His big Afro, infectious hearty laugh, and casual dress (he wore denim overalls and work shirts) would have provided a stark contrast to the sober, earnest, conservatively dressed black men who sat around President Johnson's conference table. But Carmichael's organization had decided to boycott the conference. By this time the young activists in SNCC seemed to be shifting to the left of the other civil rights groups. Their move was motivated in part by the glaring inequities they found in American society when they began working with poor black residents in Deep South rural communities. Suddenly, the lunch counter sit-ins, Freedom Rides, and other direct-action campaigns that had been a staple of SNCC's activities ever since the organization's birth did not seem so important anymore. By the time of the White House conference, SNCC activists were much more concerned about helping poor black people by fostering "radical social, economic and political change." They elected Carmichael chairman of their organization, and observers inside and outside the movement anticipated that it was just a matter of time before he guided SNCC even further to the left. They did not have long to wait. Just days after the White House meeting, Carmichael publicly proclaimed his support of a new concept: Black Power. The clenched fist and bushy Afros that many white Americans came to associate with Black Power made them so uncomfortable that when SNCC's new chairman declared, "We feel that integration is irrelevant,"[9] some white people actually breathed a sigh of relief.

Yet, many of the black leaders at Johnson's conference, such as Cecil Moore, remained willing to work with white people or anyone else if black people could benefit. Moore headed the Philadelphia branch of the NAACP, and even though he was characterized by some as "foul mouthed, vituperative, and defiant," everyone agreed that he was totally focused on improving the black economic position. His position was "I don't want a white America, I don't want a black America, I want a green America."[10] Roy Wilkins, the head of the NAACP's national office, was also at Johnson's conference. Wilkins appeared more refined than his organization's Philadelphia branch manager. A slender man with café-au-lait skin, a slender face, salt-and-pepper hair, and a salt-and-pepper mustache to match, he had been to the White House for meetings many times before this summit. As head of the nation's oldest civil rights organization, he was equally comfortable in front of television cameras or in front of the president of the United States insisting, "Jobs, schools, housing—this is the backbone of our [the NAACP's] program [and] we're just plugging away at it."[11] Then, of course, Martin Luther King Jr., of the Southern Christian Leadership Conference, was at the White House meeting that day. Everyone around the conference table agreed that King was the best known of all the black leaders. SNCC staffer Bernard Lafayette, King's choice to serve as the national coordinator of the Poor People's Campaign, succinctly observed, "Martin Luther King was a leader of leaders. . . . Martin Luther King was able to galvanize and bring all them [black leaders] together."[12]

Because of King's visibility, African American leaders at Johnson's summit were aware that by this time, King was just beginning to shift his focus from the Deep South to the urban North. He explained the reason for this change in *Where Do We Go from Here*. "The disappointment mounts," he lamented, "as they turn their eyes to the North. In the Northern ghettoes, unemployment, housing discrimination and slum schools mock the Negro who tries to hope." He acknowledged the civil rights movement's gains but reasoned, "These beginnings have revealed how far we have yet to go. The economic plight of the masses of Negroes has worsened. The gap between the wages of the Negro worker and those of the white worker has widened. Slums are worse and Negroes attend more thoroughly segregated schools today than in 1954."[13] According to King, material circumstances for the black underclass needed to be improved, but at the same time, he insisted that this was not nearly enough. King argued that the psychological oppression accompanying economic, social, and educational oppression would also have to be addressed before African Americans could truly become free:

> The tendency to ignore the Negro's contribution to American life and strip him of his personhood is as old as the earliest history books and as contemporary as the morning's newspaper. To offset this cultural homicide, the Negro must rise up with an affirmation of his own Olympian manhood. As long as the mind is enslaved the body can never be free. Psychological freedom, a firm sense of self-esteem, is the most powerful weapon against the long night of physical slavery. . . . The Negro will only be truly free when he reaches down to the inner depths of his own being and signs with the pen and ink of assertive selfhood his own emancipation proclamation.[14]

Above all, as African Americans continued their quest for freedom, King advised, they would have to find a way to make peace with their own identity. He explained, "The Negro's greatest dilemma is that in order to be healthy he must accept his ambivalence. The Negro is the child of two cultures—Africa and America. The problem is that in the search for wholeness all too many Negroes seek to embrace only one side of their natures."[15] Thus, more than six decades after W. E. B. Du Bois had cried out in frustration, "One ever feels his twoness," Martin Luther King Jr. was convinced that African Americans would never truly be free until they were able to heal that twoness and conquer the racial schizophrenia that characterized African Americans in the United States. When King spoke to the other leaders at President Johnson's summit in 1966, his words left no doubt that his vision was much broader and deeper than it had been eleven years earlier in 1955 when the Montgomery Bus Boycott had catapulted him to prominence.

Weighing heavily on King that day was the problem of divisions that had begun to appear in the ranks of black freedom fighters. He was especially worried about the young advocates of Black Power who seemed to have run out of patience. Even though he disagreed with certain parts of the Black Power philosophy, he did not doubt the sincerity of these young people. He sympathized with their disappointment at the slow pace of change in American society thus far, because he, too, was disappointed, and he articulated that disappointment forthrightly: "It is a disappointment with timid white moderates who feel that they can set the timetable for the Negro's freedom. It is disappointment with a federal administration that seems to be more concerned about winning an ill-considered war in Vietnam than about winning the war against poverty here at home. It is a disappointment with white legislators who pass laws in behalf of Negro rights that they never intended to implement. It is disappointment with the Christian church that appears to be more white than Christian." But King's criticism did not target white Americans only. He found fault with the actions of some African Americans during the black freedom struggle, black ministers in particular: "It is disappointment with some Negro clergymen who are more concerned about the size of the wheelbase of their automobiles than about the quality of their service to the Negro community." Finally, as far as King was concerned, the actions of the black middle class were particularly disappointing, because they had "sailed or struggled out of the muddy ponds into the relatively fresh-flowing waters of the mainstream, and in the process . . . [had] forgotten the stench of the backwaters where their brothers [were] drowning."[16] Thus, as he sat studying the faces of the black leaders seated around the White House conference table at President Johnson's summit, King clearly understood that their struggle was entering a new phase.

Many of King's contemporaries, black and white, inside the movement and out, were coming to the same conclusion. Most recognized that the changing nature of the struggle was accompanied by a profound shift in black attitudes. An editorial in *Life* magazine in 1966 approvingly explained that there was a "new Negro mood" among African Americans. The editor warned white Americans about what they could expect from this "New Negro." Predicting that "a new Negro readiness to fight [would] be evident . . . not just in the red-hot fringe but in a more general assertiveness and even arrogance," he advised that "whites should be prepared for this. A great deal of mutual hurt may be the price of the candid confrontation that is rending the old veil of caste. Let none bemoan the fact that Negroes no longer 'know their place.' The reason they don't is that they are in the course of occupying a new place—and about time too." That same spring, Adam Clayton Powell Jr., the flamboyant and irrepressible black congressman from Harlem, delivered the commencement address at Howard University, one of the best-known black universities in the country. During his address, Powell articulated the "New Negro mood" when he advised his audience that "the era of compromise is gone." His voice rising to a crescendo, the eloquent Powell concluded that the time for demonstrations was past and that African Americans now had to "SEEK BLACK POWER . . . AUDACIOUS POWER." The words rolling off Powell's tongue were so powerful that they almost seemed to swagger.[17]

Many black leaders were convinced that one of the main reasons for the new group assertiveness and determination was the growing frustration of the black underclass. For example, Bayard Rustin, a leftist black radical who had worked with the civil rights movement from the beginning, a close adviser to King, and one of the architects of the March on Washington in 1963, bluntly insisted that many African Americans living in the inner city felt more alienated than ever. "They are saying, 'Let's get Whitey. Let's put his head in the bowl and pull the chain.' This says something to the poor guy on the corner who can only make a living by selling pot. There are too many guys like this and we're not doing enough for him." Rustin gloomily predicted that black anger and alienation would reach a boiling point, and when that happened, "I think we're in for it."[18]

Dan Watts, the black militant publisher of the *Liberator* magazine, who agreed with Rustin about the alienation of poor African Americans, was also concerned about the actions of some members of the black middle class who were willing to work with the white power structure, perhaps

a little too closely. White use of these black collaborators, in Watts's estimation, helped to create an illusion of progress, but it was only an illusion. "It seems to me," he said, "that whatever big IBM machine decides
which Negro is going to make it in his field just isn't working right.
Invariably it picks the guy who basically hates his own race and wants to
play white man." Another angry black militant insisted that the use of
black collaborators actually exacerbated racial strife: "When the blowup
comes . . . it'll be at least partly because The Man [Whitey] feels he
has kept up on racial matters by having lunch downtown with Whitney
Young or Roy Wilkins. He mistakes what the black Anglo-Saxons tell him
for the cry of the black masses."[19] Amiri Baraka, a playwright and one of
the best-known leaders of the cultural black nationalists, issued a general
condemnation of white people: "I don't think it is necessary to make anything clear to the white man except perhaps that most of the people in the
world would be better off if the white man didn't exist."[20]

White Americans were frightened by such angry pronouncements,
but they were even more frightened when the black anger turned to violence. Of course, race riots were nothing new in America, but the sheer
scale of the Watts riot just the year before Johnson's conference had been
unprecedented. Then, when Detroit erupted barely a year after the historic Civil Rights Summit, Americans were forced to admit that the brazen
audacity of these most recent riots seemed to signal that a new black consciousness had moved into America's inner cities. Watts had been big, but
Detroit was even bigger, and the extent of the violence and destruction
took the nation by surprise; Detroit had a reputation as a big city that had
achieved racial harmony. In fact, in the months following the upheaval in
Watts, worried social scientists and fearful social critics alike had studied
America's largest cities and concluded that more urban unrest was likely.
But when they compiled a list of the cities most likely to erupt, Detroit
was not even on the list. What they thought were "the hottest prospects
at the moment," in addition to Los Angeles, were Oakland, Washington,
D.C., New York City, and St. Louis.[21]

Nobody expected trouble in Detroit because during those prosperous times for the auto industry, most Americans thought of Detroit as the
home of the Motown sound and the capital of the American auto industry where big fins, big engines, and lots of chrome ruled, and where the

employment picture for black workers was more rosy than in any other city in the country. In 1967 black workers in Detroit had a higher per capita income than black workers anywhere else in America. The city's young Irish Catholic mayor, Jerome Cavanaugh, was considered the "Golden Boy among U.S. mayors . . . who seemed to personify the surging prosperity of Detroit," and who also seemed to have the support of Detroit's huge black community.[22] Just months before Detroit erupted in the most costly race riot in American history up to that time, the city was basking in positive press: "Leaders of the Great Society and civic officials from across the country were flocking to Detroit to see how Jerry Cavanaugh did it. He was a pioneer for model cities, and his pilot programs—including anti-poverty centers, job-training centers, a youth employment project—had become the early design for federal programs."[23] But after the destruction of nearly eight days of rioting in late July of 1967, social scientists and government officials were left to wonder if any place in the country was safe from the rage that seemed to have settled over black communities in the country like a sinister black cloud.

Even corporate America was alarmed. For example, General Motors, at that time the largest corporation in the world, made an unprecedented offer. The chairman of the board sent Mayor Cavanaugh a telegram that read, "The facilities, skills and resources of General Motors and its people are available to assist in the planning required to insure the prompt and effective rebuilding of Detroit. [signed] Frederick G. Donner, Chairman of the board, and James M. Roche, President." After reading it, the amazed Cavanaugh exclaimed, "It's practically a carte-blanche offer—and coming from General Motors! That's a landmark."[24] But while the mayor undoubtedly appreciated the auto giant's offer, he was having trouble coping with bewilderment and frustration as he toured the neighborhoods in his city that had practically been leveled by enraged rioters. He said sadly, "We did the textbook things here in Detroit. We did more than any other city in police-community relations, anti-poverty, inner-city schools, job training—the whole bit. I was sure of myself, got praised, and now I can't guarantee anything." His confidence badly shaken, he lamented, "But I can't pull the covers over my head and pretend those recent events didn't happen. That's the way it is with the whole nation. None of us can pull the cover over our heads any more."[25] By this time, many white Americans wished they could ignore the new black anger, but they knew better.

Yet, there were still some people, both black and white, who stubbornly clung to hope for more peaceful change. One editorialist opined, "The vast majority [of African Americans] probably still believe that equality can be won by peaceful means and that force would be self-defeating."[26] As late as the spring of 1968, just weeks before King was assassinated, many still hoped for a peaceful solution. John Gardner, former secretary of Health, Education and Welfare, was one of those optimists. In March 1968 he articulated what many of his fellow Americans were thinking when he insisted, "Poverty is not easy to eliminate, whether the poor are black or white. In the case of the Negro it is made harder by the evil of racism. . . . I have heard the authentic voices of hatred, and the threats of violence—from white men and black. But those who hate cannot save us; they can only destroy." Gardner maintained his faith in his country's power to effect change. He advised, "We must begin with a massive resolve on the part of the great, politically moderate majority of whites and blacks—to transform destructive emotion into constructive action." In the final analysis, he warned, "We cannot have two nations, one white and one black. Every time we salute the flag we pledge allegiance to 'one nation indivisible.' One nation it must remain."[27]

Although some held on to optimism, as the 1960s came to a close— even after the passage of the Civil Rights Act of 1964 and the Voting Rights Act of 1965 and the creation of Affirmative Action—many white Americans were worried about the explosive black rage that they could not understand. At the same time, African Americans were left wondering what their relationship to this new American legal reality would be. Most wanted to believe that things would truly and finally become better, but after the long string of disappointments and broken promises they had endured, little hope remained. In that unsettled atmosphere, many of them could relate to the words of the rhythm and blues song "Ball of Confusion," by Motown's Temptations, which begins,

People moving out, people moving in;
Whyyyy because of the color of the skin;
Run, run, run, but you sure can't hide.

In line after line, the song's intensity builds:

The cities ablaze in the summertime;
and oh ohhhhh, the beat goes on.

In the song's conclusion, a driving beat combines with the Temptations' powerful voices to capture the frantic atmosphere of that era:

Great googamooga can't you hear me talkin' to you.
It's a ball of confusion.
That's what the world is today, hey, hey.[28]

Yet, regardless of their confusion about their relationship to their country, most African Americans felt a sense of loss when they first heard about the death of Martin Luther King on April 4, 1968. It was an event of such importance to African Americans that many clearly remember where they were and what they were doing at the moment when they heard the awful news. Those who were closest to King have particularly painful memories of that day. Rev. Samuel Billy Kyles, from his vantage point on the balcony of the Lorraine Motel, gazed with shock and horror at King's still form a split second after the shot rang out. He explains, "When I saw Martin lying there on that balcony, I could just feel the loss that we were going to experience. . . . I knew that would be a heavy burden to get beyond. But in a real sense we were traumatized. . . . We were in shock."[29]

Andrew Young, who raced up the steps from the parking lot below, recalls, "I realized as soon as I ran up there and saw that he'd been hit that he was dead. In fact, I saw where the bullet penetrated the tip of his chin and tore his spinal chord in half. And in some ways I was feeling that he had deserved his reward."[30] Rev. Ralph Abernathy, King's handpicked successor to head the Southern Christian Leadership Conference, raced out of room 306 as soon as he heard the shot. For a split second, he could not comprehend the scene confronting him, but as soon as the horror penetrated his consciousness, he dropped to his knees at King's side. He cried out in an anguished voice, "Martin, this is Ralph. . . . Can you hear me? Can you hear me . . . ?" King's eyes seemed to be fixed on the face of his right-hand man, but he was incapable of speech, and those bending over him were not sure that he could actually see anything. Some were shocked that the inconsolable Abernathy was trying to collect some of King's blood in a jar.[31] As Young stood there in the midst of the chaos, the memory of a recent meeting with the fallen King came to his mind: "Well, he had met with us about three or four days before. It was [the] only time I ever saw him sort of fuss at people and tell them off. He was fussing about the fact that we let him get out there by himself and that we needed to all assume more leadership responsibility, and that he always supported us in any of our ideas but . . . some of the staff didn't particularly like the idea of the Poor People's Campaign. Almost nobody wanted him to go to Memphis." Young shook his head sadly as the memory continued to play through his mind. "We saw Memphis as a distraction. And he just said that this was what he felt he needed to do and that we needed to both help him with this, but also carry more of the burden. He said, 'you don't have to wait for me to speak out on everything.' So in a sense, he had given us marching orders before his death." Later that evening, after Young and King's other close associates returned from the hospital, Young recalls, "We all got together and we decided that . . . you never let death stop the movement, because if you do, you send the message that you can kill us . . . so we were determined to send the message that the movement [had not] stopped."[32]

Former SNCC staffer Charles Jones recalls that in the weeks after King's death, he and his SNCC colleagues were equally determined to keep the movement alive. Jones was in Washington, D.C., when he heard the news, and he immediately thought about the impact of this tragedy on the future of the movement. According to Jones, by the time King was assassinated, "We had come to understand how change takes place; and it is not standing up giving the broad speeches, though that's critical because Martin had this magic that inspired everybody. But, it was the organization that got people to the meeting that allowed him to [deliver his speeches]. So we were in the churches doing the creative organizing. . . . We knew where the real power was. The real power was in organizing —the people."[33] Thus, even though Jones was personally saddened by the news, his commitment to organizing for the black freedom struggle never wavered. Longtime King associate and SNCC staffer John Lewis was not in Memphis when King was shot, but he remembers exactly where he was when he received the news. He was in Indianapolis, Indiana, campaigning for Senator Robert Kennedy, a candidate for the Democratic nomination for president in 1968. Lewis considered King's death a serious blow to the black freedom struggle because "Martin Luther King had emerged in my mind as the undisputed symbol of the civil rights movement. He was a mass leader."[34]

Birmingham native and activist James Armstrong had marched with King in the historic Selma-to-Montgomery march. He was devastated when news of the assassination reached him: "That was the hurtinest [sic] thing in my life because, well, I knew it was the end of the world." The old man pauses and stares off into the distance as he remembers King's importance in his life and explains, "Granddaddy was a man [who] I always said, taught me how to make a living, cause I grew up around him. But I met Dr. King, [and] he taught me how to live."[35] Julian Bond recalls that he and other members of SNCC had their differences with King's philosophy, but they still respected him and his commitment to the cause. "Behind his back we joked at him," Bond said, "but, you know, we loved him, and were just devastated when he died. But I immediately thought, what's going to happen to the movement now without this guy? We just lost so much; this is irreplaceable. . . . There's no substitute. There's nobody in the wings."[36]

In Selma, Alabama, Joanne Bland can still describe the precise instant she heard the news: "I was home when I first heard it. . . . I went down to Brown Chapel Church. People were already hollering and crying. . . . It was just awful." By that time Bland was one of a few black Selma students who were integrating the local high school, and the adults were concerned about the prospect of racial incidents in the wake of the assassination. "The next morning when we woke up, there was some discussion whether we should go to school . . . [but] it was decided—I guess all the parents got together and decided that we would go." However, trouble started as soon as the black students arrived at school. "It was awful," Bland reports. "Soon as we got to school, they [white students] started taunting us. . . . Most of us got sent home before the day was over." Bland laughs heartily at the memory: "They said they feared for our safety. They didn't have to fear for mine cause I was kicking some butt." Even though she was young when King was killed, Joanne Bland had seen her share of civil rights struggles by that time, so she knew how hard black people had worked. Looking back on that time, Bland declared, "I was determined not to give up anything when he died."[37]

Robert Booker, Student Government Association president and leader of student sit-ins at Knoxville College in 1960, agrees that with King's death the civil rights movement suffered irreparable damage. He explains, "I think we lost focus. He was the drum major. He told us what we ought to be doing [and] we don't have that anymore."[38] Bernard Lafayette was also concerned about the future of the movement: "King was dead. His view of the movement at that point; the future was very much uncertain. Cause we all knew that things would not be the same. Because it was like the death of a movement. The King era was over. So we didn't know what kind of leadership was going to emerge in the organization." In addition to his concern for the future of the movement, Lafayette was worried about the safety of other black leaders. He explains, "We knew that he wanted Abernathy to replace him, but we didn't know whether or not this was going to be a series of killings. So we didn't know whether other leaders were going to be killed."[39] Rev. Al Sharpton was only a teenager when King was assassinated, but he vividly remembers his reaction. He was watching television when he learned the news: "I was home with my mother. . . . I was shocked because I had already joined Operation Breadbasket. . . . My mother was hysterical. She grew up in Dothan, Alabama so she first hand grew up under segregation. I had seen it visiting the South with my parents. . . . But she absolutely grew up under it, so she took it very personally. . . . I think it was his death that helped me commit that this is really the kind of ministry I wanted. . . . I was interested in a social ministry and that's what I've done ever since."[40]

Carol Moseley Braun was also a teenager when King was assassinated. Braun, born and raised in Chicago, later became the only African American woman ever elected to a seat in the U.S. Senate. When King took the movement north to Chicago in 1966, Braun, at age fifteen, marched with him. She holds the experience as "one of the proudest moments that I can relate." During the march white hecklers began throwing rocks and bottles, and she became so angry that she was ready to throw something back, but because of King's influence, she did not. She explains, "His example in that situation gave me a glimpse into the profound philosophical underpinnings of nonviolence as a response, and why he had taken the approach that he did." This experience was particularly important at this point in her life because "Half of my friends were joining the [Black] Panthers." In fact, Braun was a friend of Fred Hampton, a Black Panther who was later killed in a shootout with Chicago police. Braun concludes, "A lot of my friends were going [in] the direction of the violent responses . . . and I think that the Dr. King experience kept me in a different path."[41] Fellow Chicago resident Timuel Black, a founding member of the Congress of Racial Equality (CORE), agrees with Braun's assessment of King's critical importance. As he puts it, "King became the symbol, the intellectual symbol and the articulate spokesperson for the feelings that we all had. Nobody could do it that well."[42]

To the east of Chicago in Detroit, Michigan, Maureen Taylor, a former member of the Detroit chapter of the Black Panther Party, was shaken when she heard about King's death. She was riding a city bus with her younger sister at the time, and the tragic news prompted her to reflect on the destructive and violent race riot that had engulfed her city the summer before. She explains her feelings at the time:

> Shock, and tremendous sadness, and fear because I saw anger on the streets of Dexter [a major thoroughfare in Detroit] that I had only seen the year before in July. . . [during the riot]. I saw that. And here it is now in April on a clear day, and I'm holding my baby sister's hand who is right next to me trembling, and I told her "just hold on, cause I don't know what to make of this cause this is so horrible, I don't know what's going to happen. And these people out here, if it wasn't for you I'd be out there with them." [We] went down a few more blocks; I just never saw anything like it.

Taylor saw people breaking out store windows and looting, but then she saw an even more frightening spectacle: "I saw people laying on the ground that already had been beaten up. I saw gangs of people roving around. Two or three people got on the bus. There were two or three white folks on the bus. They snatched one of them off. The bus driver asked, please leave these two ladies alone. I begged and pleaded." After a few tense moments, "The bus driver was given permission to drive on."[43]

In Washington, D.C., a "young black gangster" whose nickname was Spanky recalled the rage he felt when King was killed, even though he did not believe in King's nonviolent philosophy. He explained that King's death "killed a lot of hopes. . . . Don't get me wrong . . . I don't necessarily say that I would have been one of those nonviolent marchers with him, but everybody knows that he was out there trying to work this thing out the right way. But after he was killed, I said, 'What's the use?' There ain't nothing left, man. A lot of people feel that way. All hope is gone now. Nobody's going to get out there like he did."[44] Charles Jones notes that the rage felt by Spanky and other young black D.C. residents provided a fertile breeding ground for urban unrest in the nation's capital. Frowning at the memory, Jones declares, "When Martin was assassinated, among other things, the District of Columbia exploded." As the violence intensified, Jones and other black leaders knew that they had to take action. "We assembled a leadership [group]; some leadership called the Black United Front. Stokely [Carmichael], myself, [Walter] Fauntroy; and the primary issue was [that] we need to be in control of the process that rebuilds this city."[45]

The ferocity and pervasiveness of black anger at this moment in history was frightening in its intensity. Movement insider Bayard Rustin tried to explain the source: "The murder of Dr. King tells Negroes that if one of the greatest among them is not safe from the assassin's bullet, then what can the least of them hope for? In this context, those young black militants who have resorted to violence feel vindicated. 'Look what happened to Dr. King,' they say. 'He was non-violent, he didn't hurt anybody. And look what they did to him. If we have to go down, let's go down shooting. Let's take whitey with us.'"[46] Famous black photojournalist Gordon Parks offered an emotional explanation of the depth of the black anger at white society that had been unleashed by King's assassination:

He [King] spent the last dozen years of his life preaching love to men of all colors. And for all this, a man, white like you, blasted a bullet through his neck. And in doing so the madman has just about eliminated the last symbol of peace between us. We must struggle to distinguish between *his* act and *your* conscience. It is not enough any more when you ask that all whites not be blamed for what one did. You must know how we really feel—before grass takes root over Dr. King's grave. We are angry. All of us.

Parks went on to insist that he had talked to a broad cross section of African Americans, including "the Black Nationalists in Los Angeles, ministers from Minnesota and New York, [and] college students in Atlanta." As a result, he warned ominously, "Believe this, no matter what anyone else tells you: you have pushed us to the precipice."[47] Down in Selma, Alabama, civil rights attorney J. L. Chestnut Jr. was left to lament the profound impact of King's death on the future of the black freedom struggle. He explains, "Before Martin Luther King's body was cold in its grave, the white leadership was saying, 'we've had enough demonstrations and marches. We need to sit down now and talk.' They tried to sell that to Martin and never were able to do it. But the moment we buried him they [white leaders] did sell it. And the moment we gave up marching and demonstrating, we've been on the defensive ever since."[48]

The black anger, disappointment, and disillusionment were so profound that African Americans both inside and outside the civil rights movement were left in a state of profound confusion. It was at this critical moment in history that many Americans, both black and white, began to redefine King the martyr and his importance from their own particular perspective. Rev. T. Randel Osburn, one of King's movement colleagues, succinctly explains the process of the appropriation and manipulation of King's memory that seemed to start almost as soon as he was killed: "The truth of it is, after Martin Luther King was dead and you kept getting the birthday, the celebrations, and all that, everybody interpreted him. The tragedy is, everybody interpreted Martin Luther King from their perspective and from what they could do."[49]

In this atmosphere of uncertainty, trauma, and sadness, the specter of the martyred Dr. Martin Luther King Jr. hung over America like a cloud. The cloud contained the tear gas sprayed onto the black demonstrators in the South during the struggles over black voting rights and equal access to public accommodations; the napalm and the Agent Orange sprayed in the jungles in Vietnam; all the disappointments that had accompanied members of the Mississippi Freedom Democratic Party when they returned home to Mississippi after the Democratic Party refused to seat them at its national convention in 1964; and all the tears that had been shed at all the funerals of civil rights activists, both black and white, who had died for the cause. In short, in the wake of King's death, many African Americans were left wondering if the black freedom struggle could ever get back on track, because in a real sense that shot in Memphis not only killed King; it also killed what was left of black America's innocence.

Even for those African Americans who had not embraced King's nonviolent philosophy, whether they were disillusioned members of what was left of the Student Nonviolent Coordinating Committee, members of the Black Panther Party for Self Defense, or even numbers runners or gang members in black inner-city neighborhoods, King had become *the* symbol of black leadership in America. The eloquent black Baptist preacher from Atlanta seemed to have found a way to make white America listen to him. He had been the guest of presidents and kings; his advice had been sought by labor organizers and religious leaders. His commitment to nonviolence had never wavered, and he had even won the Nobel Peace Prize. But in the end, he had been the victim of the kind of white violence against African Americans that seemed to be as old as America itself. If Martin Luther King Jr. was not safe from white violence and brutality, many asked themselves, then who was? In the days and weeks after the assassination, that question reverberated through the minds of black leaders as they looked for ways to make African Americans feel both hopeful and safe in post-King America.

4. The Media and the Message

In the grim days following Dr. King's death, Rev. Ralph Abernathy was full of grief and full of insecurity about trying to fill a martyr's shoes. One *New York Times* reporter observed, "The Rev. Ralph David Abernathy did not look like a leader at that moment. Numb from lack of sleep, jowls unshaven, he spoke haltingly as some staff members gathered around to help while others drifted off to their private griefs." Abernathy's first public words in the immediate aftermath of the assassination did nothing to pierce the veil of uncertainty that had settled over the remnants of the black freedom struggle. In a voice husky with emotion, he began, "The assassination of Martin Luther King, Jr. has placed upon my shoulders the task . . ." Abernathy stopped and looked wordlessly at the circle of King advisers around him. The sadness in the room was so thick it was almost suffocating. He continued, "No, make that 'the awesome task.' The awesome task of directing the organization he established, which has given—what do we say here—'hope'?" Abernathy paused again, searching the faces of those gathered around him. But all he saw were eyes puffy from weeping and lines of grief and pain creasing the skin around closed mouths. He went on, "So much hope to the black people—to the oppressed people of this nation. Even after fifteen years of sharing the struggle with Dr. King, I tremble as I move forward to accept this responsibility. No man can fill Dr. King's shoes."[1]

Those closest to both King and Abernathy are quick to point out that Abernathy was forever haunted by the shadow of the martyred Martin Luther King Jr. A short time after the assassination, Abernathy's discomfort at living in King's shadow caused him to declare defiantly, "Don't ever get it in your mind it was Martin Luther King's dream only. It was Ralph David Abernathy's dream too. So no need of asking me to be Martin Luther King. . . . I've been Ralph David Abernathy for 42 years and each time I look in the mirror in the morning, I look better and better."[2] Despite his bluster, Abernathy was clearly insecure about the endless comparisons between his leadership style and that of the martyred King. Andrew Young reports that privately Abernathy would sometimes plead with him, "Why don't you write beautiful speeches for me like you wrote for Martin?" Young's reply was always the same: "Ralph, you know better than anybody else that I never wrote a single speech for Martin Luther King."[3] Abernathy would then go out to face the black community, the media, and the inevitable comparisons yet again.

In the wake of King's assassination, riots broke out: hellish fires consumed large portions of many black neighborhoods, and snarls of rage became fixed on the faces of black inner-city dwellers all over the country. These black people were not singing "We Shall Overcome." Instead, they were making demands. In his 1968 book *Look Out Whitey! Black Power's Gon' Get Your Mama!* SNCC field secretary Julius Lester expressed his fear that African Americans were facing a grim and uncertain future: "The old order passes away. Like the black riderless horse, boots turned the wrong way in the stirrups, following the coffin down the boulevard, it passes away. But there are no crowds to watch as it passes. There are no crowds to mourn and weep. No eulogies to read and no eternal flame is lit over the grave." Lester's description is reminiscent of the funeral procession following the death of President John F. Kennedy just five years earlier. Lester was convinced that whether anyone acknowledged it or not, the change following King's death was just as important as the political change that accompanied President Kennedy's death. Americans may not have been ready for it, but, according to Lester, "The new order is coming, child. The old is passing away."[4]

The black expressions of anger and grief were soon met with white calls for the restoration of law and order. Julius Lester observed, "If the press had ever screamed as loudly for an end to segregation and discrimination as it screamed for law and order, segregation and discrimination would be a vague memory today." The young activist continued: "'Law and order must prevail' has become the cliché of the 1960's and the biggest lie, because the American black man has never known law and order except as an instrument of oppression, and it has prevailed upside his head at every available opportunity. It exists for that purpose. The law has been written by white men, for the protection of white men and their property, to be enforced by white men for the protection of white men against blacks in particular and poor folks in general."[5] Coincidentally, 1968 was an election year, and during the campaign, Republican candidate Richard Nixon highlighted the issue of law and order, promising to make its restoration a priority. Many white Americans were receptive to the candidate's promise, and that fall a majority voted to send Richard Nixon to the White House. Nixon's victory signaled that American society had come full circle since the election of 1960, when Democratic candidate John F. Kennedy, who was perceived to be more sympathetic to civil rights issues, had barely edged out Nixon. At that point most political observers were convinced that Nixon's political career was dead. But just eight years later, Kennedy was dead, King was dead, Nixon was the president-elect, most white Americans were tired of hearing about civil rights issues, and most African Americans were tired of talking about them.

In this volatile atmosphere, increasing numbers of African Americans also came to consider law and order an important issue, but their perspective was totally different: they believed that all the white rhetoric about law and order was just a cover for a new and even more aggressive policy of black repression. Black militants were among the first to sound the alarm. For example, H. Rap Brown, Stokely Carmichael's successor as head of the Student Nonviolent Coordinating Committee, declared that African Americans were about to be exterminated. He asserted: "Remember hearing about those 500 sheep that got killed out in Colorado last summer? What do you think that was all about? *Really?* Don't you know that cracker is getting it ready? It was gas." Brown went on to explain that the gas was then transported to the East Coast. He said, "That cracker told you in his jive newspapers and television that he had to stop along the way for 'repairs' and to 'check on the safety' of that stuff." Brown scoffed, "Dig that crap! Where did he stop? Yeah—where did he stop? He stopped in Omaha, Chicago, Cleveland, Washington, Baltimore—he stopped in 37 cities that have the biggest number of niggers. *That's* where he stopped." Brown concluded,

The cracker is ready.
Back in the Pentagon, he's got a pickup list with a million niggers on it. All he's got to do is push a button, and in nine

seconds he got a telegram landing on the chief of police's desk telling where you're at. The concentration camps are waiting. And when that cracker gets done with this 1970 census, he's got all the jive he needs—where you live, what your pad's made of, whether you're using gas or electricity, how big your door is, and if he blows up your place whether any crackers would get hurt.[6]

Maureen Taylor was a member of the Detroit chapter of the Black Panther Party for Self Defense at that time; she found that a feeling of vulnerability was her constant companion during those years. "When you're brought up with this ongoing contention that says you might not live another moment. When you're brought up, surrounded . . . with all of the . . . the late sixties and early seventies and the death and destruction and the violence and the street demonstrations. . . . every day is a story about how people's rights are trampled and the way people get at this is through violence and just day after day after day." As a result, "It doesn't matter where you go. You can never escape the shadow of the plantation." She adds emphatically, "You went all the way to Vietnam, and you come back dead."[7]

Black militants were not the only ones who took the rumors of concentration camps and black genocide seriously. Numerous black politicians were alarmed about the prospect of unprecedented black oppression. One of those was Gary, Indiana, mayor Richard Hatcher. His campaign for mayor was brutal, punctuated by constant media attacks, an attempt on his life, and an attempt to bribe him. But even after he survived to emerge victorious on election day, he was convinced that his struggle, along with that of his black constituents, was far from over. He said, "It has now become a struggle for survival between civil rights and 'law and order' philosophies." Hatcher had heard the rumors that the Nixon administration was constructing a series of concentration camps, and he reasoned that if the rumors were true, it "can lead one to several conclusions, the most frightening of which is that such camps are being prepared for dissidents, maybe Black and white."[8] Hatcher's fear was based on the existence of a law that had been passed during the height of the anti-Communist hysteria of the McCarthy era. That law, the McCarran Internal Security Act, provided for the establishment of detention camps, and it further gave the president the power to authorize the attorney general to "arrest and detain . . . all persons as to whom there is a reasonable ground to believe that such persons probably engage in or probably will conspire with others to engage in acts of espionage or sabotage."[9] Under the terms of the law, people could be detained indefinitely without charges or warrants. As African Americans of this era became increasingly concerned about what many viewed as heavy-handed and brutal police treatment of black participants in recent race riots, many in the black community feared that it was just a short step from this police overreaction to invoking the provisions of the McCarran Act. Freshman black congressman William Clay from St. Louis shared the fear. He warned, "The implications of this detention provision for black people seem clear. . . . No one can predict when this nation may see fit to seize upon a witch hunt. Those of us who are sensitive to the nature of protest and to the hasty and violent reactions to dissent feel warranted in our anxiety."[10]

Even Whitney Young, the director of the National Urban League and a political moderate, was alarmed at the repressive mood under the Nixon administration. He observed, "The undeclared war on radical groups like the Black Panthers by the police has left many dead, and a feeling of bitterness in the ghetto. Shrill calls for law and order have resulted in greater oppression and denial of justice." Given this new reality, Young argued, the future looked grim. He concluded, "The national mood seems to be one of drifting toward a harsh, repressive society rather than the open, democratic one that has always been the American ideal."[11] Dr. Ralph Bunche, black Nobel laureate and distinguished undersecretary of the United Nations, agreed with Whitney Young, saying, "Black leaders in the United States do not have great confidence in the Nixon Administration to advance." Black journalist Samuel Yette was more blunt in his criticism: "The Nixon Administration is not heeding . . . the warnings that both conservative and militant Negro leaders have sounded. So engrossed is Mr. Nixon in devising a political scheme by which to give gratification to the implacable racists below the Mason and Dixon Line that he has neither the time nor the inclination to correct the injustices that give rise to frustrations and turmoil in the black slums."[12] Furthermore, Yette predicted, Nixon's "benign neglect" of America's inner cities would affect the whole country, and the results would be catastrophic.

He warned his fellow Americans, "If it [benign neglect] is the choice of the new decade—and it appears to be—then the inevitable second choice belongs to black people in America. *That choice is the style in which they—and America—will die.*"[13]

Such dire predictions were expressed frequently and forcefully by a broad cross section of African Americans. But it seemed that Nixon was too busy to listen because he was busy breaking the law on a grand scale to ensure his reelection. The ensuing Watergate scandal eventually brought down the Nixon presidency. The first hint of the president's illegal activity surfaced on June 17, 1972, when Bob Woodward, a young reporter for the *Washington Post,* received a call from his paper's city editor assigning him to cover a story about a burglary at the Democratic National Committee Headquarters in the Watergate Hotel–Office Complex. Over the next few months, Woodward, along with Carl Bernstein, another young *Post* reporter, followed a trail of political corruption and irrefutable evidence that carried them through the highest levels of federal power all the way to the presidency. With each new revelation, the Nixon White House became increasingly antagonistic to the press, but to no avail: the sordid details continued to surface at a rapidly increasing rate, leading to a conclusion that shook the American political system to its very core. Then, on August 9, 1974, Richard M. Nixon became the first and only president in American history to resign from office.

But long before the break-in at the Watergate, President Nixon had declared war on the press. "Within eighteen months of Nixon taking office, the White House staff had hired private investigators and used the FBI to spy on journalists. It had created an 'enemies list,' consisting of people who had spoken or written something considered by the staff as anti-Nixon or who had opposed Nixon in a campaign or on an issue."[14] Nixon's staff also attempted to identify journalists who were likely to be sympathetic to the president and tried to "persuade . . . [them] to write favorable stories about the president."[15] Moreover, the Nixon administration's attempt to manipulate the media occurred in the midst of growing public distrust of the press. The mood of suspicion is particularly striking because it followed a period of unprecedented admiration and trust of the media during the early to mid-sixties. That trust was inspired by public appreciation for the tenacity and heroism of journalists who reported compelling stories of hymn-singing peaceful black civil rights demonstrators being attacked by howling mobs of prosegregation white southerners and accounts of American combat troops fighting a difficult war in faraway Southeast Asia. But as the sixties lurched to an end through one crisis after another—the murders of Martin Luther King Jr. and Bobby Kennedy, the urban race riots that erupted every summer, and the antiwar protests raging on the nation's college campuses—many Americans became weary and suspicious. "Few Americans sympathized with either protesters or journalists," one scholar said, "and many wanted to believe that an exploitative press corps was duping them. Something sinister had to be behind all the turmoil and changing values of the 1960s. It had to be a few agitators and the ambitious and immoral news establishment."[16]

By the early seventies, however, the central role played by the media in exposing the corruption of the Watergate scandal turned the tide and rehabilitated the media's image. In particular, *Washington Post* reporters Woodward and Bernstein received accolades and attention from their fellow Americans. Having "disappeared from the spotlight in December 1972," the two "reemerged in June 1974 with the publication of their book, *All the President's Men*. . . . The book was a runaway best-seller, and suddenly Nixon's two antagonists were national heroes."[17] It was in this atmosphere of renewed trust and admiration that the black leaders in post-King America were forced to face the power of the national media.

Because many of these newly emerging black leaders were veterans of the civil rights movement, they were already acutely aware of the power of the press, especially the relatively new medium of television. In fact, many TV reporters of this era had received their first real television news experience reporting the dramatic life-and-death stories of sit-ins, Freedom Rides, and school integration crises. From the beginning, the eloquent and well-dressed Dr. Martin Luther King Jr. seemed to be a natural in front of the camera. However, other civil rights activists also became quite sophisticated in their dealings with reporters. For example, Congressman John Lewis, a veteran activist, knows how important the press was to the development of young leadership in the movement. He explains, "Many of us were forced to become leaders. We were young . . . and you'd be sitting in on a lunch counter, and some member of the media would walk up and put a microphone in your face, or some reporter would start [asking questions]. . . . You were forced to grow up. You were forced to be responsible. So we didn't have any choice."[18]

Congresswoman Eleanor Holmes Norton asserts, in the same vein, "The press will always focus on leadership. . . . That's the way it always has been; that's the way it always will be. There will always be, at least in a movement atmosphere, somebody who you go to to find out what's happening." Furthermore, in Norton's view, the media played a crucial role in publicizing major movement developments. For example, the demonstrations were covered, and there were documentaries, "the like of which we had not seen before," to inform the public about the movement and about segregation.[19] SNCC's communications director, Julian Bond, is convinced that the press did much more than just disseminate information. In particular, where black leadership is concerned, Bond argues, the press was in a position to influence movement development because the media was "enormously powerful . . . first by propping up figures, including Martin Luther King, to the exclusion of others. You know, King was a magnificent person, and a magnificent leadership figure, but he wasn't alone." Yet, because of the press's exclusive focus on certain leadership figures during the civil rights movement, there are many others whose contributions were never appreciated, Bond charges. "These others just disappeared. Roy Wilkins, Whitney Young, A. Philip Randolph. You know, this pantheon of just dynamic figures [were] just pushed aside."[20]

An example of the celebratory reporting on King to which Bond refers appeared in 1963 in the *Saturday Evening Post*. Published just after the Birmingham campaign, the article named Martin Luther King Jr. as "the most powerful Negro leader in America"[21] and claimed, "King endows this American struggle with qualities of messianic mission." Reese Cleghorn, the author, went on to describe King as "a short man whose thick neck and heavy shoulders convey an impression of height and power."[22] Even after his death, King continued to receive favorable publicity. On April 12, 1968, *Life* editorialized, "King was a thoroughly good man who achieved greatness by showing forth the Negro cause at its best. His was the old American cause of equal rights for all men, and King put it in a form in which this generation of Americans must face it."[23]

The favorable press coverage of King becomes particularly obvious when it is compared to the treatment of Malcolm X by the major media.

Three years before King's death, on the occasion of Malcolm X's assassination, *Life* published a cover story about the murder. The headline on the magazine's cover screamed, "Death of Malcolm X and the Resulting Vengeful Gang War." Below that headline in much larger block letters, the magazine termed the events surrounding the assassination "A Monument to Negro Upheaval." The story inside the magazine appeared under the headline "The Violent End of the Man Called Malcolm X."[24] When such articles appeared regularly, many wondered whether the press was reporting the news or attempting to influence it. Regardless of reporters' motives, however, black leaders had no doubt that the media had the power to change lives and influence movements.

Decades after the turbulent 1960s, Congressman John Lewis has not forgotten the lessons of media power he learned during his activist days; he is convinced that the power of the media has not diminished over the years. Lewis thinks the more recent media coverage he has received during his years in public office has been beneficial to his political career. He has noticed "a sense of respect, or a sense of support." People tell him, "I've never seen you before; I've never met you before . . . but, I've seen you on television. I've seen you in the newspaper." Lewis concludes, "I think the media can be a good force; especially television."[25]

In recent years cable television, satellite radio, and the Internet have dramatically extended the reach of the electronic media. Dr. Benjamin Hooks, a civil rights attorney and past president of the NAACP, claims that with cable and satellite communication, the impact of the electronic media on the careers of black leaders has increased exponentially. "The last five or six years," he says, "Ted Turner and the cable network gives you a chance to be known that you never had before. . . . Martin had to make his way without that. Thurgood [Marshall], and Roy [Wilkins] and all the rest of them."[26] The growing influence of the media on black leadership is accompanied by a growing sense of concern, however. There are many who charge that even though the earlier generation of black leadership during the civil rights movement did not have the media access that exists today, at least most of them could count on a certain amount of sympathy for the plight of African Americans. But that sympathy no longer exists. It became submerged in the volatile era of the early 1970s when Americans began to grow tired of the chaos in the inner cities, weary of the war in Vietnam, and shocked and disillusioned by the actions of their president. To many white Americans who had been sympathetic to the civil rights campaigns of the recent past, it seemed that the hymn-singing nonviolent demonstrators of the early civil rights era had been replaced by Afro-wearing Black Power advocates, glib black politicians, or worse, Molotov cocktail–throwing black rioters from the inner city. As reporters began to focus their attention on this new cast of black charac-ters, the tone of the interaction between the media and African American leadership changed: it went from sympathetic to adversarial.

Against this volatile background, countless black leaders have sparred with the press during the past four decades. Mayor Richard Hatcher of Gary, Indiana, found that his problems with the media started early, dur-ing his run for mayor in the fall of 1967. There was intense hostility directed at him by the media during his campaign. "The news media here, from the very moment that it appeared that I had any chance of winning, treated me with unmitigated hatred and antagonism, and just hostility." Hatcher reiterates, "COMPLETE HOSTILITY." He realizes that his situation was not unique: "What I found later was that in talking to people like Carl [Stokes, the first black mayor of Cleveland, Ohio] and others . . . much of what I thought was just happening to me was happening to them also."[27] As Hatcher focused on his campaign in the last few weeks before the may-oral election, he used humor in an attempt to defuse the situation, joking about the refusal of local newspapers to support him. With a twinkle in his eye, he chuckles at the memory of the speech he delivered to various groups of voters just before the election. He advised,

> You know they're [the newspapers] not going to endorse me. It wouldn't make any difference who was running against me. . . . It wouldn't make any difference if Mickey Mouse was running against me. . . . You know, now that I think about it, if King Kong was running against me, I can see the editorial right now:
>
> > Here is King Kong.
> > He is very strong.
> > Vote for King Kong,
> > And you won't go wrong.[28]

Hatcher breaks into a broad smile as he recalls, "People loved it." But the former mayor's smile fades as he thinks about the treatment he has received from the press more recently. "If you can believe this, I haven't been in office in twenty years, almost, and . . . they haven't gotten over it yet. They still write these really nasty editorials [about me]."[29]

In Hatcher's estimation, media hostility continues to plague black leaders in the new millennium, and race is not the only motivation for such hostility:

I always think of it not only in terms of race, but also in terms of class. In many ways, the media's function, I think, is to first of all head off any real revolutionary activity and so if there's someone that doesn't quite fit the mold, then I think immediately, the media sees that as a threat to the order of things, and so from that point of view, it's not only race, it is also an issue of class and so forth. I think with regards to black leadership in particular, the media has been especially hostile towards those blacks who are outspoken, and who sort of don't buy into what I call the arrangement; the arrangement being, you know, that whites are supposed to be up here; blacks are supposed to be down here, and that's the way things should be.[30]

Former senator Carol Moseley Braun also had a particularly difficult time with the press while she was in office. Because she was and remains the only black woman ever elected to the U.S. Senate, Braun's career is truly unique. She was the subject of a great deal of media scrutiny during her time in the Senate. At one point she was accused of campaign finance irregularities, and the press hounded her relentlessly. She recalls, "The Senate was the worst six years of my life. Oh it was horrible. . . . The press, they were just determined to destroy me personally, and so, from the very beginning, from the minute I won the primary. . . . It was just awful. They kept coming at me, and with every sort of character assassination. And so I spent six years really being defensive; trying to defend my integrity and my honor, and to keep myself from going to jail for that matter." Things got so bad for Senator Braun that at one point she considered resigning. "I had asked my lawyers to look . . . and see what would be involved if I did . . . just give it up. . . . And my lawyers sent me the memo back, saying that if I resign that the Republican governor would appoint [my replacement]. So now I'm looking at, okay, do I really want to turn the Senate over to the Republicans on top of everything else?" On one particular evening after a long and difficult session with her lawyers, the troubled and weary Senator Braun returned to her apartment in the shadow of the capitol building. Without thinking much about it, she turned on the television as soon as she entered her apartment. A made-for-TV movie, *The Autobiography of Miss Jane Pittman,* just happened to be on, and before long Braun became engrossed in it. The movie's main character, played by black actress Cicely Tyson, is an old black woman who lived through slavery, segregation, Klan outrages, and all sorts of economic injustices. At the end of the movie, the civil rights movement is just starting in the segregated South, and in a remarkable act of defiance, Miss Jane walks right up to the "whites only" water fountain and takes a drink. That fictional act of defiance was so inspiring to Braun that she knew she could not quit. So Braun served out her term. Before she left office, the investigation into her campaign finances was completed, and she was exonerated.[31]

J. L. Chestnut Jr., a black civil rights attorney from Selma, Alabama, has also had a difficult time with the media. He thinks "the media in this country is one of the cornerstones of the white establishment. It has its agenda. It marginalizes, demonizes, people like me. It elevates and honors people like Clarence Thomas [black ultra-conservative U.S. Supreme Court justice]. That has a very large impact throughout society. It keeps the black middle class in line. It sets goals for the black middle class."[32] Chestnut goes on to explain the method the media uses to influence public opinion. "The media, in my opinion, has not moved [any] further than this society has moved over the last 35 years. And the media—I learned a long time ago, it's not so much what . . . [is] in an editorial, it's the repetition of it. Day in and day out; . . . [it] is shaping values. And most of them are subtly anti-black." Because of his visibility as a civil rights attorney, Chestnut has sparred with journalists on numerous occasions over the years.

It's interesting to me how the media treats me. Well, I can expect the first question is, what is it that you mean that you are not a

Republican or a Democrat? [Chestnut is an Independent]. That's [the] first step to trying to demonize me in all of that . . . I'm always described as an outspoken civil rights lawyer. . . . Outspoken is a code word to whites and middle class blacks, and they pick it up too. Sometimes subconsciously, almost, they get this negative feeling about me, and I can sense it. And if I go up to Detroit or Chicago, somebody's always going to be the local reporter who comes out to do the story, and I can sense in him that he's already formed these opinions about me, and he wants to ask some outrageous question [like] how can you not be a Republican or a Democrat? You must be the devil.[33]

But attorney Chestnut also remembers a rare instance when the media, specifically the medium of television, worked in his favor. It was a time when he was invited to appear on a talk show in Savannah, Georgia, and appearing with him was the Grand Cyclops of the local chapter of the Ku Klux Klan. Chestnut recalls with a twinkle in his eye:

He was in there with a red sheet on, a red pointed hat and all of that. And he was obviously so nervous he didn't know what to do. He was sitting up on the stage smoking Camel cigarettes; one after another . . . and the host was white and gay. I leaned over and told the Grand Cyclops, I said, "brother, when this show is over with, I'm going to take you down to the corner and buy you a whole box of Camels . . . and you can smoke your damn self to death." He [the Klansman] said, "I'm not your goddamn brother . . ." He didn't know what to say and he couldn't stand the host 'cause the host was gay. . . . And at one point he told the host, [he] said, "If I had known you was a sissy, I wouldn't even come on your show." The host told him, [he] said, "If I had known you had an IQ of two, you wouldn't have been invited."[34]

At this point, the red-faced, red-robed Klansman jumped up and claimed to be a graduate of Emory University. Chestnut reached in his pocket and dramatically pulled out a one-hundred-dollar bill. He handed it to the host and said in a stage whisper, "Give him this bill if he can spell Emory."

The Klansman confidently called out the letters "E-M-E-R-E-Y." By this time, Chestnut and the host were doubled over with laughter. The furious Klansman jumped up and stormed off the stage, and as he left the studio, his red robe billowed out behind him.[35] So in this instance, the image of J. L. Chestnut was a positive one.

Despite occasionally favorable media treatment, many African Americans are convinced that this country's black leadership and the mainstream media have a problematic relationship. Some go so far as to charge that in the new millennium the media is attempting to decide who the *real* black leaders are. For example, movement activist Rev. T. Randel Osburn argues that when the white power structure identifies a black person whom it judges as acceptable, "the white folks will put you out there in the news as the leader, and they will just turn your head to all the rest of that stuff."[36] Former SNCC staffer Julian Bond agrees with Osburn's assessment. "But [the press is] propping up figures that had no demonstrated constituency. King had people in the hundreds of thousands who followed his every word. And some of these people today [have] no one. No one. All they have is the support of well-to-do right wing interests who give them access to television; to the Sunday shows; to the op-ed pages in the newspaper. But, they have nothing beyond that."[37] Black journalist Samuel Yette has an insider's view of the media's influence on black leadership choices: for example, the attitude of his Bureau Chief at *Newsweek* magazine in 1968 in the chaotic hours following Dr. King's assassination. Yette was the first black reporter assigned to *Newsweek*'s Washington Bureau, and when news of the assassination broke, the bureau chief immediately sent Yette to Atlanta. Yette was not surprised; he expected the magazine to assign him to cover King's funeral. However, as his bureau chief began to explain the assignment in greater detail, Samuel Yette was surprised, shocked, and then infuriated. He explains, "The Bureau did not want me to cover the funeral. They wanted me instead to argue against Coretta Scott King's being selected as his [King's] successor." Thinking back on that day forty years before, Yette shakes his head as he admits, "They were not that open." However, Yette is sure that "their insinuation to me was . . . they definitely felt they should have some role in the choosing of Dr. King's successor." In a clear, strong voice he adds for emphasis, "ABSOLUTELY."[38]

These days, black leaders routinely complain about what they judge as the arrogance of the press in anointing black leaders. For example, Congressman John Lewis charges, "The media, especially the white media, is too ready to identify some well known African American as a leader." But "they [the white press] don't do the same thing when it comes to white America." Lewis concludes, "So every outstanding sports figure, every outstanding entertainer is not a leader."[39] Dr. Dorothy Cotton, who was a member of the Southern Christian Leadership Conference's Executive Staff and a close confidante of King's, comments on the same phenomenon. She is convinced that when the press "anoints" black leaders, the black leadership choices are often based on the media's self-interest. "People get lifted up as leaders based on . . . what will sell and who's kind of dramatic and who makes good copy."[40]

Former congresswoman Cynthia McKinney goes a step further and argues that the media's attempt to manipulate black leadership choices has been bolstered by at least one entity within the federal government. "I think the African American community in this country has been manipulated," she claims, explaining her belief that the FBI, through its COINTELPRO program, has actively attempted to highjack black leadership choices. She insists that the media has assisted these attempts. In her words, "Corporate media were the handmaidens of the COINTELPRO program."[41] Some leaders, including Memphis minister Rev. Samuel Billy Kyles, also believe that the media influences the agenda set by black leaders.[42]

The negative bias that many of today's African American leaders see in the news is not considered a new phenomenon; it has been happening for decades. Such reporting has flourished, they believe, in a broad context of repeated attacks on black character and intellectual capacity mounted by the scholarly establishment and the medical community, going back at least a century. In the Victorian era, it was common to link assumptions about African Americans' mental abilities with "the African's birthright to sexual madness and excess."[43]Attempts to connect black sexuality and the black intellect were eventually abandoned, but there was still a stubborn insistence that African Americans were intellectually inferior. One modern scholar, Richard Kluger, reports that "by the second decade of the twentieth century, anti-Negro feeling in America was at its zenith and the social scientists had developed intelligence tests that were being avidly used to demonstrate the mental inferiority of blacks."[44] Even when those administering the tests began to realize that black northerners routinely scored higher than white southerners, they still refused to give up their cherished belief in black inferiority. Instead, Kluger observes, they concocted an argument that would both protect their assumption and explain the unexpected test results: "This [higher black scores] was due to the high mixture of white blood among the colored subjects and the likelihood that thanks to 'selective migration,' the brightest Southern blacks had bestirred themselves and moved North." This led some to conclude that "these Northern Negroes . . . were the exceptions that proved the rule."[45]

Those who championed black inferiority were often quick to argue that there was no remedy, even insisting that access to higher education would not help. For example, Howard Odum, an early-twentieth-century white scholar and native Georgian, argued in his doctoral dissertation, "The young educated Negroes are not a force for good in the community but for evil. . . . They feel manual labor is beneath their dignity; they are fitted to do no other. They sneer at the idea of work and thus spread dissatisfaction among the members of their race."[46] Gradually, over the next few decades, some scholars began to reevaluate these notions of black inferiority. Odum himself even changed his mind about twenty-five years after he wrote his dissertation. In 1936 he wrote an essay asserting that among African Americans, "there is ample evidence to indicate many manifestations of superiority, of extraordinary personality and survival qualities, of capacity for intellectual and social achievement."[47]

Black scholars had disagreed with the racist notions of white scholars all along, but they had been ignored. However, beginning in the late 1930s, as Odum and other mainstream white scholars reversed their positions, the work of black scholars like Charles S. Johnson, John Hope Franklin, and E. Franklin Frazier began to receive recognition. When Gunnar Myrdal published his groundbreaking study of black life in America, *An American Dilemma,* in 1944, many heralded it as the end of racist scholarly literature about African Americans. Yet, while Myrdal's book did not blame African Americans directly for their plight, it still portrayed them in very negative terms. In the following comments, for instance, he blends factual information with a negative bias: "The economic situation of the Negroes in America is pathological. Except for a small minority enjoying upper or middle class status, the masses of American Negroes, in the rural South and in the segregated slum quarters in Southern and Northern cities, are destitute. They own little property; even their household goods are mostly inadequate and dilapidated. Their incomes are not only low but irregular. They thus live from day to day and have scant security for the future. Their entire culture and their individual interests and strivings are narrow."[48] Thus, all through the early twentieth century, black leaders were obliged to deal with a country that embraced the idea of black inferiority and black abnormality, whether it was the victims' fault or not. The media reflected the same attitude in its depictions of African Americans.

Even in the decades following the civil rights movement, hints of black inferiority have continued to lurk in broadcasts and publications of mainstream media and in academic works. As late as 1994, fifty years after Myrdal's study and nearly thirty years after some of the most heroic and well-publicized campaigns of the civil rights movement, a book called *The Bell Curve: Intelligence and Class Structure in American Life* was published. Using arguments reminiscent of the racist arguments of a half century before, the book's authors "encouraged those people who believed that blacks were inherently inferior and [they argued] that any effort to provide the same education for blacks as for whites was impractical and ill-advised."[49] Black *Newsweek* reporter Ellis Cose claims that the authors were really asking the question, "If the races are inherently unequal, why even bother to aim for racial equality?" Cose acknowledged that "it was not the only question the book raised; it was not even the most important one, according to the authors. Yet, in one sense," he insisted, "it was the only question that mattered."[50]

A variety of scholars quickly repudiated the book's conclusions, but it was too late. The damage had already been done because, Cose points out, the merits of the authors' research and arguments ultimately mattered less than the favorable public reaction to the book's conclusions. "The volume, on its own merits, was fundamentally unimportant. Its only significance lay in what we (broadly meaning society but, more specifically and most shamefully, my own community of journalists) decided to do with it. Given the attention and respect—in some quarters verging on acclaim—accorded the authors by the press, it is not remarkable that *The Bell Curve* became a national best seller."[51] That a book like this attracted so much favorable attention means that black leaders in the late twentieth and early twenty-first centuries are still facing a negative context strikingly similar to the one that confronted earlier generations of black leaders.

Because of negative biases like these that have dogged black people in general and black leaders in particular for generations, many African Americans have argued for some time that black people need their own media outlets. For example, just a little over a year after King's assassination, James Forman, a crucial member of SNCC's administrative staff, presented a "Manifesto to the White Christian Churches and the Jewish Synagogues in the United States of America and All Other Racist Institutions" at the National Black Economic Development Conference in Detroit, Michigan, on April 26, 1969. Along with various other demands (including one for reparations in the amount of $500,000,000, which "comes to $15 per nigger"), Forman demanded black media outlets: "We call for the establishment of four of the most advanced scientific futuristic audio-visual networks to be located in Detroit, Chicago, Cleveland, and Washington, D.C. These TV networks will provide an alternative to the racist propaganda that fills the current television networks."[52] In the ensuing years, black leaders have continued to express grave concern about the scarcity of black media outlets. Rev. Samuel Billy Kyles argues that in the new millennium the dearth of black-owned media outlets in this country has "a [negative] effect on the behavior of black leadership."[53] Carol Moseley Braun agrees, and she is convinced that part of the problem is rooted in the elimination of affirmative action in federal policy regarding the ownership and licensing of media outlets in this country, particularly during the administration of President Bill Clinton.[54]

In contrast to the lack of black-owned television and radio stations, there is a strong tradition of black newspaper publishing, stretching back all the way to 1827, when the first black newspaper, *Freedom's Journal*, began publication. Samuel Cornish and John Russworm, the publishers, felt that African Americans needed their own newspaper because of the frequent and vicious antiblack articles and editorials in contemporary white newspapers. From that time to this, a variety of African American newspapers have printed news of special interest to the black community and have often provided a sympathetic outlet for the views of black leaders who have been alternately ignored and vilified by white publications. As the number of black newspapers and magazines multiplied through the late nineteenth century and the twentieth century and finally into the twenty-first century, many published only a few issues before going out of business. And even for those that were able to continue publication, the circumstances under which they were obliged to operate were often financially difficult and, especially in the South, sometimes physically dangerous. One scholar reports that "the publication of a black newspaper in the South was a hazardous occupation and still remains dangerous to some extent. The early black editors were threatened, assaulted, spat upon, inundated with vituperative remarks, and stymied by vicious gossip. Black editors complained not only of harassment from hostile whites but of mistreatment from blacks who threatened and intimidated them over local grievances."[55]

As they struggled to survive, black newspapers also had to fight for respect, both from the white news establishment and from members of the black communities that they were attempting to serve. Even though black people expected their newspapers to focus on issues of "black survival and black awareness," they still often dismissed a black newspaper as "an additional paper," nothing more than a convenient place to announce in print "the birth of the most lowly black," or the most recent black obituaries, or any other social news from the local black community.[56] Certain members of the black community were so contemptuous of their local black newspaper that they were not even interested in having it as "an additional paper." Black professionals in particular were proud when they found "colored news" in white-owned papers but had little regard for many southern black newspapers.[57] Of course, there are black papers such as the *Chicago Defender* and the *Pittsburgh Courier* that were very well received. Newspapers such as these were especially influential in the years before the civil rights movement, because they were read by many African Americans who lived far away from the cities where they were published. However, those papers were the exception.

In the years since the movement, the black press's struggle for existence and respect has continued, and there are some who charge that the newspapers have an even more difficult time now than ever, because "the civil rights movement convinced many blacks that the millennium had arrived; there was no longer a need for a black press. Subscriptions plummeted, advertisements dropped, and many presses in the Middle West and elsewhere were forced to revise their 'news formula' and downsize their newspapers."[58] Others say that as white journalists have paid increasing attention to black leaders in post-King America, black leaders have responded by seeking further attention from the white media and virtually ignoring the black press "until they get in trouble and the white people don't pay them any attention and then they come running home." African American journalist George Curry, who has reported on black leaders for both black and white publications during his long career, is convinced that many black leaders are "obsessed with trying to get coverage in the white press." Curry sadly concludes, "So colonialism is still well, and the remnants are still there, and it's still in the minds of many of our people." This is ironic in view of Curry's assessment that "the [white] news media has done a terrible job of covering black leaders," at the same time that the black press's coverage of African American leadership has continued to be "totally different. [They] tend to be more supportive."[59]

Any discussion of contemporary black media without looking at the medium of television would be incomplete. The most visible and public black entry into television was Bob Johnson's Black Entertainment Television. According to George Curry, who worked very closely with Johnson, although BET had its share of entertainment programming, it also tackled difficult topics and delved into hard news. "Even with the rump shaking, which is a legitimate criticism of BET, they had more public affairs shows than the rest of the cable industry combined. So, I said, you can criticize him [Bob Johnson] if you want, [but] that's a fact. Slowly, one by one, all those items fell out. *Emerge* [magazine], BET News, Teen Summit, down to the point where they don't have any kind of news." Curry pauses before concluding emphatically, "I don't watch it [BET] anymore."[60] (It should be noted that BET is under new management; Bob Johnson sold it to media conglomerate Viacom and thereby became the first black billionaire in America.)

Despite the scarcity of black-owned media outlets, there are increasing numbers of black journalists, both in the print and the electronic media. However, black journalists face their own issues as they write about race in a racially polarized society. Most worry about the way other black people view them, even as they measure their white supervisors' approval of their perspective. The experience of Gordon Parks, the first black photographer ever employed by *Life* magazine, illustrates the peculiar position in which modern black journalists working for white publications find themselves.

> As a reporter and photographer for the weekly LIFE, I was assigned to cover the most militant of those [black] leaders. Though they would never admit to it, Malcolm X, Stokely Carmichael, Eldridge Cleaver, Bobby Seale and others wanted to be heard through a big voice, and the magazine was just as eager to penetrate their ranks. But the black militants were like people whose houses were burning, and they suspected LIFE of being just another white arsonist. My editors also wondered whether to trust my objectivity. Eventually, all of them came to terms with their doubts. I was thrust inside those aggressive strongholds, where I had to shake off the strangeness of being considered a friendly enemy.[61]

Samuel Yette, because of his personal experience as one of the first black reporters for *Life,* understands and sympathizes with Parks's position. The two men first met when they were hired to join the *Life* staff. They were the only two black professional employees during those early days, and Parks and Yette were uncertain about a lot of things, including each other. Yette explains, "We felt each other out . . . Gordon Parks and I. . . . It was necessary for us to feel each other out because he thought I was an overly militant person. In fact, he said so." Yette had his own ideas about Parks: "I thought he was a saccharine person. . . . I thought he was a handkerchief head [Uncle Tom], and that sort of thing. But neither of us wound up being accurate."[62]

Many of the same issues that confronted these two black media pioneers over a half century ago have continued to plague later generations of black journalists, including George Curry. He began his career in journalism over a decade after Gordon Parks and Samuel Yette had sparred with each other at *Life*. Curry, a native of Tuscaloosa, Alabama, first decided to become a journalist when he was just a child. He explains, "I read the newspaper growing up, and I saw images of African Americans only when they were accused of committing a crime or if they were an entertainer or an athlete. And I thought there were so many other stories out there and the newspapers weren't telling it."[63] Today, George Curry is a well-known and well-respected journalist living in Washington, D.C., but when he talks, he talks fast, with just a hint of his Alabama upbringing in his speech. He is a man in a hurry to tell all those stories that he realized as a child needed to be told.

Curry was born just in time to witness segregation's last stand. He has vivid memories of Martin Luther King's visit to his hometown when Tuscaloosa's African American community had a bus boycott. More than forty years later, Curry exclaims, "I have never met an orator like that; and certainly one who needed no notes." After a long pause, he adds softly, "Class personified." The movement was all around him, and young Curry could not resist it. "To me, it was like you had no choice. . . . I don't see how you could not be involved."[64] When the Sixteenth Street Baptist Church in Birmingham was bombed, Curry and some of his buddies skipped school and went to Birmingham to demonstrate. Some eighteen months later, he participated in the last leg of the Selma-to-Montgomery march. Despite his excitement, however, Curry's participation was limited because of his youth. He explains, "Well you see people like Stokely, Charlie Cobb, Cleveland Sellers [members of the Student Nonviolent Coordinating Committee]. These are sharp people. People don't realize how smart they were. . . . They had rich vocabularies, great thought processes. They were activists, and so I wanted to be like them. I wish I were [born] a few years earlier so that I could have been like them." By the late sixties, Curry was a student at historically black Knoxville College in Knoxville, Tennessee, and he was well on his way to a career in journalism. After editing the student newspaper, the *Aurora,* he became just the second black reporter ever employed by *Sports Illustrated Magazine.* Two years later Curry moved on to the *St. Louis Post-Dispatch,* and then later to the *Chicago Tribune.* As he worked at these white publications, Curry was obliged to walk a fine line as he sought to tell the stories that he thought needed to be told. He explains, "This is the problem of any . . . successful black journalist is that you have to live in those two worlds;

the twoness W. E. B. Du Bois talked about. So, I wanted to write the right black stories because if I don't write them, they won't get written. But also, I don't want to be limited by that."[65]

After straddling both worlds for a number of years, Curry finally decided that it was time to work for a black publication. The young journalist made the change when he received an offer he could not refuse from black media mogul Bob Johnson: Johnson promised to give Curry complete freedom to shape the editorial policy of *Emerge,* a magazine owned by Johnson, if Curry accepted the position of editor. Curry would also be free to combine his activist instincts and his journalistic skills. He jumped into his new position with gusto. He recalls with a twinkle in his eye that one of the magazine's first issues after he became editor featured a picture of Clarence Thomas (an ultraconservative black U.S. Supreme Court justice) with an "Aunt Jemima" kerchief on his head. On the cover of another issue, Ward Connerly (an ultraconservative black opponent of the policy of affirmative action) is depicted as a puppet. Curry explains that the decisions he made about *Emerge*'s content made some people uncomfortable, but not Bob Johnson. According to Curry, Johnson "never flinched. And people would go to him and ask, Bob . . . why [do] you let George Curry do all that?"[66]

Even though Curry's experience at *Emerge* was not very long ago, it seems that opportunities for black freedom of thought and expression in the print media are now more limited. Furthermore, in an increasingly complex profession, black journalists are obliged to compete for jobs as reporters, news anchors, and editors while juggling the interests of their viewers or readers with the interests of the news organizations, black or white, for which they work. And today's black leaders wonder and worry about the agenda of members of the media, both black and white, and how that agenda will affect their image and their effectiveness.

Many African American leaders also worry about the role of black scholars in shaping public opinion on the plight of African Americans in this country, because as the number of black journalists has grown, there has been a corresponding increase in the number of black scholars. Back before the civil rights movement, the black intelligentsia occupied a vital position in the black leadership equation. They were expected to conduct research and write about topics that would advance the interests of the race. Julian Bond recalls how effectively they functioned during this earlier era: "There was a time when I knew by name the presidents of most black colleges because they were notable figures, and they were always making pronouncements about one thing or the other." Other black scholars were also important; they "use[d] knowledge to advance the race."[67]

One of those scholars who has devoted his career to research and writing about African Americans is John Hope Franklin. Today, at age ninety-two, Franklin is a professor emeritus at Duke University. He has produced numerous groundbreaking works on the history of African Americans, including his survey of African American history, *From Slavery to Freedom,* now in its ninth edition after millions of copies have been sold. Franklin attended Fisk University as an undergraduate during the depths of the Great Depression in the 1930s, and after he graduated, he followed in the footsteps of another famous Fisk alumnus, W. E. B. Du Bois, by enrolling in Harvard University, where he completed his Ph.D. in history. Franklin recalls that although he appreciated the opportunity to study at Harvard, there were things about the institution that he did not like. He recalls, "I was not awed by Harvard at all. It was just another day in my development. . . . [But] I couldn't stand Harvard. . . . It was too fancy, too presumptuous, too self-satisfied." Despite those criticisms, however, Franklin insists, "I took it seriously. It's a great university . . . so I wasn't going to go up there and think I could rest on my laurels, whatever they were." Franklin adds emphatically, "I worked."[68]

Just before finishing his Ph.D., Franklin joined the faculty at St. Augustine's College, a small, private, historically black college in Raleigh, North Carolina. When he officially finished his Ph.D., word of his accomplishment spread quickly, and the white president of the college called him in to find out if it was true. Franklin confirmed that it was, and the president's reaction was swift and vehement. Franklin explains, "He began a tirade about [how] I shouldn't think I was any better than anybody else; and just because I had a Ph.D. it didn't mean that I was going to . . . have any special advantage."[69] The young Franklin was amazed, but he was also angry. He left St. Augustine's and, after a stint at North Carolina College for Negroes (now North Carolina Central University), he joined the faculty at Howard University, in Washington, D.C., one of the premier black institutions of higher learning in this country. At Howard, he was surrounded by some of the most respected black scholars in the world, who produced important scholarship on African American issues. The dean of Howard University's Law School, Charles Hamilton Houston, was the chief architect of much of the legal strategy employed by NAACP attorneys in the cases leading up to the landmark decision *Brown v. Board of Education.*

Franklin is quick to point out that although being among so many well-known scholars studying African American issues was an amazing experience, the frustration that hung over the campus like a dense, impenetrable cloud was breathtaking. "It [Howard] was an unhealthy place because it was the last place to go." The reality of legal segregation in the academy had for years been an endless source of frustration for brilliant black scholars such as those at Howard, because it had circumscribed their careers and their lives. "Everybody sitting up there; all dressed up and nowhere to go. Great minds . . . E. Franklin Frazier, Sterling Brown, Rayford Logan, . . . Alain Locke. You name it, they were there." Sitting in his comfortable home in Durham, North Carolina, decades later, Professor Emeritus John Hope Franklin shakes his head at the memory of so much frustrated black scholarly talent.[70]

Because Franklin was much younger than these eminent scholars who had been at Howard for years, he was presented with opportunities to enter mainstream (a code word for white) academia that many older black scholars never had. So a short time later, in 1956, he became the first black head of a history department at a major white institution. Departmental politics at Brooklyn College, his new institution, were complicated and sometimes nasty, but the young black department head was able to navigate them without a problem. When Franklin's colleagues at Brooklyn College asked their new department head about the ease with which he dealt with departmental politics, he smiled and said, "I came from Howard."[71]

During the latter part of the 1960s, as more black undergraduates began attending previously all-white or nearly all-white schools, they began demanding courses that were relevant to their experience. University administrations responded by establishing black studies programs and recruiting black scholars, often from the faculties of historically black colleges and universities. At the same time, white college administrators began more aggressive recruitment programs aimed at prospective black students, both graduate and undergraduate.

In the view of some scholars, these efforts have had a profound impact on the consciousness of black scholars and the future of scholarship by and about African Americans in this country. Social critic Norman Kelley characterizes the impact this way: many post-civil-rights-era black scholars are "trained in the high falutin['] theoretical abstractions of academic feminism, cultural studies, semiotics, structuralism and post-structuralism, literary theory, and meta-theory." In Kelley's view, these scholars, whom he christens "the niggerati" (an expression coined by Harlem Renaissance writer Zora Neale Hurston), "may well be the most useless group of Negroes that black America has ever produced. None has yet matched the work of earlier generations."[72] Those scholars of "earlier generations" whom Kelley refers to, by the way, include some of the frustrated black intellectuals Professor John Hope Franklin encountered at Howard University.

Kelley insists that many of the "new black scholars" in this materialistic new millennium are less concerned about the plight of black people than they are about turning a profit. He believes "their 'political enterprise,' if one can indeed call it that, has nothing to do with people but with theory, identity, books, publications, journals, television appearances, assignments from elite journals read by whites, socialist confabs, etc. In reality, they engage in self-promotion masquerading as intellectual discourse, *positioning themselves as market intellectuals.*"[73] Kelley goes so far as to charge that some of today's best-known black intellectuals have become part of an emerging black elite that consciously and carefully distances itself from the majority of African Americans—particularly the poor. He argues that the new black scholars "have gained much more as beneficiaries of an elite patronage system that needs a smattering of dark faces to legitimize the rhetoric of meritocracy."[74]

Kelley's concern is shared by some black leaders. Senator Carol Moseley Braun, for instance, thinks black scholars do not provide the supportive intellectual context that black leaders need to organize their people: "Quite frankly, the black academics and the black intellectuals, the intelligentsia have distanced themselves so much from the real world of political action. They sit back, they criticize, they throw brickbats, and they have opinions about everything, but they don't *do* anything." Senator Braun concludes, "The people who have the knowledge and should do, don't. This has created a leadership vacuum, and [rap mogul] Russell Simmons and others have entered that vacuum."[75]

Thus, black leaders continue to face an uphill battle in terms of both perceptions and perspectives by and about African Americans in post-civil-rights-movement America—whether the perspectives and perceptions are those of black or white journalists or black or white scholars. As some continue to worry about the black image, however, many others are putting their faith in the growth of black political power in the new millennium. African Americans today have more access to the political process than ever before, and many have begun to feel that they have finally arrived: increasing numbers of black elected officials are integrating America's all-white governing bodies. And, of course, Barack Obama's successful run for the presidency puts the exclamation point on the narrative of the growth of black political power in the new millennium. Nevertheless, as those who came through the civil rights movement more than forty years ago look at the new reality of the black political position in the new millennium, they issue a warning: African Americans must never forget that the basis for this increased black political access is firmly rooted in the civil rights victories of the recent past. Members of that generation can never forget that it was only after black protesters had been beaten, jailed, and killed that Congress finally passed the Voting Rights Act of 1965. They fervently hope that in the giddy excitement surrounding the election of the first black president in U.S. history, others will not be able to forget either.

5. From Protest to Inclusion

These days, as African Americans savor the election of the first black president, they dream about the potential for change that comes with an Obama presidency. Many older African Americans want to pinch themselves to make sure they are not dreaming: they never thought they would live to see this day. Over four decades ago, African Americans were thrilled about the revolutionary possibilities that President Johnson's new Voting Rights Act promised. Most of them had thought they would never live to see that day, either, when the federal government would pass such a comprehensive voting rights bill. That is why on August 6, 1965, many African Americans celebrated when President Lyndon Baines Johnson signed the Voting Rights Act into law during a solemn ceremony at the White House.

Some of the people who attended the signing ceremony that day, such as Roy Wilkins and Martin Luther King Jr., flashed huge smiles, and the audience on the White House lawn broke into enthusiastic applause; they knew they were witnessing history. The act, stipulating "No voting qualification or prerequisite to voting or standard, practice, or procedure shall be imposed or applied by any State or political subdivision to deny or abridge the right of any citizen of the United States to vote *on account of race or color,*" enjoyed broad bipartisan support.[1] The South's large African American population was now poised to become a formidable political force for the first time since Reconstruction.

It was the actions of African American activists that had focused the nation's attention on the tragedy of southern black disfranchisement in the first place. For decades, African Americans in communities all over the South had been protesting their lack of voting rights. For example, in 1946, immediately after World War II, black Atlanta residents staged an effective voting rights campaign, resulting in a dramatic increase in the number of registered black voters in that city. In 1959, poor black residents of rural Fayette and Haywood counties in west Tennessee started their own voter registration campaign. Many of these black protesters were sharecroppers, and enraged white landowners quickly retaliated by evicting them. After they were turned out of their homes, these poor black sharecroppers lived for months in tents under miserable and frequently dangerous conditions. Their desperate plight as they subsisted in tent cities received national attention when their story was reported in the *New York Times*.

It was six years later, in 1965, that dramatic events in Selma, Alabama, grabbed the nation's attention again and generated demands for change at the federal level. On March 7, 1965, a group of demonstrators met at Brown Chapel Church in the heart of Selma's black community to begin a march all the way to the state capital in Montgomery. For some months before this, through early March of 1965, many of these same people had marched to their county courthouse every day attempting to register to vote. Day after day, the result was always the same: they were refused admittance. Finally, out of frustration at their inability to register, and anger over the murder of Jimmie Lee Jackson, a local young black activist, they decided to march all the way from Selma to the state capital in Montgomery to dramatize their disfranchisement. On that chilly, overcast Sunday, they walked through the quiet streets of Selma, wondering how authorities, especially their county's notorious sheriff, Jim Clark, would react to their march. They did not have long to wonder, because when they turned onto Highway 80, the road that led out of Selma to Montgomery, they came face to face with a wall of Alabama law enforcement officers. The officers were positioned at the foot of the Edmund Pettus Bridge, the bridge that carried Highway 80 over the Alabama River, and the marchers could not help but notice that the lawmen were wearing gas masks.

Marchers and lawmen faced each other across the great divide of southern tradition and racial etiquette. In a matter of minutes (though it seemed much longer), Alabama state troopers shot tear gas canisters into the crowd of marchers, and after the briefest pause, disoriented marchers began blindly stumbling through the cloud of tear gas. The scene was punctuated by the gagging and retching of black demonstrators whose lungs had been invaded by the tear gas. Then a new sound joined the gagging and retching: it was the staccato beat of horses' hooves hitting the pavement, mingled with the thump and smack of billy clubs striking black flesh as members of Sheriff Jim Clark's mounted posse leaned over their saddles and clubbed as many terrified marchers as they could reach. Above all of this, the sobs and shrieks of the marchers were heard.

Before they were gassed, the demonstrators had been trying to cross the Edmund Pettus Bridge. Now they were just trying to escape Sheriff Jim Clark and the other lawmen, who were chasing them. A crucial difference between these events in Selma and previous voting rights campaigns is that television cameras were on hand in Selma to record the awful scene, and as Americans watched the violence unfold on their TV sets, many were shaken and ultimately moved. In the wake of this televised violence, Dr. Martin Luther King Jr. put out a call for people of conscience to come to Selma. In response, Americans from all walks of life converged on Selma, determined to complete the march that had been stopped by tear gas and violence.

The story of this amazing response is nearly as irresistible as the spectacle of the televised violence that occurred on March 7, 1965, the day that came to be known as Bloody Sunday. For the next two weeks, the nation was transfixed by the drama of young and old, black and white, male and female, marching along side by side on Highway 80 in the heart of the Deep South in support of black voting rights. Despite the violence that had brought them together, the marchers were optimistic, almost buoyant as they walked along in the damp March chill. Mile after mile they sang freedom songs, with words such as, "Oh Wallace, you never can jail us all, you know segregation's bound to fall." The singers' determination sometimes gave way to playfulness: "You know Jack and Jill went up the hill; and Jill came down with the Civil Rights Bill." The song finished with "Don't want no shuckin', don't want no jive, Gonna get my freedom in sixty-five."[2]

Days later, when the large, enthusiastic group of marchers arrived in Montgomery, King stood in the shadow of the Alabama State Capitol Building and addressed the crowd. In the musical cadence of his black southern Baptist preacher's voice, King exhorted, "The confrontation of good and evil compressed in the tiny community of Selma generated the massive power to turn the whole nation to a new course." Near the conclusion of his speech, he asked rhetorically, "How long will it take? How long will prejudice blind the visions of men?" Full of optimism and hope, King answered the question: "How long? Not long, because no lie can live forever. How long? Not long because you shall reap what you sow. How long? Not long because the arc of the moral universe is long, but it bends toward justice."[3] The crowd went wild. All over the country, black people cheered. America cheered. This scene buoyed the optimism of those who believed in the power of their nation's political system to change black lives. Professor John Hope Franklin has vivid memories of the hopeful atmosphere of that day. He and other well-known historians were there participating in the Selma-to-Montgomery march, and the experience convinced him that revolutionary change was just around the corner. "It was something brand new," he says, "because it was reaping the benefits of first the Voting Rights Act, and the Civil Rights Act. And I thought this was moving us to another level of realizing the goals of the struggle."[4]

Civil rights movement insiders had been insisting for months that political involvement was destined to be the next phase of black activism. As early as February of 1964, more than a year before Bloody Sunday, Bayard Rustin, one of King's close advisers and one of the architects of the march on Washington, urged civil rights activists to concentrate on political strategies. Rustin conceded that "the task of molding a political movement out of the March on Washington coalition is not simple." But, he asserted, "no alternatives have been advanced. We need to choose our allies on the basis of common political objectives.[5] . . .The role of the civil rights movement in the reorganization of American political life is programmatic as well as strategic. We are challenged now to broaden our social vision, to develop functional programs with concrete objectives."[6]

Along with moderates like Rustin, there were black militants urging black political participation. Malcolm X, recognized as one of the most militant black leaders of the twentieth century in general and the 1960s in particular, made one of his most famous speeches shortly after movement insider Rustin began urging African Americans to build a political coalition. In that speech, "The Ballot or the Bullet," Malcolm advised, "The political philosophy of black nationalism means that the black man should control the politics and politicians in his own community . . . the black man in the black community has to be re-educated into the science of politics so he will know what politics is supposed to bring him in return. Don't be throwing out any bullets. A ballot is like a bullet."[7]

So, when President Johnson signed the Voting Rights Act that hot August day in 1965, many African Americans were poised to participate in the social revolution they were sure would accompany their participation in the political process. They soon realized, however, that regardless of the passage of the Voting Rights Act and sincere federal efforts to enforce it, change would be very slow in coming. When King had stood on the steps of the Alabama State Capitol Building after the Selma-to-Montgomery march and asked the question "How Long?" black people in the audience were not certain of the answer, but they hoped it would not be too long. In the years after the passage of the Voting Rights Act of 1965, though, many could answer, "A very, very long time," because in the months and years that followed, African Americans were confronted by one example after another of southern white intransigence, particularly in the rural areas. Wilcox County, Alabama, just south of Montgomery, is one of those areas. The county seat, Camden, is only thirty-eight miles from Selma. Wilcox County has a history and a tradition of plantation agriculture, large Greek revival antebellum mansions, and ruthless repression of black residents. When the Voting Rights Act was passed in 1965, Wilcox County's black population constituted nearly 78 percent of the total, and black Wilcox residents knew their superior numbers should have ushered in a historic shift in political power under the new law. However, the many lynchings, beatings, and other forms of repression that were part of the black community's collective consciousness convinced them that their white neighbors were not about to concede power without a fight.

In this atmosphere, where white residents were willing to do anything to blunt the impact of black voting strength in their county, charges and countercharges of fraud were leveled in the very first election after the passage of the Voting Rights Act, which was held on May 3, 1966. A slate of black candidates ran, including Rev. Lonnie Brown, a candidate for state senator in District 19. Black residents were genuinely hopeful in the initial stages of the campaign. Brown, a Wilcox native and longtime civil rights activist, observes, however, "Sometimes when you go into these things, you go in kind of naive." Many of the black candidates, he reports, felt empowered just by the opportunity to run for office: "[There were] two things we had in mind; if we could get those positions, and [even] if we didn't get them, we ran for them to let younger people understand that you can do it. It's there for you."[8] Throughout the campaign, the optimistic Reverend Brown continued to believe that when the election results came in, Wilcox County would have its first black elected officials since Reconstruction.

Finally, the big day came, and African American voters all over the county excitedly went to the polls for the first time in their lives. However, the excitement of Wilcox County's new black voters was tempered by a nagging sense of unease because they knew how angry and determined their white neighbors were. Despite their fears, most black voters proudly marked their ballots, and then they waited, secure in the knowledge that they far outnumbered the county's white electorate. By that evening, the anxiety had become almost unbearable as the candidates and their supporters waited to hear the vote tallies. Brown recalls, "It seems to me that up until about ten o'clock the night of the election I was leading, but that changed. What we really think happened [is that] it changed in the counting." The votes were counted in a room inside the courthouse, where no African Americans were present. When the vote tallies were complete, not a single black candidate was elected. Brown concludes, "We felt that it [the election] had been stolen." Such an overwhelming defeat in their heavily black county left black political activists reeling. Most were disappointed, some were angry, but all remained determined. Brown explains, "We were discouraged some. . . . but you got to remember, we had been discouraged all of our lives about something. So it wasn't enough to kill our spirits . . . it just intensified [our desire]."[9] Black determination notwithstanding, over the next decade and beyond, the fraud and intimidation continued unabated. It was not until 1978 that the first black candidate was elected to office in Wilcox County, Alabama, thirteen years after President Johnson signed the Voting Rights Act into law.

Later generations of black candidates in elections in other areas also suspected that dirty tricks were routinely used by the white power structure to maintain the political status quo. For example, in neighboring Macon County, Alabama, the home of the famous black accommodationist leader Booker T. Washington, Tuskegee native Johnny Ford served as the campaign manager for several local black candidates in the early 1970s. Because Ford anticipated the use of fraudulent tactics by the white power structure, he helped develop an organization of black poll-watchers in his county. As soon as the polls closed, the organization quickly swung into action. Ford explains, "Once the election was over, [we went to] the voting machines [and] record[ed] the results. [Then we] walked out of the courthouse across the street. Get on the phone, call in the results to our headquarters. That happened all over the county." But Ford and his poll-watchers did not stop there: they contacted Washington. "So we had the Justice Department there too. And we had results before they [the opposition] could do anything about it."[10]

Some thirty years after Ford and his poll-watchers revolutionized Macon County politics, James Perkins, a native of Selma, Alabama, decided to run for mayor. He was not the first black candidate to challenge white incumbent Joe Smitherman in the years after the passage of the Voting Rights Act. But up to that point, none had succeeded, and many of the town's black residents were convinced that there was only one reason: election fraud. Thus, when Perkins decided to run, he knew he had his work cut out for him, and he and his supporters took careful measures to ensure the integrity of the vote tally. "We staged security at the front and back door of City Hall because that's where the ballots were. We had someone to stay in the clerk's office all that day. All that night someone was down here watching City Hall. The next day we showed up with 15 volunteers and 3 copying machines. We copied everything that had a mark on it." At the time Perkins ran for mayor, he owned a computer company, and he had one of his programmers come to Selma to analyze the vote tally. "Then we began to sort and process that data looking for patterns and then it became very obvious what was happening. We found what we dubbed as factories; absentee ballot factories where 40 and 50 ballots were coming out of a single home. . . . We took that to the attorneys."[11] The results from that election provided the basis for a lengthy court battle, but eventually Perkins was seated as mayor of Selma. The fraud and intimidation that marred countless elections in the late 1960s continued unabated. By the early 1970s these continuing efforts to restrict black voters were carried out against the backdrop of the political dirty tricks perpetrated by members of President Richard

Nixon's administration. Because of the resulting Watergate scandal, many Americans became suspicious of all politicians. Thus, just as larger numbers of black candidates were beginning to enter the political arena, they were faced with an atmosphere of suspicion, in which charges and countercharges of all manner of political trickery were common.

When black candidates, most of them with no political experience, took the first tentative steps toward running for office, many quickly realized that their inexperience put them at a serious disadvantage. Of course, the widespread black inexperience was a direct result of the systematic exclusion of African Americans from the political process for much of their history in this country. The era of Reconstruction right after the Civil War was a notable, but brief, exception. At that time, a number of black men, some of whom were newly freed slaves, ran successfully for political office. Frederick Douglass, former slave, newspaper editor, abolitionist, and one of the best-known black leaders of the nineteenth century, recognizing the importance of this black political participation, spoke of it when he met with President Andrew Johnson. Douglass fixed the president with a stern stare, and in his commanding bass voice said, "Your noble and humane predecessor placed in our hands the sword to assist in saving the nation, and we do hope that you, his able successor, will favorably regard the placing in our hands [of] the ballot *with which to save ourselves.*"[12] When the ex-Confederates regained control of the southern states, not long afterward, black political participation was systematically halted through an effective and vicious combination of fraud, intimidation, and brutality. In 1901, after years of waning political participation, the term of the only black representative still serving in the U.S. Congress ended, and nearly three decades passed before another black congressman served in the House of Representatives.

As the twentieth century dawned, and Congress became all white again, African Americans began leaving the South in droves. Northeastern and midwestern industrial centers attracted the lion's share of black migrants, and that remarkable movement that came to be known as the Great Migration set the stage for northern black participation in the political process. Unlike their southern brothers and sisters, African Americans in the North were allowed to vote, and as the number of northern black registered voters rapidly increased, black candidates began testing the political waters in local races. Finally in 1928, a northern black candidate was elected to Congress. The new black congressman, Oscar DePriest, had left Alabama to move to Chicago in 1899. After being bitten by the political bug, DePriest became Chicago's first black alderman in 1915, and when he was elected to the House of Representatives in 1928, he became the first northern African American ever elected to that body. Even though DePriest was elected to represent the people in the First Congressional District in Illinois, many black people outside his district eagerly embraced him. As John Hope Franklin explains, "DePriest's position was peculiar. He represented not only his own district, but all the blacks of the United States. During his three terms in office he was in great demand as a speaker and was pointed out by African Americans everywhere as the realization of their fondest dreams."[13]

When Adam Clayton Powell Jr. was elected to Congress from a district in Harlem in the 1940s, African Americans responded in a similar way. Black representatives in Congress were still so scarce at that time that he, too, became a powerful leadership symbol to African Americans all over the country. Former North Carolina congressman Frank Ballance says of Powell's importance: "The person who spoke my language and advocated the issues that I was concerned about was Adam [Clayton] Powell." Even though Ballance lived in North Carolina, far away from Powell's district, the black congressman's importance to the young Ballance was not diminished.[14]

On the eve of the passage of the 1965 Voting Rights Act, other black candidates in northern areas ran for office with increasing frequency and success. One of the most notable examples is Richard Hatcher of Gary, Indiana. Even though Hatcher was born in the North (in Michigan City, Indiana, in 1915), like so many other African Americans, he had an ancestral connection to the South. He grew up hearing stories about black life in the South, but there is one story that made a deep impression on him. That was his father's account of leaving Georgia before Richard was born. According to the elder Hatcher, he was forced to leave the South because he asserted his independence by refusing to work for a local white man. Young Richard never tired of hearing the details of his father's harrowing escape, and even now Richard Hatcher remembers all the details of his father's dramatic account. "My father was very strong; head of the family," he recalls. "[He] dropped out of school in the second grade down in Georgia and basically came up North because . . . he didn't want to work for this one [white] man, and at that time, you didn't tell someone you didn't want to work for them." Hatcher pauses a moment, reflecting on his father's bravery, and continues with a smile: "Basically, [they] had to disguise him as a woman and put him on a train, and that's how he got out."[15]

Richard Hatcher's father had a profound influence on him. In particular, the elder Hatcher exposed his son to politics very early. "On election day he [the elder Hatcher] went around and picked up people and took them to the polls to vote. I would ride with him. . . . I was just three or four years old, so I just sort of grew up with the idea of politics." Another important influence on young Richard Hatcher was his exposure to civil rights activism. His civil rights involvement began when he was a student at Indiana University in Bloomington and he came to realize that there were segregated restaurants near the campus. Hatcher explains, "At that time, as long as you were on campus at IU [Indiana University], you were fine. . . . The minute you went off campus, all of that changed. You couldn't get your hair cut, you know, in the city, and you certainly could not go into any of these grills or bars or whatever."[16] Hatcher and a group of his friends reacted by picketing one of the establishments closest to the university's campus, and eventually it desegregated. Other restaurants soon followed suit. This early civil rights success seemed to whet Hatcher's activist appetite, and he soon set his sights on conditions in his hometown. When he returned to Michigan City, Indiana, for the summer, he helped organize demonstrations to desegregate local establishments.

Hatcher sees his eventual entry into politics as a natural outgrowth of his youthful activism, because when he first ran for office, he was primarily concerned about fighting the corruption that was so ingrained in city government. By this time, he had graduated from law school and was working in city government in Gary, Indiana. He recalls that his first introduction to city government was shocking and disturbing: "It was an environment of corruption. It was a way of life. You were expected—I mean if you didn't do that, they thought something was wrong [with you]. And so that's why I decided . . . we have to challenge all of this." So in 1963, Richard Hatcher ran for a seat on the Gary, Indiana, City Council. He won. Soon after he was sworn in, he was elected council president; this was an unprecedented achievement for a freshman councilman. From the outset, it was clear that Hatcher was a councilman on a mission. He recalls, "I immediately introduced an omnibus civil rights bill because at that time, you still couldn't go to [certain] restaurants here in Gary." Looking back on it, Hatcher frowns at the memory, saying emphatically, "There were places where you [black people] couldn't live."[17]

After serving on the Gary City Council for three years, Hatcher decided to run for mayor. First, he had to secure the Democratic nomination, and his campaign during the primary election was grueling and bruising. Hatcher ran against two white candidates, one of whom was the incumbent. Because everyone expected one of the white candidates to win, Hatcher says, "I was just there. I was pretty much under the radar. No one really gave me much of a chance to win at all." But he did win, and he smiles at the memory. He did not have long to savor his victory, however, because to the candidate's surprise and dismay, the local Democratic Party refused to support him—even though he had won the party's primary. The years seem to melt away, and the emotion in his voice is still raw as Hatcher explains the depth of his disappointment when his party turned its back on him: "A few days after the primary, the county chairman came out and said that he wasn't quite sure whether the Democratic Party could support me because he wasn't sure that I was a red, white, and blue American."[18] Hatcher rolls his eyes in exasperation and explains that the Democratic Party chairman questioned his patriotism because of his very vocal and very public opposition to the Vietnam war.

Undaunted, Richard Hatcher put all his energy into campaigning for the fall election. When some members of the National Democratic Party establishment heard of the young candidate's plight, they offered their support. Two of Hatcher's most prominent supporters were Ted and Bobby Kennedy. Still, even with the support of some members of the National Democratic Party, Hatcher faced an uphill battle. As he looks back on that long-ago struggle, he pauses, and then in a soft voice describes one of the lowest points of the long and difficult campaign: "It was pretty ugly. I was actually shot at . . . I came out the door one night; we were going to go to some meetings, and this car sort of roared down the street, you know, and I heard this sound. . . . You don't think it's a shot, but it went right through the screen door that I was coming out of." Hatcher adds matter-of-factly, "Fortunately, it didn't hit me."[19]

The reaction to Richard Hatcher's candidacy ranged from one extreme to the other: after being shot at, Hatcher was offered a forty-thousand-dollar bribe if he would just withdraw his candidacy. He refused. Then, on the eve of the election, two reporters from *Look* magazine asked to meet with Hatcher at midnight. Even though he had some misgivings about the clandestine meeting, he decided to go anyway. When Hatcher met with them, the two white reporters glanced furtively around and jumped at every shadow they saw as they haltingly described a plot they had uncovered to manipulate the election results the next day. After Hatcher reported the plot to authorities, the FBI got involved, and the governor of the state of Indiana called out the National Guard. To this day, Hatcher refuses to believe the governor's claims that he mobilized the guard to prevent violence at the polls. Instead, Hatcher is convinced that the governor's action was a thinly disguised attempt to intimidate black voters.[20] Yet, even though the sight of the National Guard's tanks rolling down the streets of Gary made many African American residents uneasy, it did not keep them from the polls. By 8:00 P.M. on election night, black residents in Gary were buzzing about the possibility of a Hatcher victory. The buzz grew louder and louder until finally, at midnight, the results were certified: Richard Hatcher had become the first black candidate ever elected mayor of Gary, Indiana. Furthermore, even though Carl Stokes was elected the first black mayor of Cleveland, Ohio, at the same time, Hatcher was sworn in just hours ahead of Stokes, making Hatcher the first black mayor of a major American city. The year was 1967.

Thus, at the dawn of black electoral success, in those first chaotic months after President Johnson signed the Voting Rights Act, the majority of black voters and black candidates had few black political role models and precious little experience. While northern African Americans had limited political experience, black southerners had virtually no experience at all, and in this experience vacuum, movement activists who were recognized as leaders in the South often became the first black candidates to run for political office. Yet, even though they were seen as leaders because of their ability to organize and implement a protest campaign, civil rights activists were not necessarily able to run a successful political campaign.

The transition from protest to political action was therefore often difficult and fraught with contradictions. It was that way for Andrew Young. After his participation in the civil rights movement, Young went on to serve as mayor of Atlanta, congressman from the Fifth Congressional District in Atlanta, and ambassador to the United Nations during the Clinton administration. But early in his shift from activism to politics, when he was first elected mayor of Atlanta, some of the same activists he had marched with during the movement began protesting city policies, and they decided to picket the mayor's office. Young smiles at the memory, enjoying the irony of being the target of civil rights activists whom he still regarded as colleagues and friends. At one point, Young recalls laughingly, he grabbed a sign and joined the picket line outside his office. The line between protest and politics was exceedingly fine.[21]

Congressman John Lewis is another veteran civil rights activist who entered politics. In his estimation, movement leadership and political leadership are two entirely different things: "It's a different world . . . you may be in a sense a movement leader; a leader of a cause. The movement was like a mission. It was a calling. If you're in the movement, you're never out of it. You may be out of an organization . . . it's almost like a religion . . . it was so sacred, so precious, so right, and so necessary. As an elected political leader you have to go out and ask for people's support, ask for their vote. And they can give it or not give it. . . . You can be rejected by the voters."[22] Congresswoman Eleanor Holmes Norton has also switched from activism to politics. She argues that although there are fundamental differences between movement leaders and political leaders, political leadership is a necessary complement to civil rights leadership: "We needed the same kind of pervasive leadership in all the quarters of the society that everybody else had if we were in fact going to move. We couldn't move with just a few civil rights leaders kind of pronouncing what should be done. We needed to have people in the state legislature. We needed to have elected officials throughout the society and [on] the school boards. We need to have people in the House and the Senate."[23]

Native Atlantan Julian Bond was one of the earliest leaders in the black freedom struggle to move into political leadership. Because the experience he gained while serving as SNCC's communications director allowed him to polish both his writing and his public-speaking skills, he was favorably situated to make the leap from protest to politics. In 1965, at the urging of friends and movement colleagues, Bond decided to run for a seat in the Georgia state legislature. As he thought about it, he had some hard decisions to make. First was the issue of party affiliation. Bond had been so busy as a civil rights activist that he had not given much thought to the matter. He explains, "I didn't know whether I was a Democrat or a Republican. It had never been an issue." The choice of party affiliation, particularly for black southerners in the 1960s, was not simple: even though the national Democratic Party publicly embraced civil rights, numerous southern white Democrats were rabid segregationists. And there was a cadre of liberal Republicans during this era who staunchly supported civil rights legislation. Finally, after mulling it over, Bond made his decision. "I said to myself, 'do I want to be in the party headed by Barry Goldwater, or do I want to be in the party headed by Lyndon Johnson?' And I said, 'I want to be in Johnson's party.' And I ran as a Democrat."[24]

Julian Bond won, becoming the youngest candidate elected to the Georgia state legislature that session. Because many of his new colleagues were among the most bitter opponents of the black freedom struggle, the freshman state representative had no idea what to expect. Looking back, Bond confesses, "I had a stereotypical view of what my colleagues would be like—my white colleagues. I thought they'd all be country hayseeds." He soon realized how wrong he was: "I was surprised to discover that while many were country hayseeds, some of them were sophisticated educated people with a wide view of the world." As he began to get acquainted with the other legislators, he worried that his lack of political experience would have a negative effect on his ability to represent his district effectively. "I initially thought I wouldn't accomplish much, but I'd be a voice. I'd be a loud voice and I'd promote these issues. They'd probably get rejected. Nonetheless, they'd hear about them." As it turned out, most of the issues he raised "did get rejected. . . . But we were able to do some things." To his surprise, Bond's experience as a state legislator allowed him to see the issues that were most important to him from a new perspective. Everything was not just black and white after all. "We were able to relieve some of the inequities that weren't typically black-white, but played out in the legislature as urban-rural."[25]

In neighboring Tennessee, Robert Booker was elected to the Tennessee General Assembly one year after Julian Bond's election in Georgia. Like Bond, Booker entered politics after participating in the civil rights movement. Booker's involvement had been in Knoxville, Tennessee, where he was the Student Government Association president at Knoxville College, a historically black Presbyterian school. In 1960, Booker and other Knoxville College students conducted sit-ins that desegregated the city's downtown restaurants in record time. Fresh from his victories in the local civil rights movement, Booker decided to run for the state legislature in order to continue his work for black progress. He won, but when he took his seat in the legislature, he soon became frustrated by his new colleagues' resistance to change. Forty years later, Booker grimaces at the memory. "[It was] very frustrating," he says. "Great experience, because I got to meet some great people; learned how the legislature works. But, frustrating when you thought about getting a minimum wage law passed and that wasn't going to happen in Tennessee." None of the other bills that Booker supported passed either. He sighs as he remembers the experience and concludes sadly, "So it was that kind of thing that really frustrated me, and after six years, I really got tired of it."[26]

Selma civil rights attorney J. L. Chestnut Jr. was an eyewitness to Bloody Sunday and the subsequent events leading to the passage of the Voting Rights Act of 1965. Yet, even though the real possibilities for change ushered in by the new law excited Chestnut, he realized that there were limits. "The black leadership prior to the civil rights movement," he explains, "was of necessity accommodationist, and created pretty much and nurtured by a self-serving white establishment. The civil rights movement produced a handful—I mean locally—a handful of black leaders not endorsed by the white establishment, but very soon co-opted by the white establishment. And that's true for any number of reasons. It is almost impossible to control a city *solely on the basis of political power.*" To illustrate his point, Chestnut uses the election of Maynard Jackson, the first black mayor of Atlanta. "Maynard Jackson told me years ago that the thing he learned in his first term when he was first elected mayor of Atlanta, he went in and the first day he discovered how little power was in the mayor's office, and how much real power was in the boardrooms of Coca-Cola and all these other [corporations]. And he literally made a

B-line to corporate Atlanta and [said], 'I tell you what, you give me jobs and prosperity. I'll give you peace.' And Maynard struck that deal . . . and Atlanta was on its way." Chestnut observes pointedly, "Maynard Jackson represents the kind of evolving new black leadership that came out of the civil rights movement."[27]

Dr. Joe Leonard is a slender and dapper young man with a recent Ph.D. in history from Howard University. The most famous campaigns of the civil rights movement of the 1960s were over by the time Leonard was born in 1967, but he is intrigued by the movement and the complex process of leadership formation within the black community. He is particularly interested in the transition from movement leadership to political leadership. Leonard works at the Black Leadership Forum in Washington, D.C., and is a former staff member of Rev. Jesse Jackson's Rainbow/Push Coalition. He observes, "We had black leadership at the grassroots level [during the civil rights movement]. Now the people at the grassroots level look to that black senator or state representative, or congressman and think, 'that's my leader.'" Leonard declares with frustration, "That ain't your leader, that's your REP-RE-SEN-TA-TIVE." He is careful to emphasize each one of the syllables. "That's why the House of Representatives says House of Representatives, not House of Leadership." Leonard laments, "The activists of the sixties are going into politics . . . because that's where they think leadership is." But Leonard disagrees with this notion. Instead, he argues that the effectiveness of black elected officials is severely limited because they are confronted by deeply ingrained patterns and customs in the majority white legislative bodies in which they serve. Because the institutions are so orthodox, "you will never really flourish."[28]

Regardless of the limitations faced by black elected officials, many black activists are still convinced that an African American presence in elective politics is the necessary next step to ensure the continuation of black progress. Dr. Benjamin Hooks recalls just how important legislative support was when he first became the director of the NAACP.

I became head of the NAACP in 1977. It was a tough time, but the laws were on the books. What I was faced with was the Supreme Court every year knocking it back a little bit: Bakke . . . I guess I could call a whole handful of cases; every one designed

to knock it [black legal progress] out. In the total black community they never realized what was happening. In the intellectual black community they understood it. And the way to get it
[changed] was not marches and demonstrations. . . . So we had
to go back to Congress to get Congress to pass laws to undo
what the Supreme Court had messed up.[29]

In most instances, the movement veterans who made the leap from
movement activism to the political arena were located in the South, particularly in those areas that were directly involved with civil rights movement campaigns. At the same time, however, the pace of black political
activism in the North was also increasing, but it grew outside the context of direct involvement in black protest activities that were part of
the major civil rights campaigns. Consequently, there were times when
the northern black political perspective clashed with the civil-rights-
activist perspective, making for a complex political atmosphere. For example, former senator Carol Moseley Braun found that in her native Chicago there seemed to be a natural separation between black movement
activists and black political activists. "From my perspective," she explains,
"there were almost two parallel tracks. You had the movement people on
the one hand doing their thing. But then the people who were involved
in electoral politics were an entirely different group, and they didn't often
come together." The separation sometimes led to tense times: "There
were times when there was antagonism; where the activities of the civil
rights community either embarrassed or threatened the machine politicians." However, sometimes the two sides cooperated. "There were other
times when they [civil rights activists and politicians] got together in private settings and played the old rope a dope."[30] The two groups would
pretend they were still at odds with each other while they attempted to
wring concessions from the white power structure.

Today's black politicians are separated from the civil rights movement
and the black politicians of that era by four decades or more and by new
political, economic, and educational realities. Yet, the civil rights movement of the 1960s continues to exert a powerful influence on the black
psyche; it transcends the generations. That is why many black politicians
today continue to feel a direct connection to earlier generations of black

politicians and to the civil rights movement of the previous century. For-mer North Carolina congressman Frank Ballance refers to those anteced-ents as he says, "You have to think about that history . . . as you try and uphold your responsibilities and be true to your heritage and your his-tory. So, yes, I think about Adam [Clayton] Powell."[31]

Mayor James Perkins of Selma, Alabama, can never forget the civil rights movement because he has personal experience with the results of the movement. As a child, he witnessed demonstrations firsthand. During his adolescence, he felt the pain that came with rapid change:

> When I finished high school, I was angry . . . at the world. I was bitter at the results of desegregation. The results of desegregation had taken our school away. . . . Keep in mind that after the lights were turned out and the celebrities went home, we were left to implement desegregation of our school systems and our lunch counters, and our movie theaters. . . . And it was the children who walked into the front doors of the doctors offices for the first time and insisted on being waited on, and insisted on the elimina-tion of separate waiting rooms and those types of social issues.[32]

As he recalls the turmoil of that period, Perkins's smooth, medium-brown skin gathers in deep folds of concentration between his eyebrows. "It was us. We did that. And it left scars because, you know, it was done with tremendous resistance. So, as a child, I was angry." On his journey to adulthood, and to the mayor's office, Perkins had to learn to deal with those feelings that were left over from the civil rights era. When he ran for mayor, the issue of race quickly surfaced, and through that experience, Perkins learned, "Everybody white is not against me and everybody black is not for me. There are people who don't want change. There are people who are afraid of change." Today, Perkins is determined to move beyond politics based on race in his town, which remains one of the most endur-ing symbols of the civil rights movement. He insists, "I represent reform. I don't care how you paint it, shape it, or shade it."[33]

Black politicians younger than Mayor Perkins were born too late to experience the ugly reality of de jure segregation or the uplifting feeling of civil rights activism. Nevertheless, most have enormous respect for the struggles of the black activists who came before them and paved the way for their political participation, even though they recognize that their own perspective is different from that of the civil rights generation. For example, this is the view of Kwame Brown, a thirty-three-year-old black member of the Washington, D.C., City Council:

> I looked at the political landscape, and I was always somewhat frustrated. Respectful, [but] respectfully frustrated. Because I have so much respect for the generation that came before me, but I was disappointed in the fact that we were still singing the same song. . . . I really think we're in an era where we can change that fight. . . . And I thought about it, and I came to a conclusion. . . . I said, "it's my fault. It's my generation's fault." Because a lot of [my] friends and people I know of my generation, we want to make money quick, fast, and in a hurry, and we don't want to do no work. And until we decided that we were not only going to give back, but get involved, no matter what the price was, then this world will continue to go down the direction that everyone will still not be happy with.[34]

Congressman Artur Davis, a member of the House of Representatives representing the Seventh Congressional District in Alabama, is about the same age as Councilman Brown. When Davis was growing up in Montgomery, Alabama, stories of the civil rights movement were all around him. Davis left the South to complete his education: he received both his undergraduate degree and his law degree from Harvard University. Determined to serve his region, the young lawyer made his way back to Alabama, where he worked as a federal prosecutor, served as an assistant U.S attorney, and worked on the staff of the Southern Poverty Law Center.

In 2000, when Davis decided to challenge black incumbent Earl Hilliard for the congressional seat in Alabama's seventh district, the campaign turned ugly. Some people charged that Davis could not possibly understand the historical connection of the civil rights movement to black Alabama politics, because he had been born after the movement was over. Davis bristles at the accusation. In a voice that blends his Harvard education with his Alabama roots, he argues, "I have a problem with analyses that purport to say [that] these individuals [who] are younger did not experience the civil rights movement, ergo, they [do not] relate to politics in the same way. Number one, all of us don't relate to politics in the same way. You know, the politics of Memphis and Birmingham are different; the politics of the Black Belt and Memphis are different." The young congressman's tone softens as he continues, "We were very careful in our campaign to talk about that movement [the civil rights movement] with reverence. We were very careful to talk about the contributions of that movement with reverence because that's . . . appropriate and completely accurate from a historical standpoint."[35] Despite his best efforts, Davis lost his bid to unseat Hilliard. Undaunted, Davis immediately set his sights on the 2002 election. The next time around, he won.

Davis represents an unusual district. It includes Birmingham, Alabama's largest city, Montgomery, the state capital, and several counties in the Black Belt, which is the poorest part of the state and one of the poorest regions in the country. These are the places where some of the most memorable triumphs and tragedies of the civil rights movement occurred, and they are forever linked with images of Bull Connor, the bombing of the Sixteenth Street Baptist Church, Bloody Sunday, and the Selma-to-Montgomery march. Artur Davis is sensitive to the civil rights legacy of his district, but he is also mindful of the difficult challenges he faces. He explains, "If you are historically aware of the civil rights movement, if you are historically aware of the legacy of racism, it certainly affects the way you view the world." The young congressman pauses thoughtfully. "I think you can respond one of two ways. One way is to respond with a very negative sense of pessimism and resentment toward outsiders. Another way is to . . . appreciate the progress we've made as a country and a community, and to realize the need to continue to move forward. . . . I think I was from the latter category . . . I was motivated by the history of our community and motivated by the history of the region."[36]

As younger black politicians formulate their views, their elders are watching them carefully, and they worry. Older black leaders know what it is like to be denied their basic rights because of the color of their skin, and they wonder what impact the lack of firsthand knowledge of segregation will have on the views of their young colleagues. For example, former North Carolina congressman Frank Ballance, who remembers segregation, insists, "There is a difference between people who did not experience the raw form of segregation [and those who did]. They don't understand the brutality of that system . . . so they haven't seen the dark side of America." Ballance worries that this difference in perspective could have serious consequences. "They [younger leaders] may not be as aggressive as Maxine Waters [black congresswoman from California], or some other people who have been through the fire, and through the storm."[37]

Black politicians in the new millennium are also obliged to deal with the same choice that Julian Bond faced more than forty years ago at the beginning of his political career: party affiliation. Of course, this is nothing new; African Americans have debated the issue of political party affiliation for well over a century. During Reconstruction, the newly freed slaves voted with the party of Lincoln, and the Radical Republicans were glad to have their votes. Black loyalty to the Republican Party survived in many areas until well into the twentieth century. For example, Dr. Benjamin Hooks, past president of the NAACP and a native of Memphis, Tennessee, observes that even during the early twentieth century when he was growing up, there was an important black Republican presence in his hometown. Hooks was born in 1925, and during his adolescence, Robert R. Church, a prominent black Republican, was a close friend of his father's. Hooks asserts, "If you read the life of R. R. Church . . . all during the forties, he was a part of that Republican Party effort to make . . . things better, and was beating the drum for equality, and moving forward within the system that existed at that point at a time when the Democratic Party [was not interested]. The whole Black and Tan Republican movement was about that."[38]

Yet, even though the majority of African Americans who could vote in the late nineteenth and early twentieth centuries remained safely in the fold of the Republican Party, there were exceptions. Even as early as 1928, some African Americans were becoming alarmed at the racist tone enunciated by Republican Party leaders trying to woo white southerners to their party. Certain prominent black newspaper editors were so incensed that their newspapers endorsed Alfred E. Smith, the Democratic nominee for president in 1928.[39] However, the most serious black defection from Republican ranks occurred during the Great Depression. Democratic president Franklin Roosevelt's sympathy for the black plight, and the inclusion of African Americans in his New Deal programs, prompted a massive shift of black voters from the Republicans to the Democrats. That shift became apparent by the election of 1936 and was even more pronounced by the election of 1940. In the later decades of the twentieth century, bolstered by President John Kennedy's sympathy and President Lyndon Johnson's active support for the cause of civil rights, African American loyalty to the Democratic Party remained virtually unshakable.

These days, even though the vast majority of African Americans still faithfully vote for Democratic candidates in national, state, and local elections, many black voters are becoming increasingly uneasy about what some see as blind black allegiance to the Democratic Party. Julian Bond, who always ran as a Democrat during his political career, laments, "The Democratic Party is awfully disappointing now." He quickly continues, "But it doesn't mean that the option is the Republicans, because the Republicans are worse. I'm fond of saying that in the 2002 election one party was shameless and the other was spineless, and when the shameless and the spineless compete, the shameless will win every single time." Bond is convinced that African American voters will continue to vote for the Democratic Party, "not because it's the savior, but because it's so much better than the Republicans who are terrible." He sighs in frustration as he concludes, "That's a funny situation to be in."[40]

Selma civil rights attorney J. L. Chestnut refuses to identify himself as either a Democrat or a Republican. With a twinkle in his eye, the old civil rights lawyer chuckles as he talks about the consternation that his personal declaration of independence from political party labels invariably causes. Because of his race and his civil rights background, people expect him to be a Democrat, and he never tires of surprising them by declaring that he is an Independent. His own independence notwithstanding, Chestnut worries about the impact of party labels on the fortunes of some black leaders; he cites the example of black conservative Republican J. C. Watts. During the 1990s, Watts was elected to represent a conservative and largely white congressional district in his native Oklahoma. Chestnut is convinced that Watts's Republican affiliation makes perfect sense, reasoning, "I think that J. C. Watts dealt with the reality of his situation."

The lawyer goes on to explain that "the people who had to vote for him were white. He represented their interests. And he said what he had to say. . . . But where he could help [black people], he did that."[41]

J. C. Watts grew up in a very poor Oklahoma community, where he insists that all the residents, irrespective of color, had certain important values in common. As he puts it, "The value system in Eufaula [his hometown] was much the same. Your word mattered a lot more than how much money you had in your pocket. Your honesty was more important than the house you lived in or the car you drove. Unlike in Washington, it wasn't who you knew that determined how far you could go, but how hard you were willing to work."[42] Despite these shared values, however, Watts is quick to point out that racial segregation was a part of his world. "I can remember hearing my parents and grandmother talk about race and discrimination. They weren't blind to the world around them."[43] And race mattered a great deal to young J. C. Watts; he saw definite advantages in being black. "Back in the mid-1970s when I was sporting an Afro and about to go off to college, Jesse Jackson was inspiring young African Americans like me and my brothers and sisters by telling us, "You *are* somebody." Watts insists that Jackson "was right, and so was that message then and now. 'I am somebody' is as truthful and potent a statement for my kids today as it was for me and my buddies in 1975 growing up in Eufaula. Ten years earlier, the Civil Rights Act of 1964 had been a cultural earthquake in our country, but while Jim Crow may have been officially stricken from the law books, its legacy remained in too many hearts."[44]

Years later, when J. C. Watts decided to go into politics, he chose to join the Republican Party, even though the vast majority of African Americans were Democrats and the Democratic Party had for many years been perceived to be much more sympathetic to black civil rights than the Republican Party. "My decision to become Republican wasn't based on history but on the principles that the party stands for today. By 1989, I felt I no longer had much in common with the national Democratic Party. . . . In December of that year, I switched my registration not out of convenience, but out of conviction." The former congressman freely acknowledges that some have been critical of his choice: "I knew what I was doing wouldn't be popular. It created some strain even in relationships I had built over the years."[45] He explains the source of much of the criticism he has received this way: "That refusal to be stereotyped and cast into certain beliefs and behaviors is what gets people of color who take another path, particularly a conservative path, into a heap of trouble."[46]

Watts recognizes that his party affiliation has prompted other African Americans to question his loyalty to the race over the years. But, as far as he is concerned, the reason for such questioning has less to do with his beliefs and more to do with what he labels the "group identity" of African Americans. "Like any group that has endured much, African Americans have created a strong and mutually reinforcing sense of group identity. That's not a bad thing in and of itself." However, "when the group identity becomes more important than the individual, it can blind us to valuable viewpoints, options, and opportunities."[47] He insists that black group identity is what makes many African Americans unable to see the merits of the conservative Republican philosophy he embraces. "It doesn't matter whether it is Colin Powell or Condoleezza Rice, Shelby Steele, Thomas Sowell, Clarence Thomas, or yours truly—we have all been labeled expedients, Uncle Toms, oreos, sell-outs, traitors to our race, and other equally uncomplimentary characterizations."[48]

Down in Memphis, Tennessee, Dr. Benjamin Hooks agrees with Watts's assessment of black group orthodoxy as far as party affiliation is concerned. According to Hooks:

> If a black leader decided to become a Republican, and he delivered every egg in the county . . . and every cow brought milk, he'd still be dead . . . So that Colin Powell doesn't have a chance to be a black leader. . . . If he stands up at the Republican National Convention and speaks out in favor of women's rights . . . If he stands up at the Republican National Convention and speaks out in favor of Affirmative Action . . . he ain't going to get no more credit . . . because [people] will say that's what he should have said all the time. The fact that he said it there [at the Republican National Convention], they pooh poohed it. So I think that black leadership basically is standing in its own way now because we have lost sight of the fact that we would be more powerful if we could point out to the Democrats, *you do take the chance of losing us if you don't treat us right.*[49]

Mayor Johnny Ford of Tuskegee, Alabama, is a slender man with smooth dark skin and a winning smile, and like J. C. Watts, Ford is a black Republican. But Ford did not start his political career that way. His first experience in the political arena was as a campaign worker for Robert Kennedy's presidential campaign in 1968. At that time, Ford was young, idealistic, and convinced that the liberal Democratic New York senator was just what the country needed. Kennedy's assassination on June 5, 1968, devastated Ford, who recalls in a soft voice, "All of our hopes and dreams just . . ." His voice trails off. "That was it." Some years later, when Johnny Ford ran for mayor of Tuskegee, he ran as a Democrat. But he insists that his party loyalty was always conditional: "I have never been a normal Democrat or a normal Republican, or whatever. I support whoever I think can get the job done for my people." Immediately after declaring his candidacy, Ford was first surprised, then later angered, by the reaction of the National Democratic Party. His usual smile disappears when he brings up the memory. "When I was running for mayor, I went to the Democratic Party; I went to Ted Kennedy; I went to all the powers that be. I said, 'I'm running for mayor down here in Tuskegee, Alabama. You all help me. Send me some money . . . use your influence.'" Their reaction? "I was virtually ignored." Despite Democratic neglect, Ford won the election. Smiling again, he notes, "Then once the election was over, here come the Democrats. . . . I heard from everybody."[50] But it was too late, as far as Johnny Ford was concerned. The damage had been done.

Ford asserts that as soon as the Democrats snubbed him, he immediately began to look elsewhere for support. Eventually, he began communicating with members of President Richard Nixon's administration, and he openly supported Nixon's bid for reelection in 1972. Mayor Ford is quick to point out, "My support of Nixon's reelection had nothing to do with Nixon. I was just that pragmatic." When Nixon was reelected, Ford recalls with a smile, "I could turn around now and go back to all of those guys and get millions and millions of dollars, so I supported the reelection."[51] Nevertheless, Ford continued his formal affiliation with the Democratic Party for the next thirty years, finally deciding in 2002 to change his party affiliation. By this time, he had been elected to a post in the Alabama State Legislature, and he had established good working relationships with some Alabama Republicans, including Bob Riley, a white Republican state legislator who went on to unseat Alabama's Democratic governor Don Siegleman. Ford notified the chairman of the Alabama State Democratic Party and his constituents of the change in his party affiliation and, without missing a beat, continued his political career.

Since becoming a Republican, Johnny Ford has left the state legislature to run successfully for another term as mayor of Tuskegee, Alabama. He sums up his notion of the importance of party affiliation this way:

> Tuskegee was my goal—not the Democratic Party, not the Republican Party, nationally. My top priority was Tuskegee. And so, my philosophy is; where I'm different from most people is, most people join parties so that they can be a part of the party. . . . My philosophy is I use the party and the political system for the purpose of my people to get resources. I'm just that cold when it comes to politics. . . . I have no permanent friends, and no permanent enemies when it comes to politics; just one permanent interest—that's what's in the best interest of my people.[52]

Former senator Carol Moseley Braun is a Democrat, and she has been scrupulously loyal to the Democratic Party throughout her entire career in public service. However, like Johnny Ford, Braun takes a pragmatic view of party affiliation. She learned early in her career, when she was elected to a post in the Illinois state legislature, how important it was to cultivate relationships with a variety of legislators, regardless of their political affiliation: "One of the reasons I was able to be successful as a state legislator was that I've had no compunctions at all working on and voting, supporting things that the Republicans had, or going to them for support of things that I wanted. . . . It created a kind of bipartisanship in terms of my legislative activities."[53]

Down in Atlanta, Eugene Walker was elected to the Georgia State Senate. He held that seat for a decade, from 1982 to 1992. Walker has a medium-brown complexion, the intense profile and deep voice of Fredrick Douglass, and the height and reach of NBA star Wilt Chamberlain. He was born and raised in Thomaston, Georgia, a small town just outside of Atlanta. After graduating from Clark College in Atlanta, Walker

Col. Alexander Jefferson, a Detroit native and a Tuskegee airman. Photo by Cynthia Griggs Fleming.

Congressman John Lewis is speaking at a commemoration of the
Freedom Rides. His former SNCC colleague Diane Nash looks on.
Photo by Cynthia Griggs Fleming.

Selma civil rights attorney J. L. Chestnut *[seated]* poses with
SNCC's Selma Project director Dr. Bernard Lafayette at a
commemoration of the passage of the Voting Rights Act. Photo
by Charles Thompson.

Rev. James Lawson, the architect of Nashville's nonviolent workshops and a close confidant of Dr. King. Photo by Cynthia Griggs Fleming.

Washington, D.C., city councilman Kwame Brown in his office. A portrait of one of his heroes, Muhammed Ali, hangs on the wall behind him. Photo by Charles Thompson.

Courtland Cox, a former SNCC staff member and an aide to District of Columbia mayor Marion Barry. Photo by Charles Thompson.

Eleanor Holmes Norton, a former SNCC staff member and now a congresswoman representing the District of Columbia. Photo by Charles Thompson.

Left to right: Charles Sherrod, Avon Rollins, J. L. Chestnut, Charles Jones, and Bernard Lafayette posing together during a commemoration of the passage of the Voting Rights Act. Photo by Charles Thompson.

Dr. Joe Leonard, a recent recipient of a Howard University Ph.D. in history, in his Washington, D.C., office. Leonard is a former aide to Jesse Jackson Sr. Photo by Charles Thompson.

Lawrence Guyot, who was a SNCC staff member and the first chairman of the Mississippi Freedom Democratic Party. Photo by Charles Thompson.

Selma, Alabama, activist Joanne Bland addressing an audience during a commemoration of the passage of the Voting Rights Act. Photo by Charles Thompson.

Dr. Bernard Lafayette, a former SNCC staff member, poses in front of the Greyhound bus station in Birmingham, Alabama, forty-two years after he rode a bus into this same bus station as a Freedom Rider. Photo by Charles Thompson.

James Armstrong, a flag-bearer on the Selma-to-Montgomery march in 1965, carries the flag during a commemoration of the Birmingham movement. Photo by Charles Thompson.

The only African American woman ever elected to the U.S. Senate, Carol Moseley Braun. Photo by Cynthia Griggs Fleming.

Charles Jones, a former SNCC staff member and now a Charlotte civil rights attorney. Photo by Charles Thompson.

Richard Hatcher, as mayor of Gary, Indiana, was the first black mayor of a major American city. Photo by Cynthia Griggs Fleming.

Rev. T. Randel Osburn in Birmingham, Alabama, attending a commemoration of the Birmingham movement. Osburn was a member of the SCLC staff. Photo by Charles Thompson.

Dr. C. T. Vivian, former SCLC director of affiliates and a member of Dr. King's inner circle. Photo by Charles Thompson.

John Lewis in his congressional office with a picture of Dr. King behind him. Photo by Cynthia Griggs Fleming.

Andrew Young, a former Georgia congressman, Atlanta mayor,
U.S. ambassador to the United Nations during the Carter
administration, and a member of SCLC's executive staff. Photo by
Cynthia Griggs Fleming.

Julian Bond, former SNCC communications director, poses
with Rhonda Jones, who recently earned a Ph.D. in history from
Howard University. Photo by Cynthia Griggs Fleming.

Rev. Fred Shuttlesworth poses with the author at a commemoration of the
Birmingham movement. Photo by Charles Thompson.

Journalist Samuel Yette in front of his house in Knoxville, Tennessee. Photo by Cynthia Griggs Fleming.

Dr. Dorothy Cotton, former head of SCLC's Citizenship Program, makes a point to a group of students. Photo by Charles Thompson.

Unita Blackwell, a member of both SNCC and the Mississippi Freedom Democratic Party, was the first black mayor of Mayersville, Mississippi. She is pictured here with Chuck McDew, former head of SNCC. Photo by Charles Thompson.

Rev. James Bevel, a SNCC staff member and a movement strategist, explains a concept to his student audience as Lawrence Guyot looks on. Photo by Charles Thompson.

George Curry, a nationally known journalist. Photo by Charles Thompson.

Movement veterans, gathered for a commemoration of Mississippi Freedom Summer, join hands to sing the movement anthem "We Shall Overcome." *Left to right:* Candy Carawan, Guy Carawan, Timothy Jenkins, Chuck McDew, Bettie Fikes, James Bevel, Unita Blackwell, Martha Noonan, Charles Jones, Matthew Jones, and Avon Rollins. Photo by Charles Thompson.

Congressman Artur Davis from Alabama's Seventh District. Photo by Charles Thompson.

Rev. Samuel Billy Kyles in front of the Lorraine Motel in Memphis, Tennessee. The wreath on the balcony marks where Dr. King was standing when he was shot. Kyles was on the balcony with King at the time. Photo by Charles Thompson.

Robert Booker on a bridge named for him near downtown Knoxville, Tennessee. Photo by Cynthia Griggs Fleming.

Maureen Taylor, a former Black Panther and a Detroit community activist, poses at her 40th high school reunion. Photo by Cynthia Griggs Fleming.

Rev. Al Sharpton, a nationally known civil rights activist and a former U.S. presidential candidate. Photo by Cynthia Griggs Fleming.

Dr. Eugene Walker, a former Georgia state senator and now a DeKalb County school board member. Photo by Cynthia Griggs Fleming.

Rev. James Bevel *[left]*, a former SCLC and SNCC staff member, poses with the author and Rev. Harold Middlebrook, a Memphis civil rights activist, at the fortieth anniversary of the Birmingham movement. Photo by Charles Thompson.

returned to Thomaston to teach and coach basketball in the black high school, and he immediately began to help organize a voter registration campaign in his hometown. Years later, after completing a Ph.D. in history at Duke University, he moved back to Atlanta and decided to run for the school board in Dekalb County, Georgia, where he lived with his family at the time. He lost. But Eugene Walker had been bitten by the political bug, and in 1982 he ran a successful campaign for a seat in the Georgia State Senate representing Dekalb County.

From his earliest political activities, Walker had always been a loyal member of the Democratic Party. In recent years, however, he has become extremely disheartened by the political parties in this country, particularly the Democrats. Walker explains,

> I have been so disillusioned by these parties. I don't see a nickel's worth of difference between them [Democrats and Republicans]. I'm serious. Here was one of our most popular Democrats—Zell Miller. If there's a difference between Zell and George Bush other than their name, I can't see it. The majority of the sentiments lean toward being prejudiced, being obstructionist, being evil, and being mean spirited. . . . So that is the way both the Republican and Democratic Parties [are] leaning. The people are telling the Democratic Party that used to engage in advocacy for a lot of social programs that they['ve] got to abandon that. They['ve] got to become more Republican-like.[54]

Even Barack Obama has been critical of both the Democratic and Republican Parties. A short time after his electrifying speech at the 2004 Democratic National Convention, Obama expressed his misgivings: "one party seems to be defending a moribund status quo, and the other is defending an oligarchy." He concluded sadly, "It's not a very attractive choice."[55] Of course, he spoke these words four years before he made history by becoming the successful Democratic standard-bearer in the 2008 presidential election.

The state of partisan politics in America is only one of the problems confronting black officeholders. Everywhere they look, black elected officials see complex problems. Some are new, but others have plagued black people for generations, and regardless of their party affiliation, the region of the country they live in, or the political office they hold, black elected officials are searching for solutions. Selma civil rights attorney J. L. Chestnut argues that because solutions are so elusive, "it is counterproductive to be arguing about who's Uncle Toms and all. You get a black in higher office, you use him." Chestnut stabs the air with his index finger for emphasis, then frowns thoughtfully and adds, "I don't know but one exception to that, Clarence Thomas." The old lawyer concludes with a chuckle, "I'd use him if we could; we just can't."[56]

Former North Carolina congressman Frank Ballance acknowledges the complexity of the problems in his district, but he also recognizes how the issue of race adds still another complication. He explains that "by statute, by the Constitution [we] have a responsibility to represent the district. . . . And that includes black and white folk. But historically, white folk have not represented the black community. But when black folk came to Congress, they spoke up on black issues, but they represented the white folk too."[57]

Former Georgia state senator Julian Bond, who is now a member of the faculty at the University of Virginia, agrees that African Americans these days face a wide variety of different problems. He believes that in order to reach solutions, black people need to "strengthen our institutions. Build our political strength, and turn it out on election day." As Bond reflects on the nature of African Americans' problems, he insists that one of the most critical is rooted in the nation's educational system. In his view, school systems all over the country are failing to provide adequate educational opportunities for black youth. He thinks one of the most important things black people need to do is to "correct the educational crime that's happening to our young people, and it's happening all over the country."[58]

Alabama congressman Artur Davis faces a unique challenge, because the district he represents includes both progressive urban neighborhoods and impoverished rural areas. He finds that the problems in his district fall into three basic categories. First, "there is a lack of community civic structure in much of the Black Belt . . . and it's manifested by the state of the school system, it's manifested by the lack of alternative newspapers in the area. . . . You don't have the sense of community across racial lines."

Lack of economic development is Davis's second area of concern. In his estimation, economic inequality compromises the effectiveness of political power. The final category of the young congressman's concern has its roots in a lack of long-range strategic planning. He explains, "We have not managed as a state or as a region to develop a real plan for growing the Black Belt out of its economic misery. We've had a scattershot approach." Davis reasons, "One of the challenges of anyone representing this district is to try and find some sort of a unified plan for reviving the economic prospects of the region. . . . We simply haven't done that."[59]

In nearby Tuskegee, Alabama, Mayor Johnny Ford had numerous plans for his city when he was recently reelected mayor. His top priorities were economic reform, educational reform, and building a better infrastructure. As he seeks to implement changes, Ford is convinced that he cannot do it alone: "There's no one African American leader anymore. Our solution, I think, is working together as groups and networking, and speaking as a common voice whenever we can." Yet, he does not expect unanimity. On the contrary, Ford thinks black leaders should learn how to "agree to disagree, [but] not be disagreeable."[60]

In historic Selma, Alabama, just south of Tuskegee, Mayor James Perkins believes the basic issues facing black people have not changed, but the focus of today's black political leaders has shifted. It seems to him that "the issues are the same; the focus is different. This generation; the focus is on economic development. . . . Under the prior leadership, it was political and social agendas that drove the train. We are now following economic development." He reiterates, "But the issues are the same." Furthermore, Perkins insists that no matter what the problems are facing today's African Americans, the underlying basis is always the same: race. "If you want to know if race is still an issue, I would simply say to you [that] it's probably not an issue in and of itself, but it is a part of every issue we address." As he looks toward the future, Perkins does not expect this fact to change. He has "no unrealistic expectations about race as an issue in this world. It's always been an issue, and as long as we have multicultural societies, it will be an issue."[61]

Congresswoman Eleanor Holmes Norton also finds that race is still an issue, but she is especially concerned about the plight of the black family in the new millennium, and she worries about the future:

Boys in particular get eaten alive by ghetto culture early on. They in turn grow up in communities where there are not jobs. Men without jobs will find a way to get money. . . . All that leads away from families so that men have children, but do not claim them, and we are far too passive at confronting this problem at every layer of leadership—from the ministers who see these beautiful young women in church, knowing full well they're not performing marriages, and not figuring out what to do about it. Political leadership at my level, and at every level [is] not emphasizing the black family enough. It's *the* critical issue.[62]

Former senator Carol Moseley Braun is convinced that the inaction of black political leadership stretches far beyond the crisis gripping the black family in America. She argues, "We have no agenda. . . . We don't have a cogent agenda about any specific thing that government can do on any level." Braun believes the absence of a leadership agenda can be traced directly to the mind-set of black leaders in the wake of the King assassination: "The tradition since Dr. King is to focus in on our pain. And they focus in on the pain, but they don't focus in on how to solve the problem." She charges, "They [black leaders] show up wherever there's a problem," but they don't bring any solutions with them.[63]

In addition to the problems facing their constituents, black elected officials all over the country face a tough atmosphere these days, even with a new black president. Eugene Walker describes it this way: "The thing that has really troubled me, and I think, made this political situation so different is that over a period of time . . . during the late seventies, and during the eighties, and clearly in the nineties, the Newt Gingriches of the world made being prejudiced acceptable. At one time it used to be almost sinful to describe somebody as conservative. But, later on as they got the Rush Limbaugh types in prominent positions, and they started talking about their so-called values and their conservatism, then it took the place that liberal sentiment used to take." Part of this new viewpoint, according to Walker, is that "prejudice is acceptable." In this atmosphere it is especially difficult to round up support for social programs designed to help poor people of color. What is worse, Walker argues, is that some African American politicians have actually embraced that mind-set: "As that mind-set evolved, then you've got blacks buying into [it] like the Clarence Thomas types and all the [other] people who are saying, you know, prejudice ain't all that bad. You got to get off your butt no matter what the situation is and take care of yourself. It's the survival of the fittest." Walker considers this line of reasoning tantamount to "blaming the victim. And this is so entrenched, and it's so prominent in so many places."[64]

Black elected officials who continue to champion social programs worry that they are perceived to be out of step with their colleagues in the legislative bodies in which they serve. At the same time, many of the reform-minded elected officials also worry about the impact of this perception on their ability to fund their campaign when they run for reelection. Dr. Joe Leonard explains:

> There isn't a single black congressman whose district supports them in financing. The majority of it comes from corporate sponsors. So you have Cynthia McKinney [former congresswoman from Georgia] targeted because she said something wrong because the people in her district . . . really aren't responsible for her being in. They give her votes, but somebody can come in with two million dollars and run against her and win. . . . Until we begin [to get] all these black lawyers, and all these black doctors and all these black master's degrees . . . all this black wealth, wealth that we've never had before. Until we begin to use some of [these] discretionary funds . . . [to] support our own organizations, we're in trouble. We're in trouble.[65]

Yet, despite his gloomy analysis, Leonard is optimistic because he is convinced that black people of means will soon begin to provide more financial support for black candidates, and when that happens, "We will become more revolutionary."[66]

Thus, forty-plus years after the Voting Rights Act revolutionized the electoral process in America, reviews of the records of black officeholders are mixed, and criticism of their efforts has been constant and relentless. As far back as the period right after the passage of the Voting Rights Act, Dr. Martin Luther King Jr. expressed grave misgivings about black political leadership in this country: "The majority of Negro political leaders do not ascend to prominence on the shoulders of mass support. Although genuinely popular leaders are now emerging, most are selected by white leadership, elevated to positions, supplied with resources and inevitably subjected to white control. The mass of Negroes nurtures a healthy suspicion toward these manufactured leaders. Experience tells them that color is the chief argument their leaders are offering to induce loyalty and solidarity. The Negro politician they know spends little time in persuading them that he embodies personal integrity, commitment and ability; he offers few programs and less service."[67] Despite his criticism of black political leadership, King did not discount its importance, and so he advised black people "to create leaders who embody virtues we can respect, who have moral and ethical principles we can applaud with an enthusiasm that enables us to rally support for them based on confidence and trust." Reasoning that black people have an obligation to their leaders, he insisted, "We will have to demand high standards and give consistent, loyal support for those who merit it" and be "a reliable constituency for those who prove themselves to be committed political warriors in our behalf."[68]

Others besides King were critical of black political leadership in the late sixties. For example, in Wilcox County, Alabama, Mrs. Jessie Pettway, who had been an active participant in the local voting-rights campaign, was extremely disappointed in the first black elected officials in her county. Her disappointment was particularly keen because she had been so hopeful when President Johnson signed the Voting Rights Act. Pettway and her neighbors were jubilant when they were able to register and vote for the first time in their lives. Then, when the first black elected officials in Wilcox County since Reconstruction were finally sworn in, Pettway was confident that they were on the verge of a true revolution. But it did not turn out that way. Pettway sighs heavily as she remembers her frustration: "After putting people in office then you expect them to do some of the things that would help the black folks. But, to my understanding, most of the black people we put in office, *they turn white*."[69]

Just up the road from Wilcox County, in Birmingham, Rev. Abraham Woods, one of the leaders of the Birmingham Campaign, experienced similar frustration. His view is that "so often, those blacks [who] have been elected . . . , they sort of develop amnesia to some extent about how they got where they are." Reverend Woods sighs as he continues, "Well . . . it's a very disheartening thing when they do that. But when they get caught up in the legislature or in the council, and they've got to make political decisions, those decisions that they make, they compromise, you see." Unfortunately, according to Woods, the situation in Birmingham is not unique: "Not only is that so on the local and state level, but that has been so to a great extent on the national level also."[70]

Rev. James Lawson, a close associate of King's, a major strategist of the sit-in campaign in Nashville, and one of the most important influences on the establishment of the Student Nonviolent Coordinating Committee, is also critical of black politicians. As he sees it, "The truth of the matter is that in the black community, we're facing a situation where black elected officials concentrate on staying elected." Lawson pauses thoughtfully before continuing, "[They] concentrate on the agenda that gets them favor with their peers in the government, and the historic black agenda is not at the forefront of their . . . thought."[71] Professor John Hope Franklin also worries about the agenda of today's black political leaders. But he thinks their most serious problem is their narrow focus. Franklin argues that many of today's black elected officials focus exclusively on certain issues facing their constituents, and this actually limits their effectiveness because it prevents them from "looking at the larger picture."[72]

In recent years, increasing numbers of scholars have added their voices to the chorus of critics evaluating the records of black political leaders. For example, Norman Kelley, in his recent book *The Head Negro in Charge Syndrome,* charges, "Moreover, those who are duly elected—mayors, council people, congressional representatives, etc.—have become increasingly incorporated into the state's apparatus of control and management, and are thus more accountable to those [white] powers than to those from whom they derive their legitimacy, i.e., black voters."[73] Kelley's analysis seems to bear little relationship to the bright hopes and great expectations that newly elected black officeholders had in those exciting and tumultuous days right after the passage of the Voting Rights Act. The late sixties represented a high-water mark in black beliefs that, as soul singer Sam Cook crooned in his silky voice, "A change is gonna come; oh yes it will." At the same time, all over the country black people with big Afros and big dreams were dancing to the rapping-singing sound of James Brown, the hardest-working man in show business. Brown's raspy voice, backed up by the remarkable horns and driving drumbeat of his band, The Fabulous Flames, exhorted listeners to "SAY IT LOUD." His all-girl backup singers chimed in, "I'M BLACK AND I'M PROUD." Brown preached and sang,

> We been buked, and we been scorned
> We been beaten and talked about
> Sure as you're born.
> But just as sure as it takes two eyes to make a pair,
> Brother, we won't quit
> Until we get our share.
>
> SAY IT LOUD
> I'M BLACK AND I'M PROUD.[74]

The excitement was infectious, and the message was irresistible. During the same period, rapper-poet Gil Scott Heron advised his audiences that "THE REVOLUTION WILL NOT BE TELEVISED," and in "Message to a Black Man," the popular Motown group The Temptations, known for their precision dance steps, flashy outfits, and smooth love songs, sang to their listeners, "No matter how hard you try, you can't stop me now." The recent victories of the civil rights movement had clearly tapped into a wellspring of hope and resolve that had been submerged for nearly one hundred years, and black people from various walks of life were enjoying the moment.

Buoyed by the hopes and dreams of their constituents, early black officeholders entered the rarefied chambers of those all-white, all-male governing bodies that had excluded them for such a long time. They took their seats for the first time, and many could still hear James Brown's voice, "Say it loud," and the voices of his backup singers, "I'm black and I'm proud," in the background as they rolled up their sleeves, got down to business, and tried to make a difference. These days, many of the early black officeholders look back wistfully to those hopeful times. For example, James Thomas, a member of the Alabama State Legislature from Wilcox County, recalls, "The whole perception was that we was going to be able to do miracles overnight, and I was even a little bit naive. I thought that I could just transcend everything that had taken place."[75] Rev. Lonnie Brown was one of the first black candidates to be elected to the school board in Wilcox County, Alabama, and he shared James Thomas's optimism at the time. Shortly after he took the oath of office, however, Brown realized that both black and white county residents were carefully scrutinizing the actions of the new black school board members. As Brown puts it, "Wherever there are black people in the Black Belt in office, I feel that white folks, and some black folks think that . . . just because they're black people, they're not going to do anything." But with a determined glint in his eye forty years after facing that challenge, Brown explained, "We were determined to prove them [wrong]."[76]

Although these early black officeholders started out with optimism, once they began to assume their positions, they quickly found that their great expectations collided with years of political orthodoxy in the various governing bodies to which they had been elected. Furthermore, by the time this first wave of newly elected black officials began taking their seats, the peaceful demonstrations and marches that had generated widespread sympathy for the black plight had given way to black urban unrest, crumbling urban infrastructures, white flight with the resulting financial crises, Watergate, and vocal Vietnam war protests. In this chaotic atmosphere, white legislators and their constituents were in no mood to compromise any more, and their sympathy was all used up. Amid calls for law and order, this first wave of black elected officials attempted to perform the duties of their office and fulfill the promises they had made to their black constituents. As they struggled to learn how to navigate a political system that was often hostile to them and their supporters, few black politicians were surprised by the nasty treatment they received.

What caught many by surprise, though, was the treatment they received at the hands of some of their black constituents. For example, in Wilcox County, Rev. Lonnie Brown sadly recalls being maligned by people who were more than just his constituents; they were his friends and neighbors. "It hurts for people that's been your friends and all, and that you go to church with sometimes to hate you and call you names. . . . You don't want people to be angry at you, but when you get into that kind of situation, you will have to make the tough decisions of what is right, according to what you think is right."[77] Former Illinois senator Carol Moseley Braun also remembers emotional pain accompanying her political career. In her case it was complicated by her gender and her marital status: she was divorced. She explains, "My supporters hated my boyfriend and ran him out of the country." Braun is still incredulous when she thinks about this intrusion into her personal life: "You got one person in the Senate, and you come at them cause you don't like their boyfriend? . . . On every possible front, it [her term in the U.S. Senate] was just a miserable six years."[78]

It is evident that during the early days of black political involvement, black elected officials had to work hard to survive and accomplish any of their goals in a political system that had a history and tradition of antagonism to black people and their interests. It was a very difficult experience for many, and along the way, some began to feel a sense of isolation and alienation that affected their relationship with their black constituents as well as with their white legislative colleagues. However, in the intervening years, as African Americans have developed a tradition of officeholding, it seems that a new breed of black political leader is emerging, one who is adept at this balancing act between the needs of constituents and the demands of the elective office. According to scholars at the Joint Center for Political and Economic Studies, "Black politicians under the age of 40 are, in some respects, more like their white peers than their black elders. . . . They are much more likely to have gone to integrated schools, less likely to belong to civil-rights organizations, significantly better educated and, apparently, more ambitious."[79]

One of those younger black politicians, Harold Ford Jr., a second-generation congressman from Memphis, Tennessee, agrees that they are different. He explains, "We share experiences, regardless of race, far more than previous generations." And in the minds of many, Harold Ford Jr. is a perfect example of this new generation of black politicians. Because his father served in Congress before him, Harold Ford Jr. grew up feeling very comfortable with the political atmosphere in the nation's capital. When Harold Ford Sr. was first elected, his young son stood at his side "with his right hand held high, mimicking his father's pledge." As he grew to manhood, the younger Ford attended prestigious integrated schools, and when he was elected to fill the same congressional seat that his father had occupied for twenty-two years, he stepped right into the job armed with the confidence derived from familiarity and access. In short, even before he was elected to Congress, he was a political insider. Consequently, he is convinced that the time has come to approach black political participation in a whole new way. He thinks "the old labels have lost a lot of their meaning" and that, furthermore, "rigid ideology makes it easier to resist good ideas." As a political insider, Harold Ford Jr. believes race is much less important in defining leadership than it used to be: "If you're a leader, you're a leader. The labeling of black leaders is often perpetuated by people who want to narrow a person's scope. Why let anybody shrink your reach?"[80] Some forty years after the passage of the Voting Rights Act of 1965 that made Ford's election to Congress possible, there are people who argue that his articulation of a color-blind vision of political leadership is a fitting epitaph to the long struggle of African Americans for inclusion in the political process. Others are not so sure.

African Americans continue to debate the impact and meaning of their inclusion in the political process. To most of them, race still matters a great deal. Black politicians, from Chicago congressman Oscar DePriest in the 1920s and 1930s, to Harlem congressman Adam Clayton Powell in the 1940s, 1950s, and 1960s, to Memphis congressman Harold Ford Jr. in the 2000s, continue to believe that along with the issue of race, the inherent conservatism in this country's legislative bodies has always consigned and will continue to consign black elected officials to a nebulous netherworld where they bounce back and forth between the needs of their black constituents, the interests of their white constituents, and the perks of their office. It is an awkward position in which to be. In a strange twist of fate, it seems that out of necessity the old methods of lobby and compromise that predated the civil rights demonstrations of the 1960s have reemerged as black elected officials seek to influence the majority white legislative bodies in which they serve. Dr. Benjamin Hooks explains, "the old time people that the young people had laughed at . . . [have come] back into their own." This is how Hooks describes the reemergence of the old black leadership methodology: "When the marches started most places, they made fun of the people who were in the Urban League, the NAACP, or even CORE, for that matter, as being out of step and out of date. Even to the place where Martin King became an anachronism, that he became out of step and behind. So when Martin died, and we went through this series of bad [Supreme Court] decisions . . . then the [older] leaders came back into their own because they were the ones who [could] call the senators, [or] call the congressmen."[81] Today's black elected officials do face tough choices, but most of them just keep on keeping on, accomplishing what they can as they try not to let the cynical climate in post-Watergate Washington tarnish their idealism or bruise their integrity. In the new millennium, characterized by cynicism, suspicion, and fear, the idealism and naïveté of those African Americans who were just getting involved in the political process forty years ago seem odd, almost improbable. Still, most have not forgotten their hope and their optimism.

It was during that earlier era that the young Johnny Ford and his buddies wanted to play in the city park near their neighborhood in Tuskegee, Alabama, but they knew they could not because of their color. Ford recalls, "I can remember at the age of 13 when we would go down to the public park in downtown Tuskegee, and the whites would be playing, and we couldn't go in. And we would climb up in the tree." When the white children in the park noticed the black youngsters watching them, "they would throw rocks . . . and say, 'Look at those blackbirds in the tree.'" Johnny was a lean, dark-skinned, gregarious youngster with a quick wit and a ready smile, but his smile would fade when he noticed the sign on the gate to the park that had MAYOR FRANK CARR printed on it in big block letters. Young Johnny stared at that sign a long time, and then he said to his buddies, "The mayor of this town must be a powerful dude . . . if he can keep us out of this park because my parents, your parents, are all paying taxes like everyone else. . . . One day I want to be mayor of this town so that I can open up this park and all of us can run and play." His young friends rolled their eyes and giggled as they climbed down from the tree, hopped on their bicycles, and rode to the creek. They ran the snakes off, jumped in the cool murky water, and gave their friend's prediction no further thought. Now Johnny Ford fondly recalls that incident as he sits in his office in Tuskegee's City Hall, thinking about the challenges he faces as Tuskegee's mayor.[82]

In Georgia, some years after young Johnny Ford stated his desire to become mayor, Dr. Eugene Walker ran for a seat on the school board in predominantly white Dekalb County, Georgia, because of his daughter. Walker had decided that his precocious daughter, Lisa, would be one of the black students who would integrate Dekalb County schools, so Lisa in 1978 became the first black student to attend Snapfinger School in Dekalb County, a suburb of Atlanta. After the school term started, Lisa surprised her father one day when she came home and announced that their county's school board was all white. In the days and weeks that followed, Eugene Walker could not forget Lisa's innocent observation. He was painfully aware that at his urging, his daughter was integrating Dekalb County's schools. Didn't he have the responsibility of practicing what he preached by integrating Dekalb County's School Board? Dr. Walker wondered. Eventually, he decided that in the interest of fairness, he had to try. "So I ran for the school board from Dekalb County in 1978. . . . and the impetus came from my daughter. . . . My daughter sensitized me to the need to try to get a mix in Dekalb County."[83]

Dr. Walker campaigned vigorously. He was especially sensitive about the need to attract white support in his predominantly white county. At the time he reasoned, "I can't be overly black and expect to win. I gotta tone my blackness down and attract some of these white votes." On election day, Walker was nervous, but hopeful. When the returns started coming in, Walker was pleased to see that he had attracted a significant number of white votes. His pleasure soon turned to horror, however, when he realized that his white opponent had received many more black votes than Walker had. Walker says, "I took the black vote for granted, and assumed that because I was black, black folks would vote for me. I concentrated on the whites, and that was one of the biggest political mistakes I ever made." Walker lost that election, but he learned a valuable lesson: "If you ain't hitting that white man, calling him what he is. . . . my brothers and sisters ain't gonna vote for you." Walker smiles at the memory as he concludes emphatically, "I found that out the hard way."[84]

Dr. Eugene Walker did not run again for the school board, but later when he was elected to the Georgia State Senate, he was thrilled, awed, and hopeful. However, after serving a number of terms in the Georgia state legislature, Walker decided that he had had enough of politics, because of the cynicism and dishonesty he witnessed. As he sees it, "You [are] gonna have to tell the voters what they want to hear, or cuss out everybody you['re] running against—especially white folks. If you don't do it that way, baby, you ain't gonna win. It's as simple as that. That's one of the reasons I decided not to run again."[85]

During that hopeful time in the past century when African Americans were just starting on the long road to political inclusion, many were convinced that the future was bright, all things were possible, and they would finally have the power to right some of the wrongs their people had suffered for generations. One who believed that all things were possible was young Condoleezza Rice. When she was eleven years old, Rice stood in front of the White House in Washington, D.C., and said to her father, "One day I'll be in that house."[86] She succeeded, of course. Rice was the first black woman ever to serve as secretary of state, and during the administration of George W. Bush, she was viewed by both black and white Americans as part of President Bush's inner circle. In 2002, *Newsweek* magazine even called her "the most powerful woman in Washington."[87] Rice met with heads of state, she talked to the press, she was one of the president's most trusted advisers, and she is black.

Yet, despite the very visible and very public success of Condoleezza Rice and thousands of other elected and appointed black officeholders all over the country, many African Americans are still confronted by exceedingly harsh economic conditions. In the new millennium, poor black people still worry about the black-on-black crime that is part of their everyday lives. Black parents still worry about the quality of the education that their children are receiving. Young and old, middle-class and working-class black people still worry about the high unemployment rate among African Americans and their lack of access to quality health care. Yes, in the years since the passage of the Voting Rights Act, more black candidates have been elected to office than nearly anyone dreamed possible; more African Americans have been appointed to high-level government positions than ever before, and we even have a black president of the United States now. But as the majority of African Americans struggle with the huge problems that just will not go away, many are beginning to conclude that the race of those who govern them matters less than the answer to the question, "What have you done for me lately?"

6. The Continuing Challenge of Black Economic Underdevelopment

As African American leaders focused on the cultivation of black political power in the years after the Voting Rights Act was passed in 1965, they also declared that their new political power would mean little without black economic equality. Some four decades later, the vast majority of African American leaders in the new millennium say the same thing. Alabama congressman Artur Davis succinctly explains the belief of so many of his colleagues when he insists that continued black economic underdevelopment undermines the effectiveness of black political power and produces "politics that are more segregated than ever."[1] But why are the black economic problems so stubbornly persistent? Seeking reasons, many African Americans, from scholars to social critics and from educators to politicians, look to the past. They have no doubt that the root cause is slavery. Even after legal slavery ended, they point out, black economic exploitation did not end; it just assumed new forms, effectively binding each new generation of African Americans to their ancestors.

Ever since the first African slaves were brought to the thirteen colonies, economic exploitation has defined the relationship between black people and American society. The slaves, who constituted the majority of the antebellum black population in America, not only had their labor taken from them; they did not even own their own bodies, or the bodies of their children. They were defined by America's legal system as chattel, beings with no more rights than a horse or a cow. When slavery was abolished at the end of the Civil War, many newly freed slaves held their breaths and wished with all their might that their new legal status as freed people would be accompanied by a new economic independence. Most of them were convinced that their political and social emancipation were virtually meaningless without economic independence. The actions taken by some Union generals to provide food and shelter for the slaves who managed to reach the Union lines gave many a reason to hope, at least for a while. But they soon realized that their economic nightmare was far from over: in the early months after the end of the war, Union largesse ended, and the ex-slaves were left with nothing. The dismal description provided by one freedman paints a poignant picture of black desperation: "They [ex-slaves] all did pretty well till the War was about to end, then they was told to scatter and nowheres to go. Cabins all tore down or burned. No work to do. There was no money to pay. I got hungry lots of times. No plantations was divided. . . . Everybody left and a heap of the colored folks went where rations could be issued to them."[2] Things were so bad that one ex-slave compared slavery and freedom to two snakes: "Slavery was a 'bad thing,' but freedom 'of de kin' we got wid nothin' to live on was bad [too]. . . . Both bit the nigger, an' dey was both bad.'"[3]

In the last decades of the nineteenth century, the black economic plight worsened as sharecropping, peonage, and the convict lease system replaced slavery, ensnaring African Americans in a kind of debt slavery that followed them for decades. Seeking to improve their circumstances, African Americans began leaving the South in droves by the early twentieth century. Yet, even though many were able to get factory jobs in the burgeoning industrial cities of the North and the Midwest, these transplanted African Americans generally found that racism still had a profound impact on their economic fortunes. They may have experienced a dramatic increase in wages compared to what they had earned in the rural South, but racism in the workplace relegated them to the dirtiest, most dangerous, and least secure jobs in the mass-production industries spawned by the Industrial Revolution.

In the South, the fate of a black factory worker was at least as bad, as James Armstrong learned when he worked at a steel mill in Birmingham, Alabama, in the early twentieth century. Armstrong, who later carried a large U.S. flag on the historic Selma-to-Montgomery march, is a native of Dallas County, Alabama. Before he took the factory job, he served in the army during World War II, and while overseas he got a glimpse of life without prejudice: during the war, his unit landed at Normandy one month and ten days after D-Day. Armstrong was amazed by the hero's welcome he and other black GIs received from the French. Today, retired,

Armstrong serves as a volunteer at the Birmingham Civil Rights Institute. Sitting beneath a large mural at the institute, the old man smiles at the memory and insists, "I think that you got better treatment [overseas]. . . . There are more racist-type folk in this country. Over there, color didn't make any difference."[4]

When Armstrong returned to Alabama after the war, he was in no mood to accept unfair treatment. He immediately got a job at a Birmingham steel mill, and although he was glad to secure employment so quickly, he soon became angry when he saw how badly the mill bosses treated their black employees. Afraid of losing their jobs, African American workers refused to complain, and this angered Armstrong even more. Undaunted, he protested, and the other black workers were horrified. One of them told him, "Man, they['re] going to run you away from here. You come back here from the army with that little old stuff you're talking about."[5] Of course, the steel mill bosses disregarded the young GI's protests. He was only one worker, after all. And even after increasing numbers of workers began joining labor unions, enabling the unions to exert more influence, the fate of most black workers remained unchanged, because the most powerful unions discriminated against black workers. It is because of this long tradition of economic inequality and union discrimination that African American leaders have always expressed concern about the economic vulnerability that is one of the hallmarks of black life in America.

In Chicago, the difficulties facing African American workers seeking economic equality were demonstrated to young Timuel Black in the late 1920s by black workers in his neighborhood who organized a retail clerks' union to demand better pay. Within a short time, the stock market crashed, and the Great Depression that followed ushered in an era of unprecedented unemployment and economic misery. Workers everywhere scrambled just to hang on to their jobs. In Chicago, vast numbers of workers, including the retail clerks, found themselves out of work, and nearly out of hope. The Depression deepened and the misery of black Chicagoans worsened, and it was at this point that the American Communist Party sought to extend its influence among African Americans in Chicago, as well as other cities and towns all over the country. No matter how bad things were, however, Timuel Black recalls that the Communist Party's promises for economic reform fell on deaf ears in Chicago's black community. He explains that despite their desperation, black Chicagoans, many of them recent migrants from the rural South, knew that the Communist Party was nearly all white, and they were not willing to trust their economic fate to these white men, no matter what they promised.[6]

About thirty years later in Detroit, future Black Panther Maureen Taylor realized how powerful economic concerns were when she was a high school student. Even though she lived in the North, Maureen eagerly followed news of the civil rights struggle that was raging in the South while she was a student at Cass Technical High School. At that time, Cass was the crown jewel in the Detroit Public School System. It was a large, mostly white, urban high school in downtown Detroit with a well-deserved reputation for academic excellence. Even though it was a public school, students had to compete for the coveted spots in the Cass Tech student body by taking an entrance exam. The fortunate ones who were admitted immediately noticed an air of privilege permeating the high-rise high school's halls. Taylor, whose family was blue-collar, was not surprised by the supercilious attitudes displayed by white classmates who were from comfortable economic circumstances. However, when black classmates from privileged backgrounds treated Taylor in the same condescending manner, she was completely taken aback. Because of this experience, for the first time in her young life, Maureen Taylor really appreciated the relative importance of money versus race. She explains,

> We were calling this crew [black students of means] what it is that we saw. They were elite, but we called the entire group . . . E-LITES [pronounced with a long *E* and a long *I*] because they represented a particular point of view that said that they were superior, and that they were above us because. . . . they were light-skinned with curly hair. Their mothers and fathers had positions and had resources, and the rest of us were just struggling blue collar people. . . . But then after a while it became clear that we didn't want to work with them . . . because they had these superior, condescending attitudes.[7]

Years before Maureen Taylor's experience at Cass Tech, Dr. Dorothy Cotton experienced the impact of poverty when she was growing up in

Goldsboro, North Carolina. Cotton, who later worked very closely with Martin Luther King Jr. and served for ten years as director of education for the Southern Christian Leadership Conference, was from a family of four girls. Her father did the best he could to care for his daughters, but it was hard: he was a widower who barely eked out a living working in a local tobacco factory. When Dorothy was a high school student, one of her teachers, Miss Rosa Gray, took an interest in her, and under the teacher's influence, young Dorothy blossomed. In the spring of Dorothy's senior year, Miss Gray urged her to make plans to attend the prom. The teacher could not help but notice her student's reluctance when she broached the subject. However, refusing to take no for an answer, she insisted on going home with Dorothy so she could speak to her father. Dorothy Cotton reports, "In those days . . . teachers were honored . . . citizens, highly respected. And here this teacher is at my house sitting on my porch, talking to my dad, and saying she would take care of me. And my dad said, 'I'm just not ready for my girl to go to dances.'" Dorothy did not attend her prom. However, it was some time before she finally realized why her father stubbornly refused to let her go: he could not afford to buy her a dress, and he was too proud to accept help from her teacher. As she thinks about that scene on her front porch, Cotton has the wistful look of a teenage girl wanting so badly to attend her prom, but understanding why she could not. "That had to wound his pride," she says simply.[8]

In Birmingham, Alabama, Rev. Abraham Woods also has painful childhood memories of the power of poverty. He once witnessed an exchange between his father and a local white merchant that taught him a very personal lesson. Woods was from a large family of modest means, and there were times when his father had to resort to getting food on credit at the local store to feed the family. On one occasion when the elder Woods asked a white store owner for credit, young Abraham was standing there watching. He explains, "I'll never forget the particular time my father asked him [the white store owner] to extend credit, and he wouldn't do it." The refusal was bad enough, but what happened next scarred Abraham forever. The elder Woods was desperate to get food for his family, and when the store owner refused, Abraham's father did not move away from the counter. Instead, he just "stood there very humble with his hat in his hand," hoping the store owner would have a change of heart. He did not. Time seemed to stand still as the elder Woods stood staring at the floor. Finally, "he [the store owner] just talked to him [the elder Woods] like he was a little child." Decades later Abraham Woods still gets tears in his eyes at the memory. With a deep sadness, Woods adds, "and it hurt me on the inside."[9]

Many years later, civil rights movement activists recognized just how difficult it was going to be to rearrange the economic relationship of African Americans to American society, given the reality of black political powerlessness at that time. In recent years SNCC activist and Mississippi Freedom Democratic Party chairman Lawrence Guyot has often heard young African Americans criticize the civil rights movement for failing to address the black economic plight. When students ask, "Why didn't the leadership concentrate more on economic development?" Guyot realizes that they understand little about what American society was really like in the years before the civil rights movement. In fact, Guyot and other activists of his generation were eager to wipe out the deeply entrenched exploitation that ensnared so many African Americans. But they were certain that if they confronted economic inequalities first, the movement would have been finished before it started. Guyot patiently explains, speaking of today's youths who don't understand, "Well, that means they never heard of HUAC [House Un-American Activities Committee]. Because if SCLC had organized itself in 1957 and said 'we're concerned about changing the economic climate,' it would have been killed in three days."[10]

Early movement leadership did acknowledge the importance of economic issues, civil rights veterans are quick to point out, even though their campaigns concentrated more effort on addressing black disfranchisement and segregation of schools and public facilities. One of the means they could use to address economic issues, along with segregation and other issues, was economic boycotts. Of course, the most famous example is the Montgomery Bus Boycott, which began in late 1955. Montgomery organizers realized right from the beginning that because the majority of citizens who rode the city's buses were black, they could have a powerful impact on the bus company if African Americans refused to ride. The boycott lasted an astounding 381 days, and before it was over, most African Americans in Alabama's capital boycotted the city's downtown stores, too. In addition to desegregated seating on the buses, boycott leaders demanded that the bus company hire black drivers. This major and very public economic boycott was only one of many organized by black activists in cities all over the South as the civil rights movement progressed into the 1960s. Throughout those early years, demands for employment of African Americans in formerly all-white enterprises routinely accompanied the boycotts.

Whenever they organized protest activities, whether it was the economic boycott or some other campaign, civil rights activists were always mindful that white economic retaliation against economically vulnerable African Americans was a likely result. Black participants in civil rights campaigns were routinely threatened by local white bankers who promised to foreclose on their mortgages if they tried to register to vote. White school boards assured black teachers that their participation in marches would result in dismissal. White landowners made it abundantly clear to their black sharecroppers that participation in movement campaigns would result in being dismissed and evicted. Movement leaders, along with the rank and file, knew that these were not idle threats, but in one community after another, local black residents participated anyway.

Consequently, as the movement continued, one of the most important activities of civil rights activists was raising money to help the many victims of white economic retaliation. Movement veterans sometimes became tearful at the pitiful sight of families made homeless and penniless because of their participation in civil rights campaigns. Such heartrending scenes engendered emotions from shocked outrage to profound sorrow to rock-solid determination, and by the end of the 1960s, movement leaders were articulating their concerns about the black economic plight in forceful language. In Dr. King's *Where Do We Go from Here? Chaos or Community,* this increasing emphasis on economic concerns is evident: "From issues of personal dignity they [black activists] are now advancing to programs that impinge upon the basic system of social and economic control. At this level Negro programs go beyond race and deal with economic inequality, wherever it exists."[11]

His years of experience in civil rights campaigns in the Deep South convinced King that black economic inequality was systemic: "Of employed Negroes, 75 percent hold menial jobs. Depressed living standards for

Negroes are not simply the consequence of neglect. Nor can they be explained by the myth of the Negro's innate incapacities, or by the more sophisticated rationalization of his acquired infirmities (family disorganization, poor education, etc.). They are a structural part of the economic system in the United States. Certain industries and enterprises are based upon a supply of low-paid, under-skilled, and immobile nonwhite labor."[12] King insisted that African Americans seeking to improve their economic situation had few options: "The economic highway to power has few entry lanes for Negroes. Nothing so vividly reveals the crushing impact of discrimination and the heritage of exclusion as the limited dimensions of Negro business in the most powerful economy in the world. America's industrial production is half of the world's total, and within it the production of Negro business is so small that it can scarcely be measured on any definable scale."[13] These words were published in 1967.

In that same year Stokely Carmichael, widely recognized as one of the most important architects of Black Power, charged that "the economic relationship of America's black communities to the larger society . . . reflects their colonial status. The political power exercised over those communities goes hand in glove with the economic deprivation experienced by the black citizens. . . . Exploiters come into the ghetto from outside, bleed it dry, and leave it economically dependent on the larger society."[14] "Exploiters frequently come as the 'friend of the Negro,'" he pointed out; they pretend to offer worthwhile goods and services, when their basic motivation is personal profit and their basic impact is maintenance of racism. Many of the social welfare agencies, public and private, frequently pretend to offer "uplift" services; but they end up creating a system that dehumanizes the individual and perpetuates his dependency.[15]

Two years after Carmichael and King published their concerns about the black economic plight in America, James Forman, former executive secretary of the Student Nonviolent Coordinating Committee, addressed the National Black Economic Development Conference in Detroit, Michigan. Forman delivered his Black Manifesto to a packed audience, thundering:

> We, the black people assembled in Detroit, Michigan for the National Black Economic Development Conference, are fully

aware that we have been forced to come together because racist white America has exploited our resources, our minds, our bodies, our labor. For centuries, we have been forced to live as colonized people inside the United States, victimized by the most vicious, racist system in the world. We have helped to build the most industrial country in the world. We are, therefore, demanding of the white Christian churches and Jewish synagogues which are part and parcel of the system of capitalism, that they begin to pay reparations to black people in this country. We are demanding $500,000,000 from the Christian white churches and the Jewish synagogues. *This total comes to $15 per nigger.*[16]

As movement activists formulated strategies to address the black economic troubles, King warned African Americans that the struggle for economic equality would be the most difficult struggle of all:

So far, we have had constitutional backing for most of our demands for change, and this has made our work easier, since we could be sure of legal support from the federal courts. Now we are approaching areas where the voice of the Constitution is not clear. We have left the realm of constitutional rights and we are entering the area of human rights. The Constitution assured the right to vote, but there is no such assurance of the right to adequate housing, or the right to an adequate income. And yet, in a nation which has a gross national product of $750 billion a year, it is morally right to insist that every person have a decent house, an adequate education and *enough money* to provide basic necessities for one's family. Achievement of these goals will be a lot more difficult and require much more discipline, understanding, organization, and sacrifice.[17]

As Julian Bond reflects on the development of the black freedom struggle in the late 1960s, he believes the civil rights movement failed to take King's advice. On the contrary, "The civil rights movement, whatever that is, turned its attention away from black people at the very bottom and turned its attention toward this entrepreneurial class and devoted so much energy to creating wealth, which is a good thing . . . and ignored these people [at the bottom]. I think we seriously went astray, and even the NAACP engaged in this tilt, and it was a terrible, terrible thing to do."[18] The black entrepreneurial class to which Bond refers has always existed in the midst of the struggling majority of African Americans. Throughout the history of black people in American society, black businessmen and businesswomen have created enterprises including undertaking establishments, banks, insurance companies, barber and beauty shops, and restaurants. However, because most of these small black businesses were undercapitalized and dependent on a poor black clientele, they were obliged to fight for survival alongside the black masses. Yet, a few black enterprises have done very well, and King maintained that the owners of these successful businesses had a special responsibility to the black communities that supported them:

> It is time for the Negro haves to join hands with the Negro have-nots and, with compassion, journey into that other country of hurt and denial. It is time for the Negro middle class to rise up from its stool of indifference, to retreat from its flight into unreality and bring its full resources—its heart, its mind, and its checkbook—to the aid of the less fortunate brother. The relatively privileged Negro will never be what he ought to be until the underprivileged Negro is what he ought to be. The salvation of the Negro middle class is ultimately dependent upon the salvation of the Negro masses.[19]

Some say that in the years since Martin Luther King Jr. advised African Americans to join hands across that great economic divide and struggle for the uplift of all, the economic gulf in the black community only seems to be getting wider. Julian Bond looks at the matter this way:

> The black entrepreneurial class I think exercises disproportionate weight in the considerations of black people generally, the idea being that if Joe Blow becomes a millionaire, all of us are uplifted. Well, you know what Langston Hughes used to say about Ralph Bunche. He said, "the food he eats doesn't fill my stomach." And

that's true about these people. I mean, I'm happy for them. I'm glad they're making big money. Good for them, but I don't see how it affects the rest of us in any way. But still there's this feeling that you['ve] got to pay attention to them and help them succeed and so on, which I want to do, but what about the guy who works in the factory? What about the city worker who picks up the garbage: this whole class of people we seem to have turned our back on, and shouldn't have.[20]

Bond is also convinced that some black entrepreneurs are viewed as leaders just because of their wealth, and he wonders why: "In recent years you've had the addition of business leadership figures, entrepreneurial figures. At the high end, people like Bob Johnson at BET, Earl Graves at *Black Enterprise* magazine. . . . Congratulations to them . . . but in what degree are they leadership figures? Who are they leading? Are they leading black people, or are they leading companies? There's a big difference."[21]

How then does the financial success achieved by some African Americans relate to the economic plight suffered by the black majority? To begin to find an answer, one must consider the broader context of American society's attitude toward wealthy people. Modern-day American society pays a great deal of attention to the fortunes and misfortunes of its wealthiest citizens. African Americans of means, as part of that group, are pointed to enthusiastically and often as proof that King's hope for equality of economic opportunity has finally been realized. Many African Americans question, though, whether these wealthy black people are proof of a fundamental change in American society, or simply exceptions to the continued rule of black economic underachievement. Sheryll Cashin, the author of *The Failures of Integration,* has the latter view: "The odd black family on the block or the Oprah effect—examples of stratospheric black success—feed . . . misperceptions, even as relatively few whites live among and interact daily with blacks of their own social standing. We are still quite far from the integrated equal opportunity nation whites seem to think we have become."[22]

In early 2002, a *Newsweek* article illustrated the "Oprah effect." On the cover was a large photo of three distinguished black men in well-tailored business suits and, in big block letters, the words "THE NEW BLACK POWER." These men, Stanley O'Neal, Richard Parsons, and Kenneth

Chenault, had all recently been appointed as CEOs of white Fortune 500 companies. The article inside the magazine crowed, "They're at the pinnacle of three of the most important companies in the world—Richard Parsons of AOL, Kenneth Chenault of AmEx and Stanley O'Neal of Merrill. And they happen to be black."[23] Undoubtedly, African Americans all over the country, when they saw this cover, must have wondered what impact the "BLACK POWER" of these three men could possibly have on their lives. Rev. Al Sharpton's reaction to the *Newsweek* story was to thunder:

> The inference was that we no longer need the Jesse Jacksons and the Al Sharptons. These [Chenault, O'Neal, and Parsons] are the new black leadership. Well, first of all, they're not the alternative to us, they're the results of us. Second of all, their influence does not derive from a black following, it derives from a white corporation hiring them. They have a job. They're not leading blacks, they're leading corporations . . . it's ridiculous to act like because a guy's the CEO of a company that mostly white board members voted him in that he is a black leader that influences black opinions. IT'S RIDICULOUS.[24]

The very public success of African Americans like Chenault, O'Neal, and Parsons illustrates a new American economic reality: some African Americans have more financial assets than ever. However, the masses of struggling African Americans find no comfort in the prosperity of the few, because so many members of this new black elite have enthusiastically distanced themselves from their poor black brothers and sisters. Up in Chicago, Timuel Black, in his eighties now, sadly acknowledges the widening economic gulf: "It does us as a people no good because we are not united, and [black] individuals are pursuing individual goals."[25] In Washington, D.C., Joe Leonard, nearly fifty years Black's junior, agrees with the old man. He warns, "Until we begin [to get] all these black lawyers and all these black doctors and all these black master's degrees . . . all this black wealth, wealth that we've never had before. Until we begin to use some of [these] discretionary funds [to] . . . support our own organizations, we're in trouble." Leonard repeats, "WE'RE IN TROUBLE."

Yet, despite his bleak warning, Leonard refuses to be discouraged.

He insists that there is a logical reason why African Americans of means are not supporting economic uplift for their less fortunate brethren: they have not been asked. Guided by his youthful optimism and his belief in civil-rights-movement principles, Leonard predicts confidently, "I'm almost positive that people will respond because right now we aren't asking them to do it." Instead, "We're asking them to conform and do well within the system, but we're not trying to change the system. I think if they're asked to change the system, asked to create a beloved community like Dr. King often stated, I think they will respond. . . . I truly think they will."[26]

These days, it seems that visible symbols of black economic success are so pervasive that they have become part of this country's popular culture, and this is having a profound effect on black aspirations. From bad boy rapper Snoop Dogg rapping with white corporate symbol Lee Iacocca about the desirability of Chrysler automobiles, to talk show queen Oprah Winfrey endorsing everything from bras to books, it seems that the economic interests of some African Americans are comfortably intertwined with the interests of corporate America. There are black rap artists who have started their own clothing companies and black athletes who routinely receive multimillion-dollar endorsement deals from sports equipment companies. Black school-aged youngsters see these very visible black success symbols, whose images are everywhere in America's inner cities, and they aspire to be like them. This dream seems more realistic to poor, undereducated black children than the dream of a beloved community ruled by fair play and equal opportunity enunciated by Dr. Martin Luther King Jr. long before they were born.

So, every January, black youngsters dutifully attend the King Day celebrations, and they listen to the recitation of King's "I Have a Dream" speech, but they understand that King's dream has never been realized by the people in their neighborhood. Crumbling inner cities littered with garbage, broken glass, and the broken bodies of young black children killed in drive-by shootings: this is the reality that today's black youngsters in the inner city see when they leave the program where they heard the famous speech yet again. That's why the words of rap songs like Ice T's "Fuck the Police" resonate with black inner-city youth in a way that King's words of hope and inspiration cannot.

Their concern over this widening gulf has prompted many black scholars to sound the alarm about black economic underdevelopment. For example, in her study of racial integration, Sheryll Cashin includes a discussion of how the ongoing black economic crisis exacerbates the problems of the integration process. "Blacks are about twice as likely as whites to hold lower paying service jobs," she writes, "and more than twice as likely to be unemployed." As problematic as these statistics are, however, the refusal of many white Americans to acknowledge black economic underdevelopment is equally alarming, she believes. "According to a recent survey, half of whites believe that the average black person is as well off as the average white person in terms of employment." Furthermore, "four in ten whites incorrectly believed that the typical black earned as much as or more than the typical white, even though black median household income is about 64 percent that of whites."[27]

Marc Morial, the president of the National Urban League, has reported statistics that support Sheryll Cashin's gloomy assessment: "In 2004, nearly 23% of black families of four earned incomes near or below the poverty line, compared to almost 10% [of American families] nationwide." Black individuals are also suffering, he found: "Almost 28% of single blacks fell near or below the poverty line, compared to 19% [of single Americans] nationwide."[28]

There is grave concern among African American leaders, young and old, about the continuing black economic underdevelopment. The situation is particularly serious in black inner-city neighborhoods, and some black leaders are sounding the alarm. For example, Joe Leonard warns that the unemployment rate among black men in major urban areas has reached stratospheric levels: "50 [or] 60 percent unemployment [of] African American males over 25 in New York; 64 per cent in Chicago." The young leader's voice trails off and he sits motionless for a moment, almost as if he is trying to banish the disturbing statistics from his mind. Finally, he predicts in a softer voice that dire consequences will accompany this runaway black unemployment rate. One of those consequences strikes at the very foundation of middle-class existence in this society, the ability to purchase a house. "You see home ownership [among African Americans has been] stagnant the last four years [at] 48 percent. It hasn't been that stagnant for a four year period since the 30 year mortgage was signed in '72." Because things are so bad, Leonard argues, black leaders should be much more assertive in their efforts to publicize the black economic plight in America. He laments, "Here we are trying to be civil. . . . We're not letting people feel our concerns."[29]

Others point out that efforts to address the black economic plight are complicated because it is part of a larger American economic crisis. Former congressman Frank Ballance is sure that his district in North Carolina is struggling with that larger crisis. He explains that "there are more poor white folk than there are black" and insists, "Our people don't understand." Ballance concludes, "Many times what they've [white people] been saying is that they're better than the black folk. Even though they're poor, and [they're] walking on a dirt floor, [they're] better than those nigras over there."[30] Right outside Atlanta, Eugene Walker sits in his living room frowning thoughtfully. He is concerned not only about individuals and their families; he worries that the economic well-being of all of American society is at risk. In his estimation, the monstrous and rapidly growing budget deficit that has engulfed the federal government is an economic calamity confronting all Americans. "The country's broke!" Walker thunders. With an undertone of incredulity, he adds, "And we're going deeper and deeper in the hole, and ain't nobody saying a word."[31]

Former SNCC staffer Charles Jones is particularly concerned about the inequitable distribution of wealth on a global scale, and he is convinced that certain black leaders who are willing to cooperate with a corrupt system in exchange for financial gain may have even assisted those responsible for the frightening economic imbalance. "There is a direct correlation between your character and integrity and how you play the game," he insists. "[If] you can conveniently turn away from a system screwing over you and your folks, you can be bought easily." Furthermore, according to Jones, "The system needs blacks to justify the stealing that they are going to do now [of] the rest of the assets of the world." He rubs his chin thoughtfully before adding, "That['s] 5 percent that owns more than 60 percent of the earth's wealth."[32]

Indeed, the evidence of economic distress affecting a broad cross section of Americans is all around us: older Americans, regardless of race, ponder an uncertain future as pension funds go broke; hundreds of thousands of jobs are disappearing; banks and investment firms are staring bankruptcy in the face; mortgage foreclosures are at an all-time high in a volatile housing market; bright young people graduating from universities with undergraduate, graduate, and professional degrees are saddled with thousands of dollars in student loan debts. In short, Americans from all strata of society are up against the most perilous economic circumstances in this nation's history.

Because African Americans have always faced difficult economic circumstances, even in the best of times, some social critics say that the African American economic plight in this broken economy is worse than ever. Of course, dire predictions of black economic disaster are nothing new. More than four decades ago, in the midst of the bright victories of the civil rights movement and in a reasonably stable American economy, federal officials in the Bureau of Labor were already predicting a dark future. Labor Secretary Willard Wirtz warned:

> We are piling up a human scrap heap of between 250,000 and 500,00 people a year, many of whom never appear in the unemployment statistics. They are often not counted among the unemployed because they have given up looking for work and thus count themselves out of the labor market. The rate of non-participation in the labor force by men in their prime years increased from 4.7 percent in 1953 to 5.2 percent in 1962. *The increase has been the sharpest among nonwhites, increasing from 5.3 percent to 8.2 percent in that period.* The human scrap heap is composed of persons who, as a consequence of technological development, of their own educational failures, of environments of poverty and other causes that disqualify them for employment in a skilled economy, cannot and will not find work without special help.[33]

In 1970, when black journalist Samuel Yette wrote his book *The Choice,* he was convinced that the crux of the black economic problem that resulted in such negative circumstances boiled down to one disturbing truth: "Black Americans *are* obsolete people."[34] Yette explained his assertion this way:

> Black Americans have outlived their usefulness. Their raison d'être to this society has ceased to be a compelling issue. Once an eco-

nomic asset, they are now considered an economic drag. The wood is all hewn, the water is all drawn, the cotton all picked, and the rails reach from coast to coast. The ditches are all dug, the dishes are put away, and only a few shoes remain to be shined. Thanks to old black backs and newfangled machines, the sweat chores of the nation are done. Now the same 25 million Blacks face a society that is brutally pragmatic, technologically accomplished, deeply racist, increasingly overcrowded, and surly. In such a society, the absence of social and economic value is a crucial factor in anyone's fight for a future.[35]

Samuel Yette offered this analysis of the economic relationship between African Americans and the American economy during the last century, when the militant notions and dire predictions of the young disciples of the Black Power movement filled the air. In that atmosphere, Yette's warning of black economic obsolescence struck a responsive chord in a black population tired of government promises, white backlash, and media pronouncements that racial problems were a thing of the past. Today, in the midst of declarations that equality of opportunity finally does exist in the workplace, Yette has not changed his mind. Instead, he insists that African Americans are more obsolete in the American economy of the new millennium than ever, because "the technology [that made them obsolete in the first place] has really taken off."[36]

Congresswoman Eleanor Holmes Norton also attributes black economic troubles to "structural changes in the American economy." Norton is particularly alarmed by the outsourcing of jobs in the manufacturing sector. The factory jobs "went offshore before opportunities and education had caught up," she says, adding that the well-paying jobs that are now available are positions for which the majority of African Americans are not trained. Consequently, "there's a huge void here." In the absence of realistic opportunities for good jobs, Norton explains, "ghetto culture has taken over. Boys in particular get eaten alive by ghetto culture early on. They in turn grow up in communities where there are not jobs."[37]

Recent census data and other economic statistics back up the alarming conclusions reached by Representative Norton, retired journalist Samuel

Yette, and many others. Furthermore, the black economic crisis continues to worsen, even though there are more black elected officials in office today than at any other time in our nation's history. According to one scholar, "the political growth of black elected officials has been remarkable—from less than 300 in 1965 to over 8,500 in 1995." But despite that increase, "African Americans have perhaps less public policy influence than at any point in the last four decades."[38] In the meantime, black unemployment figures continue their steady, relentless climb, "accompanied by the unprecedented phenomena of tens of thousands of African Americans in their twenties and thirties never having had a full time job." At the same time, however, "the demand for the elimination of affirmative action and other programs that economically benefit African Americans grows shriller."[39]

Thus, as many point with pride to the growth rate of the black middle class in the last quarter of the twentieth century—as much as 40 percent according to some analysts—they cannot deny the even faster growth rate of the black poor.[40] And even though the black middle class has grown, continued economic progress is in doubt because of "massive transformations in the structure of the global economy and labor force."[41] The consequences of these "massive transformations" have been dire—not only for the black poor, but for the black middle class as well, a middle class that often seems to exist just one step above the poverty ensnaring so many of their brothers and sisters.

No city illustrates these alarming economic trends more clearly than Detroit, Michigan. Early in the twentieth century, African Americans left their southern homes by the thousands to move to Detroit, where they could make more money in one day on an auto plant assembly line than they could make in a month working the land. The steady income black Detroiters earned gave them access to a comfortable middle-class existence for much of the past century. But by the late twentieth century, when the American auto industry was hit with a series of setbacks, its market share shrank at a dizzying pace, and the city began to hemorrhage manufacturing jobs at an alarming rate. Today, black Detroiters find themselves trapped in an economic nightmare. Many remain unemployed, especially since the American auto industry has been pushed to the brink of extinction. Those who are able to get jobs often can find them only in the service sector of the economy, where the pay is low and job security and benefits are nonexistent.

Data from the most recent census indicate that African Americans all over the country are working in low-paying, insecure service jobs in disproportionately high numbers. While the percentage of such jobs occupied by white workers is 13.4 percent, the percentage occupied by African American workers is 24.5 percent. That statistic becomes even more troubling when it is evaluated within the broader context of national population ratios: African Americans, who occupy nearly one-quarter of service jobs, make up only 13.4 percent of this nation's total population. In view of this dismal black employment reality, it is not surprising that the income of African American workers lags far behind that of white workers. For example, only 5.7 percent of black individuals in the workforce earn $75,000 or more, whereas 15.6 percent of white workers earn at least $75,000. Comparisons of wage earners across racial lines in other categories also show an enduring income gap between black and white workers. For example, a disproportionate number of those individuals and families who comprise the working poor are African Americans: some 8.1 percent of black workers earn $10,000 to $14,999, while only 4.2 percent of white workers earn in that bracket.[42] An assessment of black income across economic categories and across time periods reveals an equally dismal picture: "In 1970, the median income for Black households was about $22,000, while for white households it was $37,000. In 1999, African-American median household income was $27,900, the highest ever recorded, but still far less than for non-Hispanic white households [which was] $44,400, and [well] below all other race groups as well."[43]

Among the factors that have caused black economic inequality to follow African Americans from slavery through emancipation, into the twentieth century, and finally into the new millennium, one of the most important is the continued segregation of the black population. Even now, more than fifty years after the Brown decision outlawing segregation, the African American population remains concentrated in only ten states: New York, Florida, Texas, Georgia, California, Illinois, North Carolina, Maryland, Virginia, and Michigan. Until 2005, the state of Louisiana was one of these top ten states, but after Hurricane Katrina, the state's black residents were dispersed, and many have yet to return. Of the ten largest cities (100,000 people or more), Detroit has the largest proportion of African American residents in its population: a remarkable 83 percent of the city's residents are black. Detroit is followed by Philadelphia (44 percent black), and Chicago (38 percent black).[44]

As African Americans continue to live in inner cities with crumbling infrastructures, they face a host of problems that exacerbate their perilous economic circumstances. One of the most pressing of them is inadequate education. So many of the school systems in inner cities are operating in the red because gainfully employed residents have escaped to the suburbs, taking the lion's share of the city's tax revenues with them. Inner-city schools are left to scrounge for scarce resources that never seem to be enough to provide the quality of education that the children so desperately need. For example, Keiara Bell, a black thirteen-year-old native of Detroit, lives in a tough neighborhood. "She lives off Livernois, south of Davison. It's a place, according to statistics where a child younger than 18 years old is twice as likely to die as the average American child. Unemployment is more than three times the national average. A third of the children live in poverty."[45] Back during the heyday of the American auto industry, Detroit was exceedingly prosperous, and Detroit's public schools were among the best in the nation. But those days are ancient history to Keiara.

City officials in her impoverished hometown struggle to keep the schools open, and they are not always successful. Recently, they were forced to close seventy-seven schools. The other schools in the system barely remain open. Young Keiara knows all too well how troubled Detroit's school system is. "Keiara does not bring books home because there are not enough books at school to go around. They stay in the classroom and are shared by all the students at Courtis Elementary/Middle School. Their day begins with a pat down and a metal detector." Detroit's teachers do their best with the scarce resources, but it is extremely difficult. Keiara's math teacher laments, "The books are old, the substitute teachers don't come, it's a system in shambles. . . . You do what you can do, teach what you can teach, and at least see to it that they get a warm breakfast."[46]

As students like Keiara Bell endeavor to get an education in systems that are woefully underfunded, the impact on black educational statistics nationwide is alarming but predictable. For example, in 2004, a much lower percentage of African Americans (74%) than white students (81%) earned a high school diploma. That same year, only 13 percent of black men and 16 percent of black women earned a bachelor's degree. At the same time, white men earned a higher proportion of college degrees (26%) than white women (23%) that year.[47] Whether Keiara Bell is aware of the statistics or not, she undoubtedly knows that she faces an uphill struggle. But that does not stop her from planning and hoping. She "lies in bed most evenings trying to work out her escape in her mind. She's been accepted to Cass Tech, the city's premier public high school. Then Stanford, the dream goes. Then Harvard for law school."[48]

Black leaders are all too familiar with the heartrending stories of countless black youngsters like Keiara Bell who are searching for a way out. However, the leaders, in general, believe that African Americans will never find the path out of their crumbling neighborhoods or the solution to inadequate schools until the fundamental problem of economic inequality is addressed. Consequently, over the years, a variety of black leaders have offered a wide range of proposals designed to deal with black economic inequality. The most militant kind of proposal is a call for reparations, such as the demand issued by James Forman in 1969 at the Black Economic Development Conference in Detroit. He declared that "the reparations [are] due us as a people . . ." because we "have been exploited and degraded, brutalized, killed, and persecuted." Forman's was not the first demand for reparations, nor the last. However, his demand is distinguished by the inclusion of a detailed plan for spending the reparations money: "1. We call for the establishment of a Southern Land Bank to help our brothers and sisters who have to leave their land because of racist pressure, for people who want to establish cooperative farms, but who have no funds. . . . 2. We call for the establishment of four major publishing and printing industries in the United States to be funded with $10,000,000 each. . . . 3. We call for the establishment of four of the most advanced scientific and futuristic audio-visual networks to be located in Detroit, Chicago, Cleveland, and Washington, D. C." In addition to these proposals, Forman's "Manifesto" contained eight others, to fund everything from a research skills center to a national black labor strike and defense fund.[49]

Since Forman issued his manifesto, African American leaders have continued to debate the philosophical, ethical, and economic implications of reparations for African Americans. Former congresswoman Cynthia McKinney is convinced that America owes African Americans reparations, because "the disparities between black and white America are worse today than they were at the time of the murder of Dr. Martin Luther King, Jr. They are that way; those disparities exist because of deliberate public policy." McKinney also argues that in addition to the victims of the transatlantic slave trade, those who were placed under surveillance by COINTELPRO, a surveillance program of the FBI, are also entitled to reparations.[50] In Detroit, former Black Panther Maureen Taylor asks wearily, "What reparations can we get?" She pauses and then continues in the impassioned tone of one who has fought to organize black autoworkers in Detroit while plants close one after another: "And the reparations should be reparations that we demand in the name of all that have been disenfranchised by this economic animal that will take your job from you and say it's your fault; and allow you to have your house repossessed; your car repossessed; your children put out of school; your benefits taken away. And you are reduced to not having any income at all."[51]

Down in Alabama, the young congressman Artur Davis, thinking of the many critical issues that Congress must consider, finds it "hard . . . to see the space for significant debate on reparations." Furthermore, Davis asks, who should be compensated? "Those who have suffered from slavery's legacy [all African Americans]? Or only those who can actually trace their family connection to slavery?" Instead of focusing on reparations, he argues, "anyone representing this district . . . [must] try and find some sort of a unified plan for reviving the economic prospects of the region."[52]

As other African American leaders in the new millennium ponder the economic plight of their black constituents, many look for assistance anywhere they can find it. Mayor Johnny Ford of Tuskegee, Alabama, notes that when he was first elected in 1972, he already had his plan in mind. He had ten priorities, and at the very top of his list was economic development. And Ford was willing to look outside the region for resources. Because he had cultivated contacts in President Richard Nixon's administration, he went straight to Washington. He proudly declares, "I was able to get millions of dollars because of my relationship with Nixon and because I supported the president's reelection."[53] Today, in his continuing search for economic aid for his constituents, Mayor Ford stubbornly refuses to overlook any possibilities. At one point, his willingness to accept aid from an unlikely ally placed him in a ticklish situation. The Alabama State Legislature was refusing to release four hundred thousand dollars that had already been allotted by the state government to fund a day-care program in Tuskegee. Ford's attempts to navigate the state bureaucracy were both frustrating and unsuccessful, so he decided to pick up the phone and call Governor George Wallace. Most African Americans who lived through America's civil rights years will never forget the image of the very young George Wallace giving his inaugural address when he was first elected governor of Alabama. His words are etched into the consciousness of many older African Americans, who can still see the pugnacious expression on his face and hear his Alabama drawl as he declared, "Segregation now; segregation tomorrow; and segregation forever." The memory of the rebel yells of approval rising from the crowd of white Alabama supporters who were listening still raises goose bumps on the arms of many African Americans.

Mayor Johnny Ford remembers too, and when he first met George Wallace in 1970, only eight years after Wallace's very public declaration of segregation, Ford expected a man who would be "twenty feet tall with horns." But the man he encountered outside the Barber County Courthouse in 1970 was not at all like the evil presence he had imagined. Instead, the George Wallace he met was very apologetic. Ford recalls that Wallace looked him in the eye and said, "I made a mistake. I'm sorry. As a man I ask you to forgive me, and I ask African Americans to forgive me." The former symbol of segregation paused to search the smooth dark face of young Johnny Ford before he said, in a soft voice that pleaded for understanding, "I was wrong." Later, when Mayor Ford, frustrated, wrestled unsuccessfully with the Alabama State Legislature, he remembered that conversation with Wallace, who had recently been reelected governor, and he decided to ask the reformed segregationist for help. Shortly after he telephoned the governor, the four hundred thousand dollars Ford had been waiting for was on its way to Tuskegee. Because he was convinced of Wallace's sincerity, Ford supported Governor Wallace's bid for reelection in 1974. Ford recalls that Rev. Jesse Jackson criticized him for his public support of Wallace; but with a smile on his face, Ford also remembers how glad he was to receive the funds for his city's day care program.[54]

African American leaders keep seeking solutions to black economic underdevelopment, and as they do, some young black leaders wonder if black attitudes about money might be the most serious impediment to the search for economic solutions. They worry especially about the premium placed on individual economic success by members of their generation. Washington, D.C., city councilman Kwame Brown, age thirty-three, is painfully aware of the focus on the accumulation of individual wealth that seems to be the preoccupation of many people in his age group.[55] But the black emphasis on the accumulation of material goods is nothing new. Back during the civil rights movement, SNCC member Julius Lester asserted that the accumulation of material goods was actually an act of resistance. He explained,

> Every aspect of the southern social system was contrived to make a black man feel that he was less than human. That was why when he bought a car he bought a Cadillac. He wanted to feel like he was somebody. Northern liberals have always criticized what they consider materialism when they see a sharecropper's shack with a big TV antenna and a big car beside it. The Negro middle class, they claim, is more materialistic than the white. *In the black community, a Cadillac is a symbol of resistance, because its proud owner is refusing to be what the society wants him to be. His Cadillac is a weapon in the fight to tell himself that he is as much of a man as any white man.*[56]

The link between black self-esteem and the accumulation of wealth that Julius Lester described in the 1960s is recognized by scholars, and they explain it this way: "Oppressed groups often have a need to make a statement of their ambitions and status. We saw it among immigrant Jews [and] Italians, and still see it in other groups." In particular, some insist, because African Americans have "a history of disappointments that go back to slavery and broken promises throughout our lives. . . . We don't believe in 'later on.' There was the promise of freedom, the promise of land, the promise of glory—they were slow coming if they came at all. We are concerned about our mortality. We die sooner, younger, more violently. [If] there's something you want, why wait?"[57]

Councilman Kwame Brown is disturbed by the thought of young black people of his generation answering this question by pulling out their credit cards and refusing to wait. He insists, however, that his generation learned that behavior from the generation before: "That's what you guys [the older generation] taught us how to do. A lot of people were saying, 'hey . . . focus on making sure . . . that your kids [will be] better off than you were.' And the only thing people saw or could see, even to this day, it only meant one thing; that you had to have more money because, you know, we chase things."[58] Self-proclaimed hip-hop historian Todd Boyd says the emphasis on the accumulation of wealth has become so important that it is now a core value of the hip-hop generation. It is "known alternately as flossin', shinin', or better yet, 'bling, bling,'" he explains. "All these have to do with an outward celebration of one's wealth, success, and overall status in life. What in an early generation might have been called 'showing off,' has now grown into an integral part of self-expression in hip hop circles." To emphasize his conclusion, Boyd quotes Biggie Smalls, one of rap's most colorful characters. "As Biggie often said, 'Money, clothes and hoes, all a nigga knows.'"[59]

Councilman Brown and Biggie Smalls are part of the same generation. But as Brown sits in his office in Washington, D.C., he is troubled about the message in Biggie's music, and the message in much of rap music that glorifies conspicuous consumerism and denigrates women. Brown is afraid that all this black emphasis on personal wealth and consumer goods could very well impede the progress of economic uplift for the masses of African Americans.[60] Brown falls silent and looks out his office window, worrying about the economic problems that plague the African Americans in his district. He knows that somewhere out there black youngsters are riding up and down the street in their hoopties jacked up on twenty-four-inch wheels with expensive stereos turned all the way up. The volume is so high that parts of the car—the license plate, the windows, the trim—actually vibrate in time to the driving beat; and over the din, a young male black voice raps, "Money, clothes and hoes, all a nigga knows."[61]

7. Black Culture Then and Now

Young African Americans in their hoopties are just the latest link in the long chain of black cultural expression stretching all the way back to the first Africans in America. The celebration of shared black cultural values has always been one of the most potent weapons in the black arsenal of resistance to white oppression. Historian V. P. Franklin explains the basis for this distinctive African American culture: "The material conditions of the black population in this society, as well as their African background, determined their predominant cultural values. The Afro-American world view was a product of the larger economic and social processes."[1]

Franklin also explains the tight bond between African American culture and black resistance: "At the core of the racial consciousness that developed among Afro-Americans in the United States was the cultural objective of black self-determination, which operated in a dialectical relationship with white supremacy. Oftentimes, resistance and education were valued as strategies to obtain the larger goal of self-determination."[2] In the final analysis, according to Franklin, the very bedrock upon which African American culture has always rested is the objective of black self-determination, or the ability of black people to control their own destiny in a hostile white environment.

The dizzying array of ideas and images resulting from modern-day advances in mass communication technology has made many African Americans less sure than they used to be that there is a set of *shared* cultural values and a common worldview. For instance, African Americans who came of age during the civil rights movement are quick to point to hip-hop culture as a sign of the alienation of black youth from traditional black cultural values. But African American youth are acting like nearly all American youth, regardless of race, when they embrace a culture at odds with the values of their elders. Of course, this obvious generational clash of perspectives is nothing new. African Americans who came of age dur-

163

ing the civil rights movement also recall differences between their perspective and that of their elders. Tuskegee Mayor Johnny Ford says that during his younger years, he and his buddies had their own style and outlook that set them apart from their elders: "We were pretty hip ourselves when we were coming along."[3]

Courtland Cox, a SNCC staff member, observed that the clash of viewpoints between older and younger activists sometimes led to dramatic encounters. In particular, Cox recalls the confrontation between young leaders in SNCC and older civil rights leaders at the March on Washington in 1963. The tone of SNCC chairman John Lewis's speech was the catalyst that precipitated that particular clash. Eventually, the two sides reached an agreement, but before they did, Cox and the NAACP's Roy Wilkins had a contentious conversation. Cox explains, "Wilkins . . . said that he was not going to have these young people, you know, come and destroy all the stuff that he'd worked for all his life." Cox was only twenty-three at the time, but he refused to defer to the older well-known civil rights leader. When Wilkins declared that Lewis would deliver the speech over his dead body, young Courtland Cox looked the older man in the eye with a steely glare as he declared, "Well, you know, that could be arranged."[4]

In Knoxville, Tennessee, former student activist Robert Booker reports that the president of the school he attended, Knoxville College, heard about the students' plans to conduct sit-ins in downtown stores in early 1960. President James Colston was horrified, and he and other Knoxville College administrators tried to dissuade the students. "They [college administrators] told us they would prefer that we not do it. Their fear was that moneys would stop coming to the college. They had also gotten bomb threats. They were afraid that the campus would be blown up . . . so, we understood their reasoning. But, in the end we said to them, 'These are our rights. We must do this. We must bring about racial equality. We do not believe that the negotiations are going well.'" Booker and his fellow students, refusing to back down, said to the administrators, "Now, if you tell us we can't do it, what we will do . . . we will write letters to *Jet Magazine,* the *Chicago Defender,* the *Pittsburgh Courier,* and all of these national media to say that the administrator of Knoxville College refuses to let us participate." President Colston quickly responded, "Now, we didn't say that."[5]

Over in Charlotte, North Carolina, SNCC leader Charles Jones also experienced opposition from older African Americans; it was during his involvement in the sit-in movement in his hometown. Jones is convinced that the conflict was inevitable and it occurred because the students and the older black community leaders were at different stages in their ideological development. When the conflict erupted, it was difficult and emotional. For example, one incident involved a local black minister and community leader. When Charlotte students began their sit-ins, the older man, who was accustomed to speaking for the black community, "was not prepared to give up leadership, and [he] insisted on being the spokesperson and the leader." The exasperated Jones finally became so frustrated that he could not keep silent. "I remember clearly saying, 'Reggie, this is our movement.'" The older man hesitated, but Jones continued without missing a beat, "Shut the hell up and sit down. No, you don't speak for us. . . . NO."[6]

Generational clashes in the African American community have always occurred. However, such clashes these days may be more acrimonious than those of the past, and in the future the severity and frequency of discord are likely to accelerate. One reason why, according to former SNCC staffer Julian Bond, is that "We are a young people. That is, we have a big gap between people, I'd say, 50 [years old] and up, and the people who are 25 and down. The 25 and down population, as I understand it, is growing enormously."[7] Complicating this demographic reality, according to hip-hop journalist Bakari Kitwana, are two critical processes: globalization and desegregation. "Young Black Americans born between 1965 and 1984 are the first generation of Black Americans to come of age in the era of globalization."[8] In addition, he notes, "Our generation is the first generation of African Americans to come of age outside the confines of legal segregation."[9]

Furthermore, Kitwana observes that globalization has affected much more than just the mind-set of young African Americans: "The real story of globalization's impact on the hip-hop generation is revealed in the widening division between the haves and have-nots that occurred during the 1980s and 1990s."[10] As globalization caused many urban centers with large black populations to lose manufacturing jobs, the young journalist points out, the jobs that remained in inner cities were generally minimum-wage jobs. Because these jobs offered little chance for advancement, virtually no security, and pitifully low wages, they had a profoundly negative impact on the hopes and dreams of this younger generation of African Americans. "Young Blacks faced the realities of rising rates of unemployment, Black youth reliance on the underground economy, particularly the crack-cocaine explosion of the 1980s, and the simultaneous boom in incarceration rates. The great contrast between the positive and negative outgrowths of this new economy has heavily influenced the values, lifestyles, and worldview of young Blacks."[11]

Against this background of revolutionary economic change, Kitwana and other members of his generation find the lip service that America pays to the cause of equal rights particularly galling. He acknowledges, "We certainly live in a more inclusive society than existed in pre–civil rights America. However, continuing segregation and inequality have made it especially illusory for many young blacks." Kitwana mercilessly dissects the American illusion of black equality. "Countless roadblocks persist in critical areas where Blacks continue to be discriminated against in often subtle and sometimes not so subtle ways. Young Blacks are twice as likely to be unemployed as their white counterparts. Young Blacks with similar skills, experience, and educational backgrounds continue to be paid less than whites for the same jobs. More so than any other racial or ethnic group, African Americans remain segregated from whites in housing." And the list goes on, he insists.[12]

Many older African American leaders are painfully aware of the tough conditions facing today's black youth, and they worry. During the famous Birmingham campaign of 1963, Rev. Fred Shuttlesworth was the head of the Alabama Christian Movement for Human Rights. He watched Birmingham's black grade school and high school children march and sing for freedom while Bull Connor's police dogs snarled at them and the Birmingham Fire Department turned their high-pressure water hoses on them. At a time when heavy industry was thriving in America, Shuttlesworth and other civil rights leaders could look forward to the day when these young freedom fighters, along with other black youth, would have new opportunities for advancement. Contemplating the plight of black inner city youth today, who must try to make their way in a country that no longer has the industrial base of the 1960s, Shuttlesworth sighs heavily. "The terrible thing is the children. So now we need to think about how we['re] going to continue to overcome violence. The children—it's so tragic that they're swept up into it. And there's a subculture [of] drugs . . . and violence."[13]

Senator Carol Moseley Braun, knowing that black youth are confronted by extraordinarily tough conditions today and an uncertain future tomorrow, is at a loss to understand their apparent lack of interest in the political process: "These are just young people who, if anything, have more at stake with this stuff than folks like me. I got my social security. I got my retirement. I got my 401(k). I got my house. My health insurance is pretty much guaranteed. . . . My generation is past dealing with this stuff [but the younger generation is not]."[14] The financial security of younger African Americans also worries former Congresswoman Cynthia McKinney. According to her analysis, "What we are seeing is the backsliding so that my son's generation fears that, and the statistics bear it out, that he won't be as successful as me. And I won't have the wealth accumulation [that] my parents had."[15]

Although many of the black leaders who fret about the plight of young African Americans are convinced that the blame rests on society, others insist that society is only part of the problem. The other part, they argue, rests squarely on the shoulders of the young. For example, Birmingham civil rights leader Rev. Abraham Woods is persuaded that "we're in a sad state. In fact, Dr. King's dream in so many instances is becoming a nightmare . . . and black people . . . we've become our own enemies. I'm frightened about that, you see. And I see some leaders who want to identify with the young people and they put their cap on backwards." Woods asserts defiantly, "I ain't gonna put my cap on backwards. . . . I keep my hat on straight. I was taught to look like somebody."[16]

James Armstrong, also a Birmingham resident, owns a barbershop now. He enjoys his memories of the strong, committed young people who marched with him over forty years ago when he proudly carried a large American flag on the Selma-to-Montgomery March in 1965. Like Reverend Woods, Armstrong is in his eighties, and also like Woods, he reacts negatively to the styles and values embraced by today's black youth. He confesses, "I turned a boy down about two weeks ago [who] wanted to rent one of my chairs in the barbershop cause his pants was low when he come in there asking for a job." Armstrong pauses and then continues, "Maybe I should have helped him, but I turned him down cause I knew he had problems." Everywhere he looks, Armstrong sees black youngsters who are vastly different from the black youth of the past. "They got earrings in their ears, and don't know what it's for . . . they don't know where that low-pants wearing comes from. That's the ugliest thing in the world. That came out of prison." There is more, though: "They won't vote. They [are] driving a $250 car with $5,000 worth of rims on it. It bothers me."[17] Up in Knoxville, former sit-in leader Robert Booker is also uncomfortable with the way some African American youngsters look. He observes, "I look at it, and to me, it's just so awful to see young men's pants hanging down." And regarding hair styles: "I despise it to see a man with braids in his hair. I have never, ever liked that."[18]

Over in Memphis, Dr. Benjamin Hooks also sees changes in the black youth culture. As far as Hooks is concerned, though, the obvious stylistic changes are symptomatic of more disturbing substantive changes. He explains, "Today, I'm not sure . . . [young people] react in anger, or whether young people think at all. I'm not too sure. It's a new kind of a world. Values are different. What people are living for is different."[19] Down in Selma, Alabama, Joanne Bland asserts, "No, I don't even think we have a culture anymore; let alone hip hop culture. I despise them using that phrase, but hip hop really scares me. . . . the words, the boldness of it." Bland is especially troubled by the way many of these young people express themselves in public, cursing and calling each other "nigga," and she concludes, "There's no respect anymore."[20] In addition to the behavior of the young, Julian Bond is worried about the aspirations and values of black youth. He thinks of the teaching he received: "My father used to tell his children that you are people who have gotten certain advantages, and your responsibility is to take those advantages and use them [to help] people less fortunate than you. And I don't get that feeling about today's [black youth]."[21]

Robert Booker is particularly concerned about the attitude of the black students he has encountered in recent years. Booker, who is retired now, recently decided that he wanted to serve his community by becoming a substitute teacher. Yet, his eagerness to serve turned to distress during his first teaching assignment. "I certainly wanted to go and teach; I wanted to inspire, I wanted to challenge, but I never got to first base. Most of the time in those classrooms, you spend with discipline problems—telling people to sit down; stop throwing paper across the room."[22] Professor John Hope Franklin is convinced that such disrespectful behavior is based on a feeling of alienation from society, which affects so many of today's black youth. He considers it "a response to rejection. In any sense, there's a kind of metaphor of failure of American society to really envelop and include everybody; and why should they [black youth] bother with [society's rules]?"[23]

Unita Blackwell, a founding member of the Mississippi Freedom Democratic Party back in 1964 and the first black mayor of Mayersville, Mississippi, is particularly alarmed by black youths' view of older black people. When Blackwell was a young girl in her native Mississippi, everyone looked up to the oldest members of the community because they were the repositories of all the community's wisdom. "They [old people] used to have positive influence because you was the truth. You was the strength. You was the person that all of us was aspiring to be, and [now] . . . stuff done got so crazy." Furthermore, Blackwell observes, some older African Americans have had a curious reaction to this lack of respect: they have embraced the same youth culture that treated them with disrespect. As she puts it, "so now they're acting out childishly."[24] Memphis native Rev. Harold Middlebrook finds that younger African Americans not only fail to appreciate the wisdom of their elders. He worries especially about the refusal of many black youth to heed the advice and counsel of Christian ministers. "The mind-set of the younger element has no concept of what that's all about," he explains. "And they don't want to be told anything, and so they rebel against—especially once we had the rise of Elijah Muhammad and the Black Muslims in this country—then you get a large segment of young people who will rebel against anything [that] Christian ministers say."[25]

As today's black leaders fret about the state of black youth in America, most agree that there is more than enough blame to go around. Some even argue that the previous generation—the civil rights generation—is at least partially responsible for the precarious position of the young. Rev. T. Randel Osburn explains this line of reasoning in a somber voice: "This new generation of rappers . . . it's really only been a year [since] I have acknowledged that we are at fault [for] this generation. . . . I'm so frustrated with rappers and young folk not doing anything. . . . [But] it isn't their fault. It's really our fault." The reason he feels that way is that "the movement was basically led by the people who were the cream of the crop; the talented tenth; who had the most to gain from the movement being successful,"[26] and according to him, the talented tenth did not reach back to help the other ninety percent.

In the years following the movement, black leaders began to realize what a serious mistake they had made, Osburn reports. Even Dr. King "understood toward the end of his life that you couldn't separate the talented tenth from the ninety."[27] As far as Osburn is concerned, this neglect of the ninety percent produced a class of disaffected, disengaged people whose offspring formed the basis of the disaffected and disengaged hip-hop generation. Civil rights leader and close King associate C. T. Vivian also believes the attitudes of twenty-first-century black youth are directly related to the actions of their elders. But in his view, it was the successes of the movement, not the failures, that created the problem. "We delivered so much," he insists, "that the younger generation . . . thought it was all over because they thought that they didn't have to worry about the future and that they had won more than they could digest."[28]

Former Georgia state senator Eugene Walker has a different opinion. He blames more recent developments for the disillusionment and disaffection of so many young African Americans. "From where I sit," says Walker, "they've just been abandoned by their parents. Now, when I say abandoned, I don't mean the parents have run off and left them. I mean the parents have run off and left them spiritually, and with no values. . . . They let them do precisely what they want to, and these children don't know what's best for them."[29] Over in East Tennessee, Robert Booker agrees that many of the problems of black young people are rooted in problems in the black family: "Until we find a way to get at the young parents, and I refer to this as babies raising babies, until we . . . have that young parent understand, your child must do better in school. He must do better than you did, or he's going to repeat the same mistakes you made, and there'll be grandbabies having babies. . . . But, until we reach young parents, it's going to continue. That's where the problem lies; with young parents whose children are out of control." Booker sadly contemplates the matter and concludes in resignation, "How we reach them [young parents], I don't know."[30] Former SNCC staffer Charles Jones, in Charlotte, North Carolina, has identified what he considers one of the most important causes of the problems affecting black youth and their families; it is easy to diagnose but hard to cure. In a voice quivering with emotion, Jones declares, "Crack has impacted the relationship between grandma, mom, and child by, in many ways, cutting it off totally. . . . That's one epidemic that's impacting the black community to its very core."[31]

Young African American leaders, as well as their elders, also see that black young people are disaffected and disengaged. Recent Howard University Ph.D. Joe Leonard believes part of the problem facing his generation is the refusal of their parents to talk about the recent past. In his view, "The only thing . . . the one thing that African Americans of past generations needed to do and must do, they're very similar to the generation after slavery who never talked about what they endured. These kids don't know—especially in the South, which is horrible—don't know that they had to get off the sidewalk and let the white person walk on that sidewalk. If they didn't doff their hat, they'd get hit, and they'd better not stare too long. . . . They [young black people] just have no clue."[32]

In addition to the stony and stubborn silence of their elders, Leonard continues, young people of his generation are plagued by having no youth organization that could help them to cope with their circumstances. "There is no SNCC right now. That's a huge void. . . . a HUGE void." He mentions the suggestion that hip-hop could serve the way SNCC did. But "the problem is . . . there is no public policy dimension to hip hop right now. . . . There's no revolutionary act. Those four kids [who started the sit-in movement in Greensboro, North Carolina] were saying let's get arrested for something honorable." Leonard's smooth young brow wrinkles in a deep frown. "It's also hard to have any sort of movement when the leaders—spokespersons for the movement—consider themselves or call themselves what the white slave masters have always called us."[33] Somewhere beyond Joe Leonard's tastefully appointed Washington office, young African Americans are riding down the street in their hoopties, their sound systems vibrating with the lyrics "Money, clothes and hoes. All a nigga knows."[34]

Congressman John Lewis, a member of the Student Nonviolent Coordinating Committee, the organization whose demise Leonard regrets, agrees with Leonard's assessment of the group's impact on black youth. Lewis himself benefited: "SNCC served as an incubator in a sense, to help grow and develop my leadership ability." He explains the way the organization helped him: "It was the Student Nonviolent Coordinating Committee and people telling me that you can do it" that convinced Lewis he could be an effective leader.[35]

Without SNCC or any similar youth organization, it seems that young African Americans are left to their own devices as they face an uncertain future. Washington, D.C., councilman Kwame Brown fears that black people of his generation might pay too little attention to the past. He reasons, "I am extremely respectful [of the previous generation, but] we still have to create our own mind-set. How do we take all the good and continue to move it forward? You can't do that by standing still. Standing still is why we're in the condition we're in right now." Brown is convinced that a large part of the younger generation's identity rests in the struggles of the past, but he worries that many in his generation are simply tired of hearing about those struggles. "We are like one generation away from forgetting. . . . Now, that is the scary part."[36]

At the same time, Councilman Brown is concerned that African Americans who came of age during the civil rights movement have given up on black youth. "They [older African Americans] are now [at] the point where they are not willing to give young folks, my generation, another opportunity." Brown concedes that the older generation has reached out to the young in the past, but many were disappointed at the results. He thinks "what happened is [that] they tried with a couple of us, and we wanted to be cool . . . drive the fancy cars, wear the fancy suits, but we wasn't smart. We didn't put the work in to be smart, and therefore [the older] generation said, "I'm not dealing with that . . . [it is] style without substance." Because some young people are doing nothing to earn their elders' respect, the older leaders said, "forget it. . . . generation X, the hip hop folks, they're crazy."[37]

When some older African American leaders look at black youth today, they wonder what to do next. C. T. Vivian, as a leader in the Nashville movement and with King in SCLC, was able to communicate effectively with people from southern sheriffs to local movement leaders. He was especially good with the young people in the Nashville movement;

they admired Vivian's unique style of assertive nonviolence. The energetic preacher was always eloquent and never silent: he would explain the rightness of the black freedom struggle to anyone who would listen. But when Vivian looks at today's black youth, he is uncharacteristically reticent. He finally says, "The truth is, I guess, I'm trying to find out where I fit into their [young people's] thing. We should win them. And if you don't win them, you shouldn't lose them, they're too important. . . . It's a real problem."[38]

Older African American leaders worry about the effect of a serious generation gap on the development of African American leadership in the new millennium. Many fondly look back to an era when the generational differences between black leaders seemed to matter much less. For example, Lawrence Guyot and his colleagues in SNCC were able to work with older black leaders during the civil rights movement even though their perspectives were often very different. He recalls, "When I grew up, most of the people who were already leaders were quite [a bit] older than we were. [But] we didn't have an age problem. I mean Amzie Moore [an older black leader in Mississippi] didn't tell us what to do. There were some problems that we agreed on mutually solving." Guyot explains why old and young were able to work together effectively in those earlier years: "See, when I grew up . . . the extended family was a reality." But now "we're becoming more atomized," and that helps to widen the gulf between young and old.[39]

Guyot's SNCC colleague Bernard Lafayette emphasizes a different reason for the disconnect between younger and older black leaders. He believes that the context in which young leadership operates today is so different from the context in which he and his SNCC colleagues worked that it ensures a very different leadership style. "They [young leaders] are different in the sense that they probably conform more to the traditional type of leaders. . . . These new leaders . . . are people who are able to put together a political campaign and win public office. *So they are part of the system.*"[40] In contrast, black leaders during the civil rights movement, from Martin Luther King Jr. to H. Rap Brown, had to be confrontational, because they were all obliged to confront a system that did not include them.

Rev. Samuel Billy Kyles agrees, and he cites the career of Congressman Harold Ford Jr., from Memphis, Tennessee, to illustrate the point. Harold Ford Jr. is only in his thirties, and when he successfully ran for Congress, he was elected to the same seat his father had occupied for over twenty years. Kyles insists that the elder Ford had to be aggressive and confrontational in order to break down the doors of exclusion, because he was the first black congressman to occupy that seat. Kyles feels that the willingness to be aggressive and confrontational thirty years ago was a key ingredient in the identity of many black leaders at that time. More recently, he points out, the context in which Harold Ford Jr. operates is much different. "He doesn't have the baggage his dad had because his dad had to break doors down. Harold Jr. didn't have to break them down. All he had to do was walk in."[41] Yet, while being an insider has its advantages, the sense of inclusion that accompanies the insider status of some younger black leaders could be problematic, according to older leaders. Up in Chicago, Timuel Black worries that the sense of inclusion breeds arrogance. He points to the example of Jesse Jackson Jr., who is a congressman from Chicago. In Black's estimation, "he's a bit more arrogant than his father." He concludes softly, "That is typical of this younger crop of black leaders."[42]

The attitude of young black political leaders is a concern of J. L. Chestnut, a Selma, Alabama, civil rights attorney, too. Chestnut was there at the foot of the Edmund Pettus Bridge on Bloody Sunday, March 7, 1965. He heard the gagging, coughing, and screaming of the black marchers as they were blinded by clouds of tear gas, and he saw them run for their lives as they were chased by members of Sheriff Jim Clark's mounted posse and hit by their billy clubs. With his firsthand knowledge of black people's sacrifices and struggle for inclusion in the political process in mind, he maintains, "I think they [younger black political leaders] are Democrats first and blacks second. I think that's a serious mistake. I think also that they don't have what Martin Luther King and Ralph Abernathy, and people like that had. . . . I don't know of anybody [these days] who's willing to sacrifice a paycheck, much less their life." But Chestnut does not feel that the different attitude displayed by younger black political leaders is the only thing that hampers their effectiveness. "The problems we face now are qualitatively, quantitatively vastly different than what they were then [during the 1960s], infinitely more complex, and I don't see . . . any black leader who really has an understanding of that."[43]

In Atlanta, former state senator Eugene Walker is critical of younger black leaders' breadth of concern. He asserts that "when they get into office, they see their tenure being extended by bringing more people into the process . . . and they do this by having these community/neighborhood groups come in with a strong mind-set involving things that affect their little neighborhood, and not the big picture." And as long as they enjoy the support of the neighborhood groups, many of these leaders show no interest in helping their constituents see the big picture. In the final analysis, Walker laughs derisively, they are "governing by opinion polls."[44]

Alabama Congressman Artur Davis, one of the younger black leaders, worries that some of the older generation may be exaggerating the size of the generational divide. "My concern," he says, "is that we are the one political community—the black community—that is attaching too much significance to the generational changes. That we're basically taking the generational changes and making them an analytical tool that may not be an appropriate way to examine these issues at all. . . . We may be putting too much analytical weight on the generational question; way too much."[45]

Regardless of the perspective of young African American leaders these days, their young constituents, rich or poor, urban or rural, northern or southern, appear to embrace either all or part of what has come to be designated as hip-hop culture. According to hip-hop commentator Bakari Kitwana, "Today, more and more Black youth are turning to rap music, music videos, designer clothing, popular Black films, and television programs for values and identity."[46] In fact, hip-hop cultural images have become so popular among large segments of America's young people, irrespective of race, that it seems the sights and sounds of hip-hop are everywhere. Black youth especially have been drawn to hip-hop because "whereas previously the voices of young Blacks had been locked out of the global age's public square, the mainstreaming of rap music now gave Black youth more visibility and a broader platform than we had ever enjoyed before. At the same time, it gave young Blacks across the country who identified with it and were informed by it a medium through which to share their national culture. . . . In the process, rap artists became the dominant voice of this generation."[47]

Cornell West, in his widely publicized book *Race Matters,* writes about hip-hop's effect on white young people in this country. He asserts that white youngsters, both male and female, imitate and emulate "black male styles of walking, talking, dressing and gesticulating in relations to others." West finds this behavior a cruel irony, because "just as young black men are murdered, maimed and imprisoned in record numbers, their styles have become disproportionately influential in shaping popular culture."[48]

But as the black young people who embrace hip-hop struggle to define what it means to be young and black in post-civil-rights America, certain events of the more recent past have indelibly marked their perspective:

> Ask any young Black American born between 1965 and 1984 where they were on September 13, 1996, and most can tell you. Ask them where they were six months later on March 9, 1997, and you'll get recollections as crystal clear as a baby boomer reminiscing on his or her whereabouts upon hearing of the assassinations of President Kennedy, Martin Luther King Jr., or Malcolm X. The September 1996 death of twenty-five-year-old Tupac Shakur was followed by memorials in New York City, Los Angeles, and several cities in between. Likewise the March 1997 death of Christopher Wallace, aka Notorious B.I.G., did not pass without the recognition of his peers. The twenty-four-year-old was commemorated with a statesman-like funeral procession through his old stomping grounds.[49]

The importance of these events to the younger generation of African Americans is generally not recognized by their elders. And at the same time, the majority of younger African Americans are at a loss to understand the reverence that so many older black people feel for civil rights leaders like Martin Luther King Jr. and the civil rights struggles of the 1960s.

Of course, on an intellectual level, black young people understand that King is important because formal recognition of the civil rights leader's contributions has become part of the culture of this nation in general and the black community in particular. However, many black young people are unable to connect with King's message of peace, love, and nonviolence. From their vantage point in America in the new millennium, where they are surrounded by images of violence against African Americans, they have trouble understanding the civil rights leader's total commitment to nonviolence. Even the fact of King's violent death tends to support a view that so many of these young people already accept: black life is cheap in America.

Yet, even with a perspective very different from their elders' views, black young people have not refused to participate in the continuing struggle for African American equality. Rap mogul Russell Simmons is one example: "A . . . telling sign of maturation and accepted responsibility among hip hop's leadership class was its embrace of anti-Bush/get-out-the-vote activities in 2004. Russell Simmons began the effort with his Hip Hop Summits, a series of arena-sized gatherings that brought local political leaders, rappers, and their young voting-age fans together in a pep rally environment. Although these events began in 2003, well before the election cycle, young adults were required to register to vote in order to gain entry, creating a sense of voting's importance that stimulated discussion of the issues and activism." Other rap artists, such as P. Diddy, are also engaged in voter registration/awareness campaigns. Diddy named his political initiative Citizen Change, and one of the promotional tools he used was the provocative T-shirt slogan "Vote or Die!" And the activism of some members of this generation goes far beyond get-out-the-vote campaigns and political rallies hosted by celebrities. Hip-hop commentator Nelson George reports, "Away from the bright lights of album release parties and MTV awards there is a growing cadre of young men and women, hip hop generation folk, who are doing grass roots organizing on a local level for little pay and not much credit."[50]

Nevertheless, older black leaders remain concerned about what many view as the negative aspects of hip-hop culture, especially the negative portrayal of black women. "Rap made slang aimed at women like 'skeezer,' 'hootchie,' 'chickenhead,' and the ubiquitous 'bitch' staples of the African American lexicon."[51] Of course, a profoundly destructive consequence of such portrayals of black women is the damage it does to the self-image of generations of young black women still forming a sense of their own identity. Nelson George, referring to the derogatory terms for black women, explains, "They've become so commonplace that many young women use them freely to attack other women and, even more alarming, to describe themselves. It is one thing to be sexually assertive; it is another to buy into men's negative language about yourself. Whereas hip hop has spiritually and financially empowered African American males, it has boxed young women into stereotypes and weakened their sense of worth."[52]

Today's black leaders express a range of reactions from concern to alarm and from irritation to infuriation when they discuss the characterization of black women and girls contained in the lyrics of numerous rap songs. Tuskegee mayor Johnny Ford, even though he sees many rap songs as simply an expression of youthful exuberance, is dismayed by the black female images some of the songs contain: "The thing I do not agree on is this vulgarness. I have serious problems with that; cursing; calling our ladies names."[53] Joe Leonard is much younger than Ford, and he grew up listening to rap. Yet, even though the music appeals to him, Leonard also dislikes the negative view of women in some of the lyrics. According to Leonard, "In 50 percent [of the songs], I think, the women are bitches." He worries about the impact this could have on black progress because, he argues, "No country, movement, [or] civilization has ever prospered that either did not own their own land, or did not have a high regard for women. If anything, they've always protected them from other people . . . protected women and children."[54]

Congresswoman Eleanor Holmes Norton insists, "Nobody should mistake that [rap] for what black culture was," and she declares, "To the extent that we get into the profanity and the degradation of women, and eventually everybody else that they can think of, this is not gonna live. That kind of thing will not survive." In the meantime, though, Norton worries about black leadership's response: "I fault black leadership for not finding ways to both speak to these children and to make it clear that this is not our culture."[55]

Black journalist Samuel Yette agrees with Norton. His feeling is that "it's terrible, terrible in that we . . . we're into hoes. Any woman, any man who cannot respect where we come from, really, really, REALLY is missing the boat."[56] Former SNCC staffer Lawrence Guyot agrees that rap denigrates women: "I think the hip hop movement has in some instances been quite misogynist, and quite a little bit anti-female beyond misogynism, and that's a fact."[57]

Older African Americans are puzzled when they hear these attacks on black womanhood. What could possibly motivate them? they wonder. Nelson George is convinced that belittling black women is a reaction to increasing black female assertiveness. He argues that black women artists, writers, and intellectuals in post-civil-rights America fired the opening salvo with the publication of books like *Black Macho and the Myth of the Superwoman, The Third Life of Grange Copeland,* and *The Color Purple.* These books all contain images of powerful and complicated black women, but they also emphasize the faults and weaknesses of the black males who are part of the narratives. Many black men were angered by these less-than-flattering portraits of black manhood, George explains, and in this contentious atmosphere, the war was on. "An indirect yet high-intensity cultural war between the African American sexes has spanned the post-soul era. It is a war in which the shots have been fired with words, with books, magazines, and poets on one side, and MCs and movies on the other."[58] Rap, as it developed, took part in the battle: "[Rap's] records articulated the general assumption that black males were under attack by white racism and, to a great degree, by black women. The perception of women as gold diggers has been rife within hip hop since Kool Moe Dee's 'They Want Money' in 1989, which was one of the first popular singles to make women as financial predators its subject, and Doug E. Fresh and Slick Rick's 'La-Di-Da-Di' back in 1984, which was cited by *The Source* as the first rap record to refer to a woman as a 'bitch.'"[59]

To many people, just as these attacks on black women are perplexing, so is the apparent reluctance of young black women to defend themselves and denounce the way they are portrayed. Hip-hop commentator Bakari Kitwana observes, "Interestingly, Black women intellectuals of the hip-hop generation have not launched a concerted public attack on sexist Black men (not even rappers) to the extent that the previous generation did."[60] An attempt to understand this attitude must consider an earlier tradition of negative male views of black womanhood and black females' reluctance to defend themselves then. During the civil rights movement, black women often experienced black male criticism, but it was aimed at black women's leadership capabilities, as opposed to their morals and their character. It was still destructive to the black female self-image. Some of this earlier criticism was blatant, and some was much more subtle. Black militant leader Angela Davis, who experienced the blatant variety, explains, "I ran headlong into a situation which was to become a constant problem in my political life. I was criticized very heavily, especially by members of [Ron] Karenga's [US] organization, for doing a 'man's job.' Women should not play leadership roles, they insisted. A woman was to 'inspire' her man and educate his children."[61] SCLC's Dorothy Cotton also encountered negative male evaluation of her capabilities. Although it was more subtle than what Davis endured, it was frustrating and infuriating nevertheless. Cotton recalls, "There was this consciousness that the females always . . . you were the secretary if you worked with all these men. You . . . made the coffee and took care of any food preparation. . . . I remember how as an executive staff person, I was Director of Education. But when they needed someone to get coffee, I was asked because I was the only woman at the executive staff table." Dr. Cotton frowns as she recalls those SCLC staff meetings of long ago. Yet, even though she was treated unfairly, Cotton was reluctant to complain. "It [unequal treatment] didn't strike me early on. . . . Women played right into that expectation." She quickly explains, with a laugh, "I have a whole different consciousness now. I, too, have evolved, and would now . . . tell these men how to make coffee." Cotton's mood turns serious again: "But, at the time it didn't seem [unfair]; I was happy to serve them."[62]

The experiences of women like Angela Davis and Dorothy Cotton are separated from the experiences of today's black women by more than four decades. Yet the earlier women seemed just as reluctant as their modern sisters to criticize the treatment they received. Their reticence is based to a large extent in the historical denigration of black men by American society. Black women of the civil rights generation were sensitive about America's attempts to emasculate black men. Women were painfully aware that as slaves, black men had been prevented from having complete control over their own families. Even after slavery ended, black men had to fight their way through a thicket of stereotypical images portraying them as less than human, and less than men. Thus, by the time of the civil rights era, many in the black community had become convinced that the liberation of black

people was possible only if black men were finally able to assert themselves and reclaim their full manhood. In that atmosphere, black female
civil rights activists, even those who were leaders, were often reluctant
to defend themselves against the black male chauvinism that seemed to
gather strength once the Black Power era started. "Above all, race loyalty
undoubtedly overshadowed gender issues in the minds of most African-
American civil rights activists of this era. They wanted to lead, but they
did not wish to assert themselves at the expense of their men. Such a position was fraught with contradictions."[63]

Black women activists from the civil rights era have a great deal in
common with today's black women: both groups came of age when
young black women were forced to cope with attitudes that circumscribed their existence and ultimately affected their ability to develop any
leadership capabilities they might have. In both instances, black women
were obliged to deal with a black community that is patriarchal in its outlook. And both then and now, black women have been sensitive to the
plight of black men who struggle to operate in a patriarchal society while
their manhood is under attack. In such an atmosphere, black women
have faced tremendous pressure to defer to black men for the good of
the race.

Operating within a community that is hypersensitive about protect-
ing the self-image of its men has had the effect of limiting black women's
leadership options. Black women leaders have nevertheless emerged, but
the positions they have held have often been less formal than men's positions, and they have been located in settings like the black church and the
black community. Belinda Robnett's study of black women's leadership,
How Long; How Long? contains a useful analysis of the development of
black women's leadership within this restrictive environment as well as a
clear explanation of the interaction of formal and informal leadership categories within black female leadership.

Returning to the topic of black youth culture, Lawrence Guyot insists
that even with all the negative aspects of hip-hop, there are some positive
ones, and these should be cultivated because "that's where the people are
. . . and we got to take the better parts of that [hip-hop] and use it. Now,
Russell Simmons has done a fantastic job of bringing politics into that
movement."[64] Courtland Cox, who, like Guyot, was on the SNCC staff,

also sees a positive side to hip-hop culture. But Cox believes the most positive part of the culture is the way it is marketed: "I'm not a big fan of hip hop music, but I think they have done better than we have done in a lot of ways. . . . I think that . . . they understand business, and they control their intellectual property much better than we did."[65]

It is ironic that many of today's African American leaders who worry about the impact of black youth culture in the new millennium were on the other side of a similar debate during the civil rights movement. Forty years ago and more, they were the young people who were challenging the cultural perspectives and perceptions of their elders. But the earlier challenge was carried out in the context of a debate between scholars over the nature of black popular culture. Scholars on one side of the debate insisted that demonstrative, exuberant African cultural traits and modes of expression, retained over more than two centuries of black life in America, were the hallmark of African American popular culture. On the other side were scholars who claimed that the African experience was too distant in the past to influence black popular culture. And almost from the beginning it seemed that African Americans who aspired to middle-class status were more often inclined to distance themselves from especially exuberant forms of African cultural expression than their poorer brothers and sisters. By the 1960s, as integration became a legal fact of life in American society, the black cultural debate continued, and by this time, some charged, class overtones had assumed increasing importance. One scholar explains that many black proponents of integration preached "adherence to white middle class norms";[66] they thought the ability of black people to integrate successfully into American society depended on shedding all vestiges of their African background. In short, "Some middle-class integrationists in the South and elsewhere semiprivately complained that many black people were obstreperous and embarrassing. They were crude and unsophisticated and needed to be culturally 'refined' if the civil rights efforts were going to be successful."[67]

Many African Americans remain convinced today that there is a direct link between black popular culture and black advancement. That is why some older African Americans who look at the popular images presented by today's black youth culture, images that challenge black and white middle-class notions of propriety, shake their heads in dismay. Rev. Abraham Woods, in a voice that reflects the depth of his feelings, explains, "They're looking like thugs, hoodlums, and rascals, you see. And King did not die for that, you see . . . and so it's really frustrating with me."[68]

African Americans of Woods's generation who feel alienated from young African Americans on account of their demeanor are painfully aware that part of the basis of this black youth culture is an institution that black people have feared for generations: prison. As increasing numbers of black youth are incarcerated with little hope for a future outside the criminal justice system, some aspects of prison culture seem to have become bound to black youth culture. Hip-hop scholar Bakari Kitwana explains, "As hip-hop culture became more commercialized in the late 1980s and early 1990s, primarily through the success enjoyed by rap music, aspects of prison culture became more apparent in rap music and Black youth culture, from the use of language and styles of dress to extensive commentary on crime and prison life. . . . With so many Blacks entering and exiting prison this influence is inescapable."[69]

To older African American activists like Abraham Woods and Unita Blackwell, these black young people swaggering down the street in their baggy clothes with sagging pants and without belts, freely cursing and calling each other "Niggas" might as well be aliens from outer space. Despite his distress, however, Reverend Woods has some sympathy for black youth who have been ensnared by the prison system. He explains that the white authorities "think of ways that when we learn to get to this goal line, then they come up with something else, you see, and they still put us in prison because prison is an industry now." Woods insists that the drug laws, especially, are designed to punish black defendants more severely than white defendants: "They have drug laws which are tailor made for our people. You have just a little crack [more widely used by African Americans] and a whole lot of cocaine [more widely used by white addicts]. There is a big difference in the time . . . you see." Woods concludes sadly but emphatically, "SO EVERYTHING HAS CHANGED AND NOTHING, NOTHING HAS CHANGED."[70] Yes, he is sympathetic toward young African Americans caught up in the prison machinery, but Reverend Woods simply cannot condone the intermingling of prison culture and black youth culture.

Most black leaders concede, aside from their opinions of the black youth culture, that rap's potential impact on the culture and worldview of

America and the rest of the world is enormous. Some of the most prominent rappers have managed to become major players on the world's cultural stage. Bakari Kitwana explains this important development: "Rap
music has given young Black males a primary avenue through which to
access public space—something that they have long lacked."[71] As black
leaders contemplate the possible extent of rap's influence, many of them
are very uneasy. They are convinced that one of the major influences on
commercial rap in particular is rooted in something alien to the black
community and inimical to its interests. Former congresswoman Cynthia
McKinney explains, "I think the type of . . . hip hop that we see largely in
the white-owned media, and definitely in white-owned distribution channels and marketing channels is the successful culmination of the strategy
[to] prevent the adherence of young blacks to a black nationalist ideology." However, McKinney is careful to distinguish early rap from the rap
music of today:

> Hip hop began as a way for frustrated young black kids to talk to
> each other and talk to their parents' generation who bothered to
> listen. And so you had the positive, although it may have been a
> message of anger, a message of frustration, a message of visual-
> izing the kind of activities that we wish we didn't have to con-
> front. But this was a method of communication by young people
> to communicate to us what their existence was like. And so it
> transmogrified from "fight the power, don't believe the hype"
> messages— strong political content—to "I want to lick you all
> over." That's what happened. And if you look at it, when the
> message was "fight the power, don't believe the hype," it was
> black-owned. It was black-distributed. And as soon as the mar-
> keting executives of the huge multinational conglomerates got
> involved, then the character changed, the message changed.[72]

Rev. Al Sharpton also insists that the roots of early hip-hop culture
and rap music were planted in a positive medium that celebrated blackness. Over time, however, the positive was eclipsed by the negative as
rap became increasingly commercial. As Sharpton sees it, the creation of
"gangsta rap that actually celebrates misogyny and criminal behavior is

alien to our culture [and] is also sponsored by outsiders to our community." To illustrate his point, Reverend Sharpton compares the rap music of today to the rhythm and blues music of earlier generations. He insists, "In the sixties and seventies black culture was pretty much owned by blacks; Motown [and] Stax Records. . . . Now even all these down street rap, hip hop, they're owned by white corporations. Black people are not sponsoring that." Sharpton pauses, then speaks again, his voice reaching the dramatic crescendo familiar to so many Americans who have seen him on the evening news whenever a story about race is reported: "So, is this a new generational expression, or is this some sponsored . . . thugism that really has little to do with our community, and therefore doesn't help us?"[73] Young D.C. city councilman Kwame Brown, a member of the hip-hop generation, acknowledges that the impetus for some of today's rap music comes from outside the black community. "It comes from other people who control the industry that push them to put out this type of music." But in many cases, according to Brown, the message in the music is less important than making a profit:

> For the hip hop generation it's all really about entrepreneurship and wealth creation. Now, that has been an area in which they could see that no matter where you are, who you are. [Whether they have] money, no money, no education, education, they could visually see themselves participating in that wealth creation somehow. . . . The things, they're chasing things . . . [They ask themselves] how's the fastest way to get [those things]. Create a record label. You know, they put so much time and energy into creating a rap and a beat. And it's really not the rap and the beat because they create these songs in five minutes. It's the ability to sell it or get someone to buy it . . . [and] next thing you know, you're a multimillionaire.[74]

"We're creating our own destiny," Brown exclaims. "There are so many entrepreneurs within the hip hop movement itself." At the same time, Councilman Brown worries about the value system engendered by this emphasis on wealth creation, because he is sure it corrupts the values of some of those involved. He declares bluntly, "We have some people in the hip hop generation that are out of their ever-loving minds."[75] Dr. Joe Leonard is also part of the hip-hop generation, and like Councilman Kwame Brown, Leonard is convinced that much of the emphasis of today's rap artists is on developing a profitable business. "The people that are involved in hip hop are business people," and he warns, "So . . . it's inherently susceptible to compromise."[76]

Hip-hop scholar Bakari Kitwana is impressed by the generation's attraction to wealth:

Everyone wants to make it big. For many, the American Dream means not just living comfortably, but becoming an overnight millionaire while still young. Many of us can't imagine waiting until we are forty, or even thirty-five, for that matter. This desire for wealth is accompanied by a sense of entitlement. That a handful of hip-hop generationers have achieved the dream makes the possibility real, despite the odds. Professional athletes and entertainers routinely secure million-dollar contracts. . . . It's nearly impossible to find a kid on the block who doesn't think he can be the next Puff Daddy or Master P, Chris Webber or Tiger Woods. Although such attitudes existed in previous generations, with the hip-hop generation, it is a near obsession.[77]

Even though it unduly emphasizes wealth creation and conspicuous consumerism, hip-hop is a bona fide cultural movement, insists Dr. Joe Leonard. "It's a cultural movement. All the cultural markers are there: language, dress, music, to a certain degree, literature. All of those cultural markers are there, and they are changing culture worldwide."[78]

But Leonard also asserts that members of his generation need much more than a cultural movement: they need a social movement to build on the progress of the previous generation. He laments, "But it [hip-hop] is not a social movement. It's a cultural movement because they lack those other devices to become a social movement."[79] Former SNCC staffer Julian Bond is convinced that the most important measure of hip-hop's importance to black people can be found in the answer to the question, What has this movement done to advance the interests of black people in the new millennium? According to Bond, the answer is "not enough," because it all comes down to a question of leadership: "You know, these rap guys may be singing about the ghetto, but what are they doing? And to be a leader, it seems to me, you have to do [something]. You have to speak, but you have to do. They don't do anything. They're not engaged in any respect. That's true of black athletes. That's true of black entertainers. Again, that's a generalization. Some people are [doing something], but . . . the majority are disconnected from the struggles of their people."[80]

Opinions about black youth, rap music, and hip-hop culture differ widely among today's black leaders. Yet it seems they can all agree that rap music and hip-hop culture's influence—whether they see it as positive or negative—is pervasive. Many also fear that the impetus for commercial rap music and hip-hop culture is more closely wedded to the boardrooms of corporate America than to the black communities that the culture claims to reflect. This suspicion leaves many older African Americans feeling that the long-standing connection between the culture of black youth and the culture of their ancestors has been weakened.

From television ads to radio broadcasts, and from billboards to Internet ads, images of black youth that are concocted in America's boardrooms are everywhere, and they are selling things: everything from their latest rap CDs to chewing gum, and from automobiles to soft drinks. Because the vast majority of African American youth enthusiastically embrace these images, they will continue to spread all over the globe, with only minimal input from members of this country's African American communities. Without a doubt, the lines of cultural transmission in the black community that have always linked the younger generation to their elders have been redirected. Thus, as black leaders seek to plan a strategy for the continued advancement of African Americans, they are faced with the challenge of dealing with the power of corporate America and the electronic media that may have already captured the hearts and minds of the next generation of African Americans.

8. Black Community and Black Identity

In this new electronic world, where images of blackness are manufactured and manipulated in corporate boardrooms, where black faces are seen in high places—from the Congress to the television networks to the White House—and where previously all-white schools and neighborhoods have a black face or two, African Americans question what it means to be black and American. At the beginning of the twentieth century, noted black scholar, activist and social critic W. E. B. Du Bois also struggled to understand what it meant to be black and American, and he confessed, "One ever feels his twoness,—an American, a Negro; two souls, two thoughts, two unreconciled strivings; two warring ideals in one dark body, whose dogged strength alone keeps it from being torn asunder."[1] Du Bois ended his explanation of the psychic pain suffered by African Americans in 1903 with this declaration: African Americans just wanted it to be "possible for a man to be both a Negro and an American."[2]

Now, in the early years of the twenty-first century, Randall Robinson, a noted black activist and the founder of the activist organization TransAfrica, is convinced that African Americans are still battling the "warring ideals" and the "unreconciled strivings" that Du Bois felt. Robinson asserts, "We [African Americans] have been largely overwhelmed by a majority culture that wronged us dramatically, emptied our memories, undermined our self-esteem, implanted us with palatable voices, and stripped us along the way of the sheerest corona of self-definition. . . . We [African Americans] alone are past-less, left to cobble self-esteem from a vacuum of stolen history."[3] At least in Robinson's opinion, African Americans in the new millennium have not yet achieved a oneness with American society. Instead, it seems that there are additional fault lines fracturing the twoness, even more than existed over a century ago, as African Americans continue their centuries-old struggle against alienation and low self-esteem in a society that *claims* to be color-blind. The current black struggle is further complicated by the profound demographic changes American society is undergoing in the new millennium because of increased multiculturalism and illegal immigration.

Throughout their long struggle to cope with a hostile American society, African Americans have relied on a strong sense of community. In the early 1970s, a sixty-one-year-old black woman, Mrs. Hannah Nelson, insisted that the black community in a hostile white society was based on a feeling of connection based on race: "Black people think of themselves as an entity."[4] Many African American leaders reflecting on their upbringing cite the importance of a nurturing black community to their early development. Congresswoman Eleanor Holmes Norton, a native of Washington, D.C., found this to be true: "I think the black community here [was] very important; the way the black community in the District saw itself because no one could tell when segregation would be lifted." Because of the positive influence of that community, Norton contends, "It never occurred to us that we were inferior." On the contrary, "We thought that people who believed in segregation were poorly educated . . . and since education was liberation, we simply went about [the business of] being educated."[5]

Like Norton, Chicago resident Timuel Black remembers a supportive nurturing black community in his city. However, Black observed, when he was a young man in the 1920s, that the black community did not always treat black migrants from the rural South the same as native black Chicagoans or even longtime black residents. He explains, "You get this separation [between recent migrants and other residents]. And there's no way for them to become urbanized except through their experiences . . . and meanwhile, they get exploited: economically, politically. . . . And you get certain black leaders . . . who benefit by helping to exploit [the migrants]."[6] In Detroit, Maureen Taylor benefited from a black community that was two hundred miles and forty years removed from the Chicago of Timuel Black's youth. By the time Taylor was a teenager, the civil rights movement of the 1960s was revolutionizing race relations in America, and even though the movement was happening in the South, Taylor felt the shockwaves in her community. "We were raised in an atmosphere and an environment charged with politics," she explains, "charged with the concept that all people are created equal." Taylor smiles at the memory of her youthful idealism as she continues, "And our attitudes were that once we finished high school, we were going to go to college. [We] never questioned—we were going to change the world . . . and it was never a question [of] looking back."[7]

Former Georgia state senator Eugene Walker found that the close-knit black community of his youth successfully sheltered him from the worst aspects of the virulent racism that characterized rural Georgia in the 1930s and 1940s. Because of his community's positive influence, Walker insists, "I never sensed the negative impact of racism. I knew it was there. We were segregated, but we always thought we were superior. . . . So I've never felt inferior about anything. NEVER."[8] Julian Bond is also a native Georgian. In fact, when Walker was first elected to the Georgia State Senate, Julian Bond was his seatmate. But while Walker was growing up in rural Georgia, Bond was living on black college campuses because his father, Horace Mann Bond, was a scholar and a black college president. Bond's earliest memories are of the campus of Fort Valley State, south of Atlanta. Later, his family moved to the campus of Lincoln University in Pennsylvania, and then back to Georgia and the Atlanta University campus. The atmosphere in these black campus communities was exciting and invigorating to Bond, who explains, "A steady stream of black leaders came to these places." He grew up in the company of such notable scholars as E. Franklin Frazier and W. E. B. Du Bois. "These people were constantly in my world."[9]

Dr. Joe Leonard, who grew up more than two decades later and several hundred miles west of Julian Bond, has vivid memories of the importance of the black community in Austin, Texas, that nurtured him. Leonard was born in 1967, after the major battles of the movement had been won. Yet, he argues, Austin was still a dangerous place: "Black boys in Texas could still be harmed, and I always felt insulated in the community. If anything, my parents never had a curfew for me as long as I was in my neighborhood. But they feared me going downtown, or someplace where whites could harm me."[10]

Selma, Alabama, where Mayor Joe Perkins spent his childhood, also had a supportive black community. One of the most important characteristics of that community, Perkins feels, was the influence of the black business and professional class. "The images of black leadership that I

embraced during my childhood were local religious and business personalities; some, in fact, in my own family. . . . The black community was *the*
community and so they [religious and business personalities] were the
local leadership in the community." The community leaders were exceptional people, who inspired young Joe Perkins and many others in Selma's black community because they demonstrated "courage. These men
and women stood up and stood out when their lives were on the line."
The influence of these individuals on the lives of members of Selma's
black community was crucial because, "at that time, our community, our
neighborhood made up our world, in many instances. And very rarely did
you move beyond those boundaries."[11] Fellow Selma native Joanne Bland
succinctly describes the Selma black community of her youth as "my area
of love."[12]

Memphis, Tennessee, was home to Rev. Harold Middlebrook, who
later headed the Southern Christian Leadership Conference's Danville,
Virginia, Project. He also found leadership important in the black community of his youth. But he insists that the leadership in that setting was
quite different from leadership among his white contemporaries: "You
know in the white community there were certain people in the banking
community and others who were the economic leaders . . . and the lines
are very clearly drawn. . . . We did not have that in the African American community when I was growing up—this dichotomy." Middlebrook
describes how the two communities were different: "They [members of
the white power structure] said to the ministers, 'you're the spiritual leaders, so stay out of the political arena.' [But] we never had that. In the
African American community they were one and the same." However, he
is convinced that just as the presence of effective black leadership was a
critical component of a healthy black community, the existence of a nurturing black community was essential to the production of effective black
leadership. "Leadership developed from an innate . . . there was a person
in every community in Memphis. There was a person—not elected by
anybody—but this was the person that everybody looked to." Middlebrook observed that these leaders were always willing to serve the community: "This person organized the clean-up, paint-up, fix-up campaign
in our community. This was the person who, if somebody died, organized
to get the food to the house and the flowers to the funeral."[13]

Down in Mississippi, Unita Blackwell also noticed the impact of out-standing individuals on the process of community-building where she grew up. "It was good people," she explains, "They didn't have wealth or anything. They just had knowledge. And the greatest thing that can happen to you in life is to have these kinds of people around you."[14] In nearby Memphis, Tennessee, Dr. Benjamin Hooks, too, emphasizes the importance of black individuals in the community. These people pro-vided the encouragement, support, and instruction that was particularly important to young African Americans in their midst so that they would "be able to live within the system without losing your manhood or your womanhood or your sense of dignity," according to Hooks.[15]

Black leaders as a group seem to agree that a sense of community is essential; and whether they are older or younger, rural or urban, north-ern or southern, many African American leaders in the new millennium fondly recall the black community of the past that exerted a powerful positive impact on their lives during their formative years. In the days before statutory segregation was dismantled, the unadulterated blackness of these communities undoubtedly gave their members a sense of belong-ing that was particularly comforting in view of the sinister sea of white opposition that seemed to surround them both figuratively and literally.

In post-civil-rights-movement America, as the country tries to adjust to a new legal, social, and political reality for African Americans, black leaders are taking a fresh look at these communities that have always been so helpful in combating racism and the sense of alienation that accompa-nies it. Maureen Taylor recalls that in the years immediately following the civil rights movement, chaos and violence seemed to take up permanent residence in the black community in Detroit. She frowns as she describes the grim reality. "When you're brought up surrounded . . . with all of the . . . the late sixties and early seventies and the death and destruction and the violence and the street demonstrations. . . . Every day is a story about how people's rights are trampled and the way people get at this is through violence." Taylor shrugs her shoulders wearily: "just day after day after day."[16]

Yet, despite the trauma suffered by black communities everywhere during these difficult years, some black leaders are still optimistic about community survival in America after the civil rights movement. Eleanor

Holmes Norton embraces this optimism; she is convinced that a form of the traditional black community continues to exist as an oasis for African Americans who are still navigating a sea of white hostility. Norton insists that "generally you go into [a black] community; the kind of music, the kind of food, the kind of way people talk, the ambience. You're right at home then, and that's in any northern city or any southern city." However, she concedes that "there have been some changes that none of us embrace."[17] Down in Georgia, Eugene Walker also believes that the black community still survives, but with an important difference: "Blacks are not as monolithic as we used to be. We've got so much diversity within the black community [now]."[18]

Others are less certain of the health of the black community. Professor John Hope Franklin is alarmed about the state of black communities in the new millennium; he worries that the loss of community among African Americans could have a damaging effect on black identity. Franklin urges, "We've got to rethink where we are, what we are, and what we want to do, and what we want to be."[19] Rev. Fred Shuttlesworth, who assesses black community today similarly, stabs the air with his index finger for emphasis, proclaiming, "The cities, the ghettoes remain ghettoes because unless you get the money to build them up and do things. . . . This is a part of the culture we live in now." Shuttlesworth's voice rises in frustration: "There shouldn't be ghettoes in America with the money we waste."[20] African Americans who live in the ghettoes, especially the youth, share Reverend Shuttlesworth's frustration. Randall Robinson, in his book *The Reckoning: What Blacks Owe to Each Other,* quotes a young black inner-city resident who explains, "It's sad but us young brothers, it's like we don't . . . nobody takes time to really let us know what a community is really about . . . how we supposed to look out for one another, how we supposed to respect one another, and talk to each other, and things like that."[21]

Black journalist Samuel Yette insists that many of the black community's problems stem from a loss of unity: "I think there was more community [unity]," but now things are different because "we're less able to communicate on the different levels. It just means that we're unfortunate and that we're not perceiving or receiving the togetherness that we had [in the 1960s]."[22] Former senator Carol Moseley Braun also insists that black communities have problems. In her estimation, the problems need to be addressed immediately by "cleaning up our neighborhoods, getting security in our neighborhoods, [and] electing people to school boards."[23] Rev. Harold Middlebrook thinks the problems with black communities have developed in the midst of a black leadership vacuum. In his view, the roots of the problem go all the way back to President Lyndon Baines Johnson's War on Poverty in the 1960s. At that time, there was hope that Johnson's poverty programs would provide much-needed help to struggling black communities that had been ravaged by the effects of long-standing job discrimination, unequal education, and recent destructive race riots. However, according to Middlebrook, whatever positive benefit black communities derived from these poverty programs came at a very high price: the destruction of grassroots leadership: "After the poverty program ended we lost that leadership that grows out of the community." Middlebrook continues, "What happened, I think, is that we sent people into communities as the experts, the trained experts. And they were the people who were to do the organizing and the work. And once the government's focus changed, you had destroyed leadership that had developed naturally out of the community, and said to them, 'you're untrained, you don't know.' And so you had put them down in the minds of the people, and all of a sudden there was nothing left in those communities as the cement and the glue to hold those communities together."[24]

Thus, black communities in the new millennium are struggling with a new set of issues and problems. At the same time, however, the black individuals who make up these communities also face a critical adjustment in the new millennium: they must define their identity in the context of legal desegregation. Many black leaders, particularly those who were part of the civil rights movement, are persuaded that as African Americans search for a new concept of themselves, their search is complicated by a history of ambivalence on the part of some and self-hatred on the part of others. C. T. Vivian says that the majority of the black people he met at the beginning of the civil rights campaigns of the 1960s "did not love themselves."[25] Timuel Black, a founding member of CORE in Chicago, explains that it has been difficult for African Americans to see their blackness as an asset because for generations most white Americans have embraced an unshakable belief that black people were inferior. That, according to Black, "meant that survival and success for blacks meant distancing yourself from things black."[26]

Down in Mayersville, Mississippi, civil rights activist Unita Blackwell is convinced that even though more than four decades have passed since black people confronted segregation, they are still battling ambivalence about their blackness. Blackwell, who is dark-skinned, insists that many African Americans still connect darker skin with black inferiority. She charges, "See, what done happened . . . if you think about it, we come through each level of brainwashing. . . . [Until] we look down on one another on account of the color of their skin." Blackwell pauses, reflecting on the absurdity of discrimination by African Americans based on skin tone. The smooth dark skin of her brow wrinkles in concentration as she asks, without expecting an answer: "How in the world [are you going] to be accepted and you don't like yourself?" The seventy-two-year-old activist concludes, "That is the ingredient that goes into this that keeps this chaos going."[27] Data from a recent census appear to corroborate Blackwell's assertion: "That census for the first time allowed Americans to choose from as many as six racial categories. Blacks chose to be black *and* something else more than twice as often as whites chose to be white and something else."[28]

There are other black leaders who have a more positive view of black identity formation in post-civil-rights America. Mayor Johnny Ford participated in civil rights demonstrations when he was a young adult, and in 1970 when soul singer James Brown sang or rapped, "Say it loud; I'm black and I'm proud," it resonated for Ford as it did for others of his generation. As he looks back on this part of his life, and as he assesses his place in the nation, the pride in Ford's voice is unmistakable: "I'm a southerner . . . I'm an African American first. But, I'm a southern African American." His tone invites no further questioning.[29] Alabama congressman Artur Davis was not even born yet when Mayor Ford participated in the civil rights movement and listened to James Brown. However, the young congressman feels that his identity is directly connected to that movement that changed the South so much. Davis complains, though, that people often assume that because of his youth he is "psychologically distant from the movement." Davis disagrees, "That's just not the case." He goes on to point out that during his campaign, he was "very careful to . . . talk about that movement with reverence."[30]

His chronological distance from the civil rights movement was not the only issue that young Artur Davis was obliged to confront during his campaign for Congress as he sought to define himself to the people of the Seventh District. Davis's opponent, black incumbent Earl Hilliard, was particularly critical of Davis's Harvard law degree. He also raised questions about his young opponent's blackness. Davis explains his opponent's line of reasoning: "He [Hilliard] said that the Ivy League schools were being used as recruitment tools for anti-black candidates. His rationale was that the kind of blacks that go to Ivy League schools are predisposed to be brainwashed; to be turned against the black establishment." But not only did Hilliard question Davis's race loyalty, he went a step further and questioned the motives and the allegiance of those African Americans who supported Davis. The congressman recalls, "His other analysis was that we had carried white areas and we had carried black areas where black people worked for corporate America, and that they had been brainwashed . . . to vote for candidates like me." In short, according to Artur Davis, incumbent congressman Earl Hilliard questioned whether he, Davis, was really a black man at all: "Hilliard's campaign essentially was, he's not really black. He doesn't sound black, he doesn't look black, he doesn't act black. He's not really part of our community."[31] Artur Davis faced the thorny dilemma that confronts so many young African Americans as they take advantage of the opportunities opened to them because of the civil rights movement: once they walk through those doors of opportunity, they often find themselves in situations that create a financial, social, and economic gulf between them and the black majority they leave behind, and they are obliged to come to terms with their own identity in this new context.

In Washington, D.C., young city councilman Kwame Brown also feels connected to the civil rights movement of the 1960s. In fact, because Brown's activist father named him after Stokely Carmichael/Kwame Ture, Brown lives with a constant reminder of this connection. Recently, just before Stokely Carmichael/Kwame Ture died, his old friends and colleagues from the movement gave a banquet in his honor. Ture's young namesake Kwame Brown attended the banquet, and he was struck by the power of the connection between the civil rights veterans at the banquet and his own identity. Brown explains, "I was sitting in that room and I started to think about these individuals. It wasn't like they received the economic reward or the financial benefit [for their activism]. And when I looked around the room, packed [with] a thousand people. I started to realize why I am where I am."[32]

Although Brown relates so closely to the civil rights activists of the past, he is careful to assert that this is only part of who he is: "I am extremely respectful of the previous generation, [but] we still have to create our own mind-set." Councilman Brown is afraid, however, that many members of his generation do not sense any connection between themselves and the activists of the past. He fears that African Americans may forget who they are. Furthermore, he charges that instead of emulating the courageous example set by young black activists of the past, young African Americans his age have other priorities, such as the urge to accumulate wealth.[33]

Over in North Carolina, former congressman Frank Ballance is particularly disappointed at the attitudes of some black elected officials. In his estimation, many of them do not identify as closely as they should with the black community. "This is my issue with some of my colleagues. When they get elected, they're so proud to be in office that they don't do what they said they'd do; that's to advocate for the community."[34]

Lawrence Guyot is sure he understands why a rift seems to be developing between some prominent African Americans in leadership positions and the black community. Because Guyot was heavily involved in the Mississippi movement and was chairman of the Mississippi Freedom Democratic Party, he vividly remembers the dangerous atmosphere during Freedom Summer in 1964. But he also remembers how movement leaders at that time felt a sense of unity with members of the black communities they served. In post-civil-rights America, however, Guyot argues, there are new avenues of advancement open to those African Americans who are willing to turn their backs on the black masses in order to curry favor with the white power structure. Guyot explains bluntly: "The need for people to be the Top Darky in the nation is very alluring. It's very profitable, it's very public, a lot of doors are opened."[35] Guyot is not the only black leader worried about "Top Darkies." As J. L. Chestnut sits in his law office in Selma, Alabama, he also expresses concern about the tendency of some black people to promote themselves at the expense of other

African Americans. The old lawyer speaks thoughtfully, "America is complex, and there are forces in America that reward and elevate blacks who have that kind of state of mind. That's one way to get ahead. To show white people that I'm not one of those people always hollering black this and black that. I'm not a professional victim myself. I believe that we ought to be color-blind, that sort of talk will . . . it will get you a long way in white America, even today." Chestnut pauses, and then with a twinkle in his eye he adds, "Clarence Thomas [ultraconservative black Supreme Court justice] is nobody's fool. Had he gone in the opposite direction philosophically, you never would have heard of him."[36] Rev. James Bevel, a veteran strategist of some of the most memorable campaigns of the civil rights movement, points out, "When the system opened up, they [certain black leaders] started trying to be successful to white people [instead of] continuing doing what we were doing, which was the complete liberation of our people in this nation."[37]

Of course, there have always been African Americans willing to cultivate relationships with powerful white people in order to advance their own agenda: from slaves who betrayed fellow slaves plotting a revolt, to African Americans after the Civil War who openly supported white authorities that imposed Jim Crow segregation on the South, to African Americans in the North who seemed to be more closely aligned with white political machines in big cities than with their own communities. Frustrated African Americans who have felt betrayed by these people over the years have assigned them a variety of names: Uncle Tom, Handkerchief Head, Oreo, Clean Negro, Representative Colored Man, Top Darky, Tea Bag Negro, Flagship Negro, and the list goes on. However, the legal and social context in which these accommodationists have operated has shifted dramatically over time. Before the civil rights movement of the 1960s, African Americans were *all* obliged to function in a country that embraced statutory segregation based on race, and that severely limited their educational, political, economic, and social options. Even black people who lived in the North suffered from the effects of racial discrimination, because statutory segregation was replaced in their region by de facto segregation. In such an atmosphere, many were convinced that their very survival depended on some degree of cooperation with the racial reality of the time.

Rev. Abraham Woods once worked with a black man who taught him a hard lesson about black accommodation and economic survival in the early-twentieth-century South. At the time Woods was a young, idealistic student at Morehouse College in Atlanta. (Woods attended Morehouse at the same time that Martin Luther King Jr. was enrolled there.) World War II had just ended, and the signs of black impatience with the continuation of racial segregation were everywhere. The president of Morehouse at that time, the famous black theologian Dr. Benjamin Mays, always preached to his young charges, "I would not be a Jim Crow Negro." Atlanta was a thoroughly segregated city at that time, and Mays worked hard to inspire his students to go out and change things. Woods recalls that Mays advised on more than one occasion "[I would not take] the wings of a bird and [go] way up in the roof of a theater just to see a picture. . . . I would not go to a restaurant where they would not let you in the front door . . . [instead they make you go] to the back to a hole in the wall and get you a sandwich." Then, Mays would repeat his admonition, careful to pronounce every syllable: "I WOULD NOT BE A JIM CROW NEGRO."[38]

A short time later, while young Abraham Woods's head was filled with Dr. Mays's powerful words, he took a job at the Varsity, an old and very well-known drive-in restaurant in Atlanta, to earn money for his school expenses. He realized very quickly that the white customers who patronized the restaurant were especially fond of one of the other black waiters, an older man named Sam. There were many times when white customers would not allow Woods or any of the other young waiters to take their order. Even if Sam was busy at the time, they were willing to wait. When Woods observed Sam's behavior around the customers, he understood why white customers preferred the older man, and what Woods saw sickened him. He sighs heavily at the memory. "Sam got a lot of that business. They waited on him. What Sam would do, when he'd go to a car he'd [say] "YASSIR, YASSIR." [He was] tap dancing, and dancing a jig, and this sort of thing, and he'd just laugh. And they'd give him a big tip." The other waiters, who were young black college students like Woods, were also embarrassed by Sam's behavior. One day, Woods had had enough, so he decided to confront the older man. He describes what happened next: "The place closed and we double-teamed Sam . . . we were thinking about beating him up." But when Woods looked into the old man's eyes, he knew he couldn't go through with it. So instead, he tried to reason with Sam. "I said, nigger, we're embarrassed about you. We're ashamed of you. . . . You're going up dancing to these cars, and kowtowing to these [white] folks. . . . You're an embarrassment to all of us." The two men stood looking at each other for a long moment; the young college student and the old family man. Finally, Sam asked, where [are] y'all from?" Woods answered, "I'm from Morehouse." Another young black waiter who was standing next to Woods answered, "I'm from Clark [College]." The older waiter smiled as he said, "I ain't from no house." Then Sam asked his young challengers, "How much money y'all got?" With his voice rising, Woods answered quickly, "That ain't what we're talking about. We're talking about you being an embarrassment." Barely controlling his temper, the old waiter said, "Look . . . I came here to get these white folks' money. . . . Y'all can do like you want to, be all sophisticated and dignified. . . . But I'm not crazy. I'm gonna do what I have to do to get that money. I got four or five times as much as y'all got." The two younger waiters just looked at Sam, but they did not say anything more. As Reverend Woods thinks about that long-ago confrontation with Sam the waiter, he concedes, "There have to be some black folks who know how to talk that talk in order to get what the [white folks] got." He refers to such people as "ambassadors to the white folks." Woods declares, however, "We just could not condescend to that."[39]

Of course, the America that confronts African Americans today is not the same as the America that eagerly embraced legal segregation when Sam the waiter was dancing his jig. Yet, even though the country has changed, there are some who charge that while certain African American leaders do not literally dance a jig, they figuratively dance as fast as they can in an effort to advance their own interests; and the stakes have never been higher. Eugene Walker is alarmed by the impact people like this are having on the position of African Americans in the new millennium. He explains, "They're very dangerous. But we've got to overcome them. The real danger to me lies in the fact [that] our people see that this is an avenue for advancement. [Black people think] I can abandon the cause and surrender to the strategy that's necessary to get to be a Colin Powell or a Condoleezza Rice: What's good for me, and that's where we're losing this battle. We have so many people that's jumping off the bandwagon, going over there, getting what they can . . . it's a sad commentary." The despair in Walker's voice is unmistakable as he concludes, "We have difficult days ahead of us."[40]

In Detroit, Maureen Taylor's appraisal of the impact of black collaborators on the position of other African Americans is even more pessimistic than Walker's. Taylor calls them Tea Bag Negroes: "These are your middle-class spokespersons that they [white authorities] keep in the Salada [Tea] box." Taylor explains how the system works:

What they [white authorities] do, when they're looking for, when they need acceptable middle-class representatives to get a point across . . . what they do is, they keep these people in a box, like Salada Tea comes in a box and when you want a tea bag, and you want the tea, you go to the box. So what they do is they keep these people, they keep them in a position of being able to have access to resources and opportunities. Now when the body politic begins to stand up and say, "wait a minute, I want my chance . . . there's something wrong with my standard of living, there's something wrong with my quality of living. I want to make a change." And noises of opposition begin to rise . . . they open it up, and they see which kind of tea bag they need, and they pull out the Salada Tea bag, the Negro tea bag, and . . . the water's already hot. And they put that tea bag in there, and they dip that Negro in there three or four times, and that brown comes out, and then these Tea Bag Negroes start saying, "you're right. Power to the people. What we got to do is organize . . ." They use all the proper phrases . . . They have the script already. . . . People can be confused by this because they're using the right phrases, the tea is brown, and you think, okay, this one is going to work for me. . . . We're moving ahead, it won't be long now. And then, you know, the water cools off and then they take that tea bag out, [and put it back in the box].[41]

Maureen Taylor's assessment emphasizes a critical characteristic that sets these people apart from earlier generations of the black collaborators: their color is no longer an impediment to their advancement in American society. On the contrary, it is the fact of their color, and their willing-ness to use it against their own people, Taylor argues, that makes them so desirable to the white authorities who reward them handsomely.[42]

Congresswoman Cynthia Mckinney agrees that there is a group of black people, many of whom are leaders, who regularly collaborate with the forces of oppression. But she does not regard the existence of this group as an accident or an unfortunate coincidence. Instead, she argues, their existence is the result of a deliberate strategy by the federal government. She refers to the collaborators as Clean Negroes, and she explains, "What's the definition of a Clean Negro? A Clean Negro, I believe, . . is inauthentic leadership. . . . It's inauthentic black leadership . . . black leadership selected by them [white government officials] before black people have the opportunity to select their own leader."[43]

As African Americans face the new millennium, they are surrounded by multiple conflicting images of African Americans. In this information age of instant communication via the Internet, text messages, cable television, and satellite radio, African Americans are bombarded with images of black people who appear to be well-connected, influential, and successful. All too often, they are christened "Black Leaders" by the media. But whether they are corporate CEOs, television personalities, movie stars, supreme court justices, rap stars, or successful athletes, the masses of African Americans are left to wonder about the motives and allegiance of these people. Are they the "Clean Negroes," the "Top Darkies," the "Tea Bag Negroes," the "Uncle Toms," or the "Ambassadors to the White Folks," that some black leaders fear, or are they sincere African Americans trying to help their people? The truth is often hard to discern, particularly in the context of an America that desperately "craves to see itself as beyond race, beyond boundaries, beyond the ugly parts of its past."[44]

Moreover, black attempts to understand the relationship, if any, of prominent successful African Americans to the fate of the masses of black people in this country is also complicated by the celebrity-worship that seems to have gripped modern American society. Some social critics charge that "the kind of society we have become [is] one that feeds on celebrity like locusts on crops and creates stars out of nothing but bright lights and hype."[45] African Americans all over the country are left shaking their heads as they see images of bad boy rapper Snoop Dogg selling

Chryslers with that quintessential white corporate symbol Lee Iacocca, or Oprah Winfrey on the cover of a *Newsweek* that calls her one of the most powerful women in America, or Condoleezza Rice on the evening news sitting next to the president of the United States at a cabinet meeting. Are these people black leaders, or are they what Rev. Al Sharpton refers to as leading blacks?

As they are bombarded by images of prominent African Americans, black people in the new millennium, young and old, northern and southern, rich and poor are left to wonder, just as an earlier generation of African Americans during the civil rights movement wondered, about the loyalties of certain black people in their midst. That crucial question of identity and allegiance is eloquently expressed by the words of the civil rights movement song "Which Side Are You On?" Originally a labor union song, it was adapted to the civil rights movement and became especially popular after CORE's director, James Farmer, and the Freedom Riders added verses during their dangerous journey in 1961. The refrain consists of the poignant question, "Which side are you on?" repeated four times. As their buses carried them closer and closer to certain confrontation with the forces of segregation in the Deep South, the Freedom Riders sang bravely,

> My daddy fought for freedom and I'm a freedom's son.
> I'll stick right with this struggle until the battle's won.
>
> Don't Tom for Uncle Charlie, don't listen to his lies,
> 'Cause black folks haven't got a chance unless we organize.
>
> They say that in Hinds County, no neutrals have been met.
> You're either for the freedom ride, or a Tom for Ross Barnett.
>
> Oh people can you stand it, oh tell me how you can.
> Will you be an Uncle Tom or will you be a man?[46]

In subdued voices the Freedom Riders finished their plaintive plea, "Which side are you on?" as their buses took them to the next terminal and the confrontation with segregation that was waiting there for them. This musical plea of the Freedom Riders from over four decades ago still resonates with many African Americans as they face a new millennium.

When they look around them at the disparate images of African Americans in the media, and they hear the cacophony of black voices—some speaking to them, and some claiming to speak for them—advocating a variety of positions on every conceivable issue, black people these days wonder just as the Freedom Riders did, "Which side are you on?"

9. A Crisis of Victory

As black leaders face an uncertain future in a society undergoing profound technological, economic, and cultural changes, many are worried about the condition of African Americans in the years ahead, and they wonder what kind of agenda to pursue. Just over forty years ago, as the civil rights movement drew to a close, and as Dr. Martin Luther King Jr. lay dying on the balcony of the Lorraine Motel, black leaders believed they knew exactly what black people needed to do: they needed to continue the struggle, of course. But what did that mean? In the intervening years, while black leaders have worked to answer this question, the civil rights movement has been transformed from a live movement to a historical event that is assigned just a page or two in most American history textbooks. But the image of Martin Luther King Jr. has grown to be larger in death than it ever was in life; every January, a "grateful" nation celebrates and embraces the memory of King as a dead martyr more enthusiastically than it ever embraced the wisdom of King when he was a live preacher and activist.

These days, scholars who study the black leadership agenda that emerged right after King's death tend to agree with political scientist Robert Smith, who argues that by the mid-1970s, black leadership had reached a consensus on its goals. The goals included an employment program that "guarantees the right to useful and meaningful jobs for those willing and able to work" and reform of the welfare system so that recipients will have "a guaranteed annual income." Among the other goals are national health insurance, tax reform, increased funding for all levels of education, and minority business initiatives.[1] However, as today's black leaders struggle to achieve these goals, they have been criticized by scholars who insist that the leaders have failed to achieve any meaningful accomplishments that will improve the position of African Americans. Many scholars are convinced that on all fronts, black leadership in the twenty-first century is a colossal failure. The titles of recent studies of black leadership scream in frustration: *We Have No Leaders: African Americans in the Post-Civil Rights Era,* by Robert Smith; *The Head Negro in Charge Syndrome: The Dead End of Black Politics,* by Norman Kelley; *The New H.N.I.C.: The Death of Civil Rights and the Reign of Hip Hop,* by Todd Boyd; and *Enough,* by Juan Williams.

In *We Have No Leaders,* a critical study of black leadership published in 1996, Robert C. Smith describes one of the most important characteristics of late-twentieth-century black leadership this way: "The most striking change in black leadership composition . . . is the decline between 1963 and 1990 in the percentage of civil rights and 'glamor personalities' . . . and a sharp increase in the percentage of persons who are elected and appointed officials in government."[2] Smith argues that as this trend developed, it eventually created a major obstacle to the effectiveness of black leadership. "The incipient incorporation of black leadership into systemic institutions and processes has had the perhaps predictable consequence of further isolating black leadership from the community it would purport to lead." In addition to the increasing isolation, Smith identifies what he considers an even more ominous development: "This process of incorporation has encouraged the creation of a new cadre of authentically *white-created* black leaders."[3] Many of the members of this new group of white-created black leaders, Smith insists, form the nucleus of the ranks of modern black conservatives. He describes these people as "a well-financed group of black conservative spokespeople who, while lacking an ideological or organizational base in the community, have, nevertheless, because of their access to white elites, money and media, constituted yet another force for centrifugalism."[4]

In an article that probes the origins of the modern black conservatism alluded to by Smith, political scientist Hanes Walton Jr. points to a particular moment in history when the group of black conservatives coalesced: December 12 and 13, 1980, at the Fairmont Conference. The purpose of that conference, which was planned by an adviser to president-elect Ronald Reagan, was "to establish a cadre of blacks of some prominence who could speak to a new thrust in domestic policies in regard to black Americans, with the hope and anticipation that they would emerge as alternative leaders to the civil rights group."[5] Walton is one of many scholars who insist that partly because of the group's origins and partly because of the group's ideology, there is a rift between the black community at large and this modern group of black conservatives. It is important to note, however, that the term *black conservative* can be somewhat misleading, especially in today's political climate. According to one social critic, the style of conservatism in vogue today, which "first came snarling onto the national stage in response to the partying and protests of the late sixties," is vastly different from the political conservatism of the past. "While earlier forms of conservatism emphasized fiscal sobriety . . . [this new form] mobilizes voters with explosive social issues—summoning public outrage over everything from busing to un-Christian art."[6]

Ironically, the cultural values that today's political conservatives espouse are basically the same as the core cultural values that the majority of African Americans have embraced for generations: opposition to abortion, reverence for Christianity, belief in the importance of the family. The major exception is political conservatives' attitudes regarding race. Whether they are discussing programs like affirmative action or school desegregation, today's political conservatives, black or white, generally disagree with the majority of African Americans. Thus, the belief of most African Americans in the aggressive pursuit of racial justice sets them apart from most twenty-first-century black political conservatives—many of whom have publicly and vigorously denounced the best-known programs aimed at remedying past racial discrimination.

Black conservatives are not the only ones out of sync with the black community. Robert Smith insists that many African Americans elected to federal office, regardless of their political ideology, find themselves being pulled further and further away from their constituents. "The institutional norms and folkways of the House [of Representatives] encourage exaggerated courtesy, compromise, deference and above all loyalty to the institution. And the black members of Congress are probably more loyal to the House and their roles in it than they are to blacks."[7] Rev. James Lawson agrees with Smith's assessment. He remembers the halcyon days during the civil rights movement when "99 if not 100 percent of us" agreed "that we must end slavery and all of its systems." Lawson labels this "the historic black agenda." Now, he charges, black elected officials "concentrate on staying elected," instead of on "the historic black agenda."[8]

Another criticism of black political leadership is found in Norman Kelley's scathing assessment of political and intellectual black leadership in modern America. In his 2004 study, Kelley argues that black political leaders have increasingly become situated on the other side of a great divide in the black community of the new millennium, because "as the 1960s black freedom movement moved 'from protest to politics,' community and protest leaders became incorporated into 'the routines of the country's political system,' and consequently, 'Black leadership has been fully incorporated not only into the political scheme of things but into the white overclass.'"[9]

As destructive as this leadership trend is, self-styled hip-hop historian Todd Boyd argues that none of it matters; he thinks the trends in African American leadership that have developed since King's death are of no consequence. Boyd asserts that there is a new group of African American leaders in the new millennium and that previous generations of black leaders are no longer relevant to the continued struggle of black people: "Well, there is now a new generation of Head Niggas in Charge and they hail from hip hop culture." In his view, "hip hop [is] something far beyond music, and far greater than the fashion, language, and ideology that expresses it. Hip hop is an unrivaled social force; it is a way of being. It is a new way of seeing the world and it is a collective movement that has dethroned civil rights and now commands our undivided attention. . . . The people who form the hip hop generation are the new HNIC [Head Niggas In Charge]."[10]

The tone of many of the newest studies of black leadership in America is strident, harsh, and critical, but this is nothing new. Even during the glory days of the civil rights movement, a time that many think of fondly as the golden age of black leadership, there was no shortage of critics; and many of them were black. For example, history professor Harold Cruse, in his seminal work *The Crisis of the Negro Intellectual,* is extremely critical of the civil rights movement and its leadership. Cruse's book was first published in 1967, three years after the passage of the Civil Rights Act of 1964 and only two years after the passage of the Voting Rights Act of 1965. Thus, when his book first appeared, many were still basking in the glow that seemed to emanate from these two major pieces of legislation that had the potential to revolutionize American society. But Cruse was not impressed: he argued that the civil rights movement's effectiveness was compromised because "the Black Revolution" was "nothing but an alarmist slogan—a rebellion without ideology." He further charged that ineffective leadership was largely responsible for the movement's failure: "The leadership of the Negro movement is incapable of devising new tactics and strategies for new situations."[11]

Professor Cruse was not alone. Journalist, social critic, and satirist George Schuyler, a contemporary, offered an even more harsh criticism of civil rights leaders in general and Dr. Martin Luther King Jr. in particular. In 1964, just before King was scheduled to receive the Nobel Peace Prize, Schuyler wrote, "Dr. King's principal contribution to world peace has been to roam the country like some sable typhoid Mary, infecting the mentally disturbed with perversion of Christian doctrine, and grabbing fat lecture fees. . . . His incitement packed jails with Negroes and some whites getting them beaten, bitten and firehosed, thereby bankrupting communities raising bail and fines to the vast enrichment of Southern 'law' n' order.'"[12]

Even though they have seen criticism of black leadership before, however, today's black leaders are still stung by the negative assessment of their motives, their capabilities, and their accomplishments. And as they seek to chart their own course to continue the black freedom struggle in the way that they think is most effective, most of today's black leaders cannot help but recognize that the specter of the martyred Martin Luther King Jr. is usually hovering somewhere in the background. Every January, the nation celebrates King's birthday, sort of. There are parades, programs, commemorations, and even special sales in department stores. A monument to King will soon be erected on the mall in Washington, D.C., and some time ago, his face was stuck on a U.S. postage stamp. Whether all this attention is the sign of a grateful nation or a collective guilty conscience, the consequences for today's black leaders are unmistakable. Constantly and consistently, consciously or unconsciously, most are compared with Dr. Martin Luther King Jr. and the kind of movement he led. White Americans do it, and African Americans do it. How are today's black leaders affected? They are alternately exhausted and pessimistic, defensive but determined.

As today's African American leaders look toward the future, most acknowledge that it is firmly grounded in the recent past; they express a variety of hopes and fears, frustrations and anxieties. Congressman John Lewis, serving in Congress in the new millennium, is one who developed his leadership style out of the civil rights movement. He was practicing it in Selma, Alabama, on Bloody Sunday, March 7, 1965, when he led a column of marchers up to a menacing line of Alabama state troopers wearing gas masks. Civil rights attorney J. L. Chestnut was there at the foot of the Edmund Pettus Bridge that day, and he watched the drama unfold. Chestnut frowns at the memory of that long-ago confrontation. He insists, however, that "John has not moved from where he was forty, thirty-five years ago in the streets of Selma. He's still an integrationist; black and white together and all of that. Whites in many instances got an agenda. Black folks got another agenda. . . . [But] John is in a class by himself. John Lewis is an icon. Blacks and everybody else will forgive John [for] the things they wouldn't forgive anybody else, because John is an authentic hero."[13] John Lewis has not forgotten the leadership lessons he learned. He characterizes his leadership philosophy this way: "Leaders must lead. Leaders must have a vision." He declares that Martin Luther King set the leadership standard for so many African Americans of his generation because, "Martin Luther King Jr., more than any other American of the twentieth century, had the ability or the capacity to get a greater diversity of people to follow him."[14]

Others of Lewis's generation also routinely reflect on King as *the* leadership role model for their generation. For example, SCLC's Rev. T. Randel Osburn believes that King's strength was in his ability to inspire unity among disparate elements of the black freedom struggle. "When Martin Luther King was alive, all this negative stuff was [in] existence and real, but because Martin Luther King was so close to the black church, he understood [that] any time those fellas started [bickering], he would go out and take on a George Wallace [to] point up the issues, and those folk would all join in behind him." Furthermore, Osburn charges, these days, "nobody's articulating where the problems are, and so you got all those so-called fighters." Osburn's voice rises in frustration as he adds, "And they fight you."[15]

Memphis minister Rev. Samuel Billy Kyles agrees that King's leadership was invaluable to the black freedom struggle at that time. However, he insists that because of the changes ushered in by King's leadership, the possibility that there will ever be another black leadership figure like him is remote. "Dr. King's leadership made the Voting Rights Act possible. But with that ability for black people to influence the political system, it opened the door for the kind of leaders like Harold Ford Jr. And this meant it shifted the climate so that a leader like King could never happen again." Kyles reiterates, "Black leadership can no longer be defined as who is *the* black leader. That will not happen again. That bullet in 1968 ended that. There will be individuals who will blossom out . . . but to have *a* black leader, *the* black leader; I don't think it will happen again."[16] Over in Knoxville, Robert Booker feels that black people have been suffering the consequences ever since the unique characteristics of King's leadership died with him. "He [King] was the drum major. He told us what we ought to be doing. We don't have that anymore."[17]

Back in Memphis, Dr. Benjamin Hooks believes that despite King's loss, black people have continued to make progress: "Since his [King's] death, we've made some remarkable strides, but what has happened since his death has been wrapped up in things he did before his death." And, according to Hooks, the circumstances of King's death have actually added even more luster to his memory. "If he had died at the age of 60, I'm not too sure what his legacy would have been. Everybody who dies [prematurely] is a martyr. It makes a difference; [it] enlarges their scope, so that he became obviously larger in death than he was in life. There's just no question about that." The old lawyer pauses and then continues in a voice laced with resignation: "History continues. It doesn't start or stop. It just keeps rolling on, and men contribute greatly to it."[18]

According to Hooks, these later contributions in the years after the movement were directly connected to the civil rights victories of the past. He explains: "Mr. Thurgood Marshall made the statement that we've now passed the Voting Rights Act, we've passed the Civil Rights Bill, but now comes the hard part; implementing it and making it work. And implementation; you don't get the headlines. I came along as a national leader at a time when we were struggling to make the thing work." Hooks says softly, "And you don't get credit for making it work."[19]

Former North Carolina congressman Frank Ballance also sees the function of black leadership now as very different from King's time. "[In the] sixties, we had very VERY vocal leaders. . . . Actually, they were more outgoing and pushing harder than the leaders are now. Now, people are a little more moderate in their approach. They won't say, 'you're a racist SOB.' [Instead, they'll say] 'well sir, you don't respect diversity.'" Smiling, he explains, "Everybody wants to be politically correct."[20]

Rev. Fred Shuttlesworth, a veteran civil rights activist whose name is most closely associated with the Birmingham campaign, is particularly concerned that black ministers should play more of a leadership role in the new millennium. Of course, Shuttlesworth recalls the crucial impact of black ministers during the civil rights movement, and he believes that black progress in the new millennium is dependent on the leadership of black ministers again: "Unless you encourage folks to resist evil; unless you're encouraging folks to fight for justice, [nothing will change.]" He concedes that the world confronting black leaders now is very different from the leadership context in which he and his contemporaries operated. These days, he points out, there are new opportunities for personal advancement that can be very tempting. "Position, money, and power change people," Shuttlesworth explains. The old minister gets a faraway look in his eyes as he concludes, "It's difficult to remain the same thing when opportunities come all around. You have to really . . . be guided by the Spirit."[21]

In too many cases, some say, black leaders are unable to resist the new opportunities. One of those who worries is Col. Stone Johnson, a tall, very dark, very lean man who is well into his eighties now. During the tumultuous Birmingham campaign in 1963, Johnson was a resident of the city, and he was one of the group of black men who volunteered to guard Rev. Fred Shuttlesworth's house because of the many threats against the activist-preacher's life. With Shuttlesworth's courage, determination, and tenacity from forty years ago still fresh in mind, Johnson is disappointed when he looks at the younger black leaders who have come along more recently. He even goes so far as to charge that "they [the white power structure] bought 'em [all] off but one or two."[22]

Dr. Bernard Lafayette is another veteran of the civil rights movement in Alabama who remembers the crucial importance of Shuttlesworth, King, and the other ministers back during the 1960s. He also recalls how inspiring those dramatic confrontations between good and evil were to the clapping, singing, ordinary brave black people who supported their efforts. These days, according to Lafayette, leadership is not as exciting. It is not as dramatic, because the nature of the struggle has changed. Back in the sixties, he notes, "we were fighting to get in. Now, what do you do when you get in?"[23] Of course, this is the central question now confronting the first black president of the United States.

Thus, different challenges face black leadership in the new millennium. Lafayette argues that for this "struggle from the inside . . . it's their [the black leaders'] involvement at the local level that I think is important. That's where your leadership really comes from . . . at this point."[24] Mayor Johnny Ford of Tuskegee, Alabama, suggests that as African Americans continue their struggle for full inclusion in American society, their leaders will be drawn from local communities. He argues, "There's no *one* African American leader anymore. Our solution, I think, is working together as groups and networking, and speaking as a common voice whenever we can." But even as he urges unity, Mayor Ford understands that disagreements are inevitable, and so he advises African American leaders to agree "to disagree, and not be disagreeable." In an effort to promote cooperation, Ford helped to establish the National Conference of Black Mayors. Because there are so many black mayors in this country—over five hundred, according to NCBM's estimates—and because the majority of African Americans are urban residents, Ford is convinced that his organization can have a powerful and positive impact on African Americans in the new millennium.[25]

Rev. Al Sharpton, who also thinks African Americans need to build networks and encourage unity, plans to spend much of his time in the near future continuing to build his organization, the National Action Network. But while he does so, Sharpton will keep on being a very visible media personality. He hosts a national radio talk show (he explains, "We need somebody to challenge the Rush Limbaughs"); and he is often consulted by the national media for comments on newsworthy events involving race.[26] Former SNCC staffer and Mississippi Freedom Democratic Party chairman Lawrence Guyot is also concerned about strengthening black unity in the new millennium. Over four decades ago, he saw and experienced the barbaric brutality of the white racist authorities in Mississippi during the height of the civil rights movement, and he still insists with a determined glint in his eye: "I'm an integrationist; and I'm an integrationist because I'm a pragmatist." Guyot knows that the stakes are high for African Americans in the new millennium, and so he carefully advises, "What we've got to be very clear on . . . is that . . . we should combine as many of us as possible . . . without consideration of sexual orientation, age, religious denomination, and move forward. . . . I believe that there are a lot of folks that are voting against their self-interest in this country, and I want to be part of the leadership that makes the argument of why not vote in your self-interest rather than vote against it."[27]

Former senator Carol Moseley Braun is less optimistic. Particularly worried about the role of politics and critical of black leadership in this area, she asserts that many black leaders do not have a plan for black participation in the political arena. "I think the nice thing would be to have an agenda." Braun reiterates, "If there's a problem, it's that we have no agenda. . . . We don't have a cogent agenda about any specific thing that government can do on any level. . . . If you ask any of our so-called leaders . . . where is the agenda for the black community, they won't be able to tell you."[28] Congresswoman Eleanor Holmes Norton, in contrast, is convinced that there is a black political agenda. In her estimation, one issue should form the centerpiece of that agenda in the new millennium, and that is the fate of the black family. Norton argues that the black family is in crisis because desperate conditions in black inner cities have led to an environment that is hostile to it. She explains that even though out-of-wedlock births are out of control and absent fathers have become far too common, ministers, politicians, and other black leaders are "not emphasizing black family enough. It's *the* critical issue." The congresswoman sits in her tastefully furnished congressional office, surrounded by the visible symbols of power of one of the most powerful countries on earth, but she still agonizes over how to address the fundamental problem of the crisis of the black family. "I believe the void in black leadership is greatest on this most difficult of issues which is family . . . and I think it's greatest because [we] don't know how to get a hold of it. It's not like a policy issue. It takes a number of actors moving together, and somebody's getting them together and it takes invading the culture and speaking about it."[29]

Washington, D.C., city councilman Kwame Brown's office is down the street from Congresswoman Norton's. As he thinks about why African Americans have not made more progress, he looks to the black victories of the past. Brown appreciates their importance but worries that too much emphasis on those past achievements has paralyzed black people in the present. He exclaims in frustration, "We can't have great things happen and then 15 years of nothing, really. And we're still celebrating the airport in Atlanta. We're still celebrating minorities getting contracts when Marion Barry was mayor [of Washington, D.C.]. . . . How can we still be celebrating something [from] 1986 instead of moving. . . . I want to create something that continues to move the conversation forward." Councilman Brown pauses to look out the window of his office, his expression reflecting his concern about the city he loves and the constituents he represents. In a low voice, the young councilman laments, "I'm faced with these kids in crumbling schools. . . . I'm faced with that right now. I'm faced with [a] health care [crisis]."[30] Brown falls into a long, deep silence that conveys a deep frustration.

Brown begins talking again, slowly at first. But his youthful optimism begins to take hold, and the pace of his speech quickens: "The first thing we need are individuals that are willing to take on the same characteristics of the individuals in SNCC, or the individuals within the whole movement. I think the values don't change. . . . What may change is what we're fighting for." As he thinks about the contexts of the black freedom struggle forty years ago and the challenges confronting black leaders in the new millennium, he frets about a growing disunity among African Americans. Furthermore, he believes this disunity is often exacerbated by the special recognition accorded certain individual black leaders: "Obama; I mean, he's there. . . . you have Harold Ford Jr. I mean, those are all great, but if everyone's in their own little world, it don't make a difference. . . . We need unity. We need a network like we used to have."[31]

The celebrity status of certain black leaders and the cynicism this seems to engender also bothers former Georgia state senator Eugene Walker. He mentions Rev. Jesse Jackson. Walker asserts, "So, when you talk about black leaders today, blacks just laugh at Jesse and them because they claim he's just looking for a handout for himself and for the rest of us." In discussions of the state of black leadership in America today, Jackson's name is often mentioned. But when Eugene Walker evaluates

Jackson's leadership capabilities, he does so from the background of a personal association with the famous preacher: Walker was Jackson's Georgia campaign manager when he ran for president in 1988. Walker recognizes that Jackson has unique talents: "The dude is one of the best speakers I've ever heard. . . . He can paint a portrait of a situation or circumstance better than anybody I've ever seen, and that's a significant gift he has." However, black opinion of Reverend Jackson's leadership capabilities is split. Walker says, "It's a mix. You got a lot of blacks that [think] Jesse can do no wrong . . . he'll always be the victim," while others see Jackson as an ineffective leader who does not represent their interests. Frowning, Walker advises, "We need individual leadership. [Black] people have got to be taught to make better choices. It's as simple as that." His words are stern, but his deep bass voice softens a bit as he reminds African Americans of their responsibility for their own fate regardless of the state of black leadership. Walker intones, "There is no way you can lead me where I don't want to go."[32]

As black journalist Samuel Yette thinks about the state of black leadership today, he mentions Louis Farrakhan. Back in 1995, when Farrakhan issued a call for one million black men to join him for a march in the nation's capital to dramatize the issues facing black men in America, the turnout was remarkable. Yette argues that, notwithstanding the charges of male chauvinism leveled at the Million Man March's organizers, Farrakhan had a responsibility to use this massive show of support as a basis for organizing African Americans for social change in the new millennium. However, according to Yette, Farrakhan squandered this unprecedented opportunity. "Farrakhan . . . I think he missed an opportunity at the end of the Million Man March to rally black people—all complexions and colors. I think he missed an opportunity to rally around and . . . I don't think he did what should have been done at that time." Yette argues that black people cannot afford any more squandered opportunities, because there are precious few opportunities for black advancement left: "I feel like we're at a place where; well, it's a little like the North Pole in that we are approaching a point where we cannot reverse it. And I think that's a fearful place."[33]

Historian Manning Marable insists that the Million Man March's success "had less to do with Farrakhan's reactionary ideology than with the deep desire among African American people to move their communities forward."[34] In the final analysis, former SNCC staffer Charles Jones argues, no matter how much enthusiasm and excitement individual leaders generate, effective and responsible black leadership cannot exist without an organized black community. Jones states bluntly: "When you organize the people, the leaders can't get away with no shit. . . . When you organize, these young leaders—or even older leaders—can't get away with ripping people off."[35]

Over in Memphis, Dr. Benjamin Hooks also assesses black leadership in the new millennium. He is particularly concerned about the precarious political circumstances facing African Americans. As he sees it, most African Americans have become virtual captives of a Democratic Party that does not appreciate them, and black leaders are not offering any guidance to their black constituents on this crucial issue. Dr. Hooks explains, "So I think that black leadership basically is standing in its own way now because we have lost sight of the fact that we would be more powerful if we could point out to the Democrats—you *do* take the chance of losing us if you don't treat us right." Hooks insists that the vast majority of black leaders are caught in this trap of unconditional loyalty to the Democrats; he includes himself: "I think that in a sense, we're standing in our own light, [and] that includes me. And we know it, but we're scared to move."[36] Manning Marable expresses a similar conviction: "The most critical mistake in black politics was the tendency to emphasize electoralism at the expense of activism. For 30 years, since the end of the Civil Rights Movement, African American leadership increasingly came from elective offices. *The vast majority of these officials were Democrats tied to a political party that had begun to distance itself from black interests and issues.*"[37]

No matter how complicated the issues are these days, some leaders remain optimistic. Down in Mayersville, Mississippi, Unita Blackwell sits in her living room looking out on a rural Mississippi landscape that has changed very little in the forty years since she worked with the Student Nonviolent Coordinating Committee. Although she can't forget the brutality that she and her fellow activists suffered at the hands of Mississippi authorities, she still remembers the infectious excitement of the young people in SNCC: how bright they were and how eager they were. And even though the young people who came to Mississippi four decades ago are now in their sixties and seventies, Blackwell still sees them as those slender young men and women who came to her state to defy segregation. With a smile and a faraway look in her eyes, she reminisces. "I hadn't ever seen students [who acted like that]. . . . I hadn't ever seen that many blacks at that level of education. . . . I was just overwhelmed." When Blackwell introduced her husband to the young activists, he took one look at them and said they were crazy. They could not possibly be in their right minds, Mr. Blackwell reasoned, because any black person willing to defy segregation in Mississippi in those days had to be crazy. But when he looked at those young people, he smiled and said, "It's about time." After all these years, Mrs. Blackwell's faith in young black people has not diminished, and she is convinced that, hip-hop culture notwithstanding, some of today's young African Americans are strong, stubborn, and independent just like the young people in the movement forty years ago. "It's cool to be an individual [now]," she points out.[38] Blackwell has no doubt that today's strong black youth will continue the black freedom struggle.

Over in Selma, civil rights attorney J. L. Chestnut beams as he declares, "I am optimistic. I've been there. I know what black folk can do. And I see things slowly but surely coming into place like they never have before."[39] Sitting in his office in his old neighborhood in Charlotte, North Carolina, former SNCC staffer Charles Jones is also optimistic and determined. "I am still committed to the Beloved Community. I am still committed to organizing around the core issues, and am doing it. I still have faith in this counterbalance between good and evil . . . every now and then, the good guys will win." Jones breaks into a broad smile: "I believe that the glass is half full. . . . I have to believe that."[40]

As black leaders look around them at the dawn of a new millennium, many cannot help but marvel at the visible changes in the status of African Americans. Rev. Abraham Woods, down in Birmingham, Alabama, in his eighties now, thinks about how segregated his city was in the past and concedes that some things have changed—dramatically. Woods explains, "Well, I guess the idea was that we won victories and victories . . . and that we had desegregated. . . . We now can become registered voters." The old preacher smiles slightly: "The hands that pick cotton can now pick presidents and governors and things of that kind." Woods's smile fades abruptly as he continues, "And many people just thought that we had accomplished quite a bit and so they settled back on their laurels, I guess. And maybe, there was not the dynamic kind of leadership [anymore]."[41] Up in Washington, D.C., young Joe Leonard, who was recently recognized by *Black Enterprise* magazine as one of the up-and-coming young black leaders on the national scene, agrees with Reverend Woods's contention that the civil rights movement was responsible for some important victories for African Americans and that with those victories has come a sense of complacency. "We've had so much success," he exults. "Seventeen per cent of the [black] population now has a BA [degree]. Three per cent [have] masters degrees. We have a million African Americans, according to the census, [who] have [a] masters or higher." Leonard pauses for emphasis, and then his voice reaches a crescendo. "ONE MILLION. That's success. . . . We've gotten our stacks large." As a result, Leonard argues, "we're conservative. We're afraid to be revolutionary."[42]

In addition to having a revolutionary outlook, African Americans need to pursue the right kind of education, Leonard asserts. "There need to be courses on activism to teach another generation. I've watched these white conservative Christian churches. They create their own universities and law schools. . . . [But] where are our universities? There's not a program that teaches activism, strategies, or tactics or classes, or all of these different things." Leonard raises his voice: "WHERE IS THE UNIVERSITY?" Even though it has not happened yet, his youthful optimism keeps him hoping that in this new millennium African Americans will become more revolutionary, and that they will begin to concentrate on developing activist strategies and tactics to facilitate black advancement. But when that day finally comes, Leonard worries, black people will need the right sort of leaders, and he is not at all confident that there are enough of them to go around. He explains, "There were more leaders in the sixties, just true leaders. I mean, people who put their lives on the line . . ." Leonard's voice trails off, and he shrugs in resignation, leaving unspoken his fear that black leaders in the new millennium do not have the same willingness to make the ultimate sacrifice that their predecessors had.[43]

Up in Chicago, Timuel Black sits alone in his apartment thinking about the remarkable changes he has seen during his lifetime. Among them is a long string of victories. When the eighty-year-old first came to Chicago as a youngster, he quickly realized that African Americans had a lot more freedom in this big midwestern city than they did in his native Mississippi; but he also learned that African Americans were still not completely free even in the North. He recalls how black Chicagoans organized to resist the de facto segregation in their city, and he smiles as he remembers how hopeful he was when he participated in the founding of CORE in 1942. Just the organization's name—the Congress of Racial Equality—gave him hope. He was jubilant when the U.S. Supreme Court decision *Shelly v. Kramer* struck down restrictive covenants that had barred African Americans from Chicago's traditionally white neighborhoods. Black has a broad grin as he recalls his joy on hearing about each successive southern civil rights campaign in the 1960s. Then came the Civil Rights Act of 1964, the Voting Rights Act of 1965, President Lyndon Johnson's War on Poverty, and his executive order establishing the policy of affirmative action. The pace of legal change was dizzying, and Black shakes his head slightly at the memory.

But in Black's mind, all these legal changes pale in comparison to that night in 1983 when he and other black Chicagoans realized that they had elected their city's first black mayor, Harold Washington. They finally had a visible symbol of their new black power in the mayor's office in city hall. However, another memory pushes into Black's mind: the tragic image of the overweight, overburdened Harold Washington slumped over his desk in city hall, dead before the end of his first term. The thought of that tragedy in Chicago's city hall decades ago reminds him that on the heels of so many black victories in recent years has come a string of tragedies that have combined to form a crisis of epic proportions that is facing African Americans in the new millennium.

The masses of African Americans still live on the fringes of the American economy; black people are overrepresented in the ranks of the poor. They are also overrepresented in the ranks of the incarcerated. African Americans have a long and troubled relationship with America's criminal justice system, and in the years since the civil rights movement, that relationship has shown no signs of improvement. Even before the decade of the sixties was over, the Republican Party in particular, starting with the administration of Richard Nixon, publicly aligned itself with the forces of law and order. As black incarceration rates reached stratospheric levels, many African Americans became convinced that the Republican "War on Crime" was really a war on black people. From the advent of President Nixon's war on drugs in the late 1960s to the use of the infamous Willie Horton campaign commercial by the Republican National Committee during the 1988 presidential campaign, it seemed that the message was clear: Republicans would not be soft on crime or soft on black people. In 1986 and 1988, during the administration of Ronald Reagan, federal sentencing statutes were passed that ensured unequal treatment for black people accused of a drug offense. These laws established sentencing guidelines for powder cocaine and crack cocaine that could not have been more different: "The result of these laws is that persons convicted of federal crack offenses, who tend to be African American, receive much harsher penalties than those convicted of powder cocaine charges, a much larger proportion of whom are white. For example, someone convicted in federal court of distributing 5 grams of crack cocaine automatically receives a 5-year, mandatory minimum sentence, while it takes 500 grams of powder cocaine to trigger a 5-year mandatory sentence."[44]

Of course, the resulting dramatic rise in black incarceration rates must be considered against the backdrop of rising incarceration rates for Americans in general. However, "While everyone is affected by the nation's quadrupling of the prison population, the African American community has borne the brunt of this incarceration boom. From 1980 to 1992, the African American incarceration rate increased by an average of 138.4 per 100,000 per year."[45] When Democrat Bill Clinton was elected president in 1992, many African Americans were hopeful that a Democratic administration might be more sympathetic to this black incarceration crisis. They were soon disappointed, however, when Clinton signed the Violent Crime Control and Law Enforcement Act of 1994. The new law provided increased funding for the construction of more prisons, and this plus repressive laws already on the books ensured that "policies passed during the Clinton Administration's tenure resulted in the largest increases in federal and state prison inmates of any president in American history."[46] During the Clinton presidency, young African Americans were hit particularly hard: "Nearly 50 percent of America's prison population is Black with hip-hop generationers making up a significant proportion of that population."[47]

These days, whether African Americans are in prison or not, and whether they live in the inner city or the suburbs, they tend to suffer serious illnesses at higher rates and they have less access to health insurance and quality health care. As recently as 2004, only 55 percent of African Americans were covered by employer-sponsored health insurance plans. That same year, 78 percent of white Americans were covered by such plans. At the same time, African Americans are stricken much more frequently by the most common forms of cancer, and they routinely have lower survival rates than white Americans. For example, "In 2004, African American men were 2.4 times more likely to die from prostate cancer, compared to non-Hispanic white men." And the bad news continues: African American men were 30 percent more likely to die from heart disease than white men; African Americans were 1.5 times as likely to have high blood pressure, and African American adults were 50 percent more likely to have a stroke than white adults. In 2005, African Americans made up 47 percent of all HIV/AIDS cases even though they account for only 13 percent of the nation's population. Black children do not fare any better than adults: in 2004 the black infant mortality rate was 2.4 times that for white Americans. In short, African Americans are dying in larger numbers and at earlier ages than white Americans from many causes, including stroke, cancer, asthma, influenza, pneumonia, diabetes, HIV/AIDS, and homicide.[48]

Meanwhile, Snoop Dogg is out there rapping in cyberspace and on MTV, making commercials and making millions. Oprah Winfrey continues her reign as the black media mogul of the twenty-first century. There are others, too: from black actors to black comedians and from black musicians to black athletes. They constitute a new black elite—wealthier than any previous group of African Americans has ever been. No doubt their laudable achievements have ensured their personal success. Yet their stories do not indicate black success as much as they represent exceptions: in the twenty-first century, despite all the victories of the recent past, African Americans face a crisis of unprecedented proportions—they are powerless, broke, sick, and incarcerated.

As black leaders all over the country look forward to an uncertain future, the crisis of their people weighs heavily on them. Young and old, northern and southern, liberal and conservative, each proposes strategies and solutions based on his or her own particular perspective, life experiences, and value system. Nevertheless, even as they contemplate the difficulties facing their black constituents, African American leaders have to smile at the miracle that happened in November. A black president: most never thought they would live to see that day in America. In Chicago, the adopted hometown of America's first black president, eighty-year-old Timuel Black savors the Obama victory. It is a potent symbol of the triumph of black leadership that cheers him up. But Black frowns as he worries about the deepening crisis facing his people and his new black president. Then the frown lines in the old man's face relax, the optimism that has sustained him over a lifetime in the black freedom struggle reasserts itself, and Black predicts confidently, "Often, crisis facilitates the rise of black leadership."[49] He falls silent as he muses and waits for new victories to come out of the crisis facing African Americans in the early years of the new millennium.

Epilogue

America is fighting two wars on the other side of the world, where military forces battle the tenacious Iraqi insurgency and determined Taliban guerillas. Improvised explosive devices lurk on the side of the road. Long periods of boredom punctuated by short bursts of anxiety and danger are the constant companions of the brave young Americans who proudly wear their country's uniform. Many of these young people, who had never seen combat before, are hardened and haunted by the exigencies of war, the sight of missing limbs and sightless eyes. Meanwhile, back home, America faces the most serious crisis since the Great Depression of the 1930s. Banks are failing. The country is losing manufacturing jobs at an alarming rate as the big three automakers in Detroit stare at ribbons of red ink on their balance sheets. Foreclosure rates are skyrocketing—forcing many Americans to ponder the awful prospect of homelessness. Pensions are disappearing as older Americans who just a short time before had been contemplating a pleasant retirement now hunker down and try to keep their jobs just a little bit longer. It seems as if the country is teetering on the brink of a precipice, and Americans are desperately looking for a leader to rescue them before their civilization tumbles over the edge.

Therefore, on November 4, 2008, the long lines at polling places all over the country were no surprise to anyone. Because the lines were anticipated, many jurisdictions offered the option of early voting during the weeks leading up to election day, and countless citizens eagerly took advantage of the opportunity. So for weeks before November 4, there had been high drama at polling places everywhere. The lines were long both for early voting and on election day—snaking around the sides of buildings and spilling out into parking lots. And despite the long lines, the crowds were orderly. The wait was three, four, five hours or more. In Georgia, voters waited as long as ten hours at some polling places. Americans going to the polls realized how much was at stake. But for

African Americans, this election was especially significant. Of course they had sons and daughters in the wars in Iraq and Afghanistan. They had watched jobs disappear, and many had lost their own jobs. They had watched the value of their homes plummet, and they had seen their pensions disappear.

But on November 4, African Americans going into the voting booth were moved by something beyond the deepening crisis enveloping their country. Despite all the despair around them, the powerful symbol of one of their own within striking distance of the White House was a cause for rejoicing. As they stood in the privacy of the voting booth pulling the lever or marking their ballot for Barack Obama, some could almost sense the spirits of the black politicians from Reconstruction, over one hundred years ago, nodding their approval. They could almost hear a chorus of amens from the spirits of voting rights activists who gave their lives in the struggle for black enfranchisement, only four decades ago. The voting rights movement of the 1960s was not really so very long ago, but it occurred in an America that seems light years away from this one. Nevertheless, many Americans still have vivid memories of that final voting rights struggle that took place in Selma, Alabama, in 1965, when African American demands for the right to vote were met with tear gas and billy clubs. Before that campaign ended, three activists lost their lives—Jimmie Lee Jackson, James Reeb, and Viola Liuzzo—and Martin Luther King Jr. was moved to declare, "The arc of the moral universe is long, but it bends toward justice." It was right after that that the Voting Rights Act of 1965 became law, laying the cornerstone for the foundation of an Obama candidacy forty-three years later.

On November 4, 2008, in Selma, Alabama, Joanne Bland thought about that struggle for black voting rights four decades earlier as she went to the polls. Even though she was just a child in 1965, she clearly remembers the chaos and fear and the hope and exhilaration of the remarkable movement as if it had happened yesterday. As she approached her polling place, she saw a line stretching around the side of the building. Bland has lived in Selma all her life, and she had never seen such a long line on election day. But she did not mind waiting. Bland's granddaughter Jasmyn stood patiently by her side as the two of them inched forward. Joanne realized that because she decided to vote before taking her granddaughter to school, Jasmyn would almost certainly be late; but she also realized what a historic election this was, and she wanted her granddaughter to witness it. In a tone laced with forty years of emotion, Joanne Bland describes the exhilaration she felt when she finally was able to cast her vote for Barack Obama: "I finally got up to the front. [I] signed my name and got my ballot. I explained to Jasmyn that I could just draw [a] line for the Democratic Party and vote for all the Democrats on the ballot, but I did not want to do that. I wanted to draw a line next to Mr. Obama's name. I did just that. I sat immobile for a few seconds to savor the moment and what it meant to me." Once Joanne finished marking her ballot, she "let Jasmyn place it in the ballot box. We both got 'I voted' stickers, and I took her to school only a few minutes late."[1]

The historic moment savored by Joanne Bland, her granddaughter Jasmyn, and African Americans all over the country had arrived only after a long and bruising primary season and general election campaign. During the months and weeks leading up to the election, there were the inevitable and never-ending hints that Barack Obama was somehow not quite a "real" American. Some of his detractors pointed to his "exotic" ancestry—he is the son of a black Kenyan father and a white Kansas mother—as a reason to question his authenticity. Others pointed to his name, Barack Hussein Obama, as proof that he is not really "one of us." Then there were some who insisted that many of the ideas he espoused were way outside the American mainstream: because of his discussion of economic inequality, some detractors branded him a socialist and others called him a communist.

However, many social critics insist, the most sensitive issue of all in this campaign was Obama's race, because while the reality of a black man running for the presidency of the United States seemed too good to be true as far as African Americans were concerned, others were not so sure. Yet, because racial issues are still so emotional for many Americans, it was uncertain that there would be an open and honest discussion of race during the 2008 presidential campaign. But even before the primary season was over, some incendiary remarks made by Obama's longtime pastor, Rev. Jeremiah Wright, surfaced. Suddenly, it seemed that the Obama candidacy was doomed by the very racial divisions the candidate had tried so hard to transcend. On March 18, 2008, Barack Obama addressed

Wright's troubling remarks and the issues they raised: "The fact is that the comments that have been made and the issues that have surfaced over the last few weeks reflect the complexities of race in this country that we've never really worked through—a part of our union that we have yet to perfect. And if we walk away now, if we simply retreat to our respective corners, we will never be able to come together and solve challenges like health care, or education, or the need to find good jobs for every American." As the young candidate continued, he was not afraid to mention racial injustice: "We do not need to recite here the history of racial injustice in this country. But we do need to remind ourselves that so many of the disparities that exist in the African American community today can be traced to inequalities passed on from an earlier generation that suffered under the brutal legacy of slavery and Jim Crow." Obama concluded with a challenge to his listeners to strive for a more perfect union: "I have asserted a firm conviction—a conviction rooted in my faith in God and my faith rooted in the American people—that working together we can move beyond some of our old racial wounds, and in fact we have no choice if we are to continue on the path of a more perfect union."

African Americans heard that speech fearfully. Would the issue of race steal this dream from them? As the favorable reactions to Obama's race speech came pouring in, black people all over the country breathed a sigh of relief. It seemed that the gifted young candidate had been able to accomplish the impossible: articulate the issue of race in a public forum in a way that satisfied the majority of black Americans and also reassured white Americans. Yet, despite his masterful speech, the whispered clandestine debate about whether Barack Obama was truly "one of us" continued. Finally, during the last weeks of the campaign, well after Obama had won his party's nomination, the whispers became louder and louder until they erupted into full-fledged shouts at some McCain-Palin rallies. The Republican candidate and his vice-presidential running mate leveled increasingly shrill attacks on Barack Obama, and the atmosphere at their rallies became more and more hostile and, some feared, threatening. From the audiences at some McCain-Palin rallies came shouts such as "Kill him," or "Off with his head," or "Bomb Obama."[2] Hearing about the threats, many African Americans shuddered, particularly those who were old enough to remember an America in which people who leveled similar death threats at African Americans were often able to carry out their threats with impunity.

Despite the efforts of some detractors to vilify Barack Obama, a black groundswell of support grew steadily throughout the campaign as huge numbers of African Americans embraced the young black candidate. In the beginning, to be sure, many African Americans were skeptical about Obama's chances and initially supported Hillary Clinton. For example, at the beginning of the primary season, John Lewis of Georgia publicly and enthusiastically supported Hillary Clinton. But after the majority of his constituents voted for Barack Obama, Lewis switched sides; like so many others, Congressman Lewis began to believe that an Obama victory was possible. Thus, as election day approached, increasing numbers of African Americans began to believe they were about to witness a historic black victory. The hope prompted some to look for the roots of the potential victory in the recent past.

African Americans of the civil rights generation, especially, are convinced that the roots of Obama's success are planted squarely in the civil rights victories of the 1960s. One of the most important of these victories occurred in August 1964, when an interracial slate of delegates representing a new political party and a new dream made their way to the National Democratic Party convention in Atlantic City, New Jersey. These were humble people, who were representing the brand-new Mississippi Freedom Democratic Party. Some of them, such as Fannie Lou Hamer, had been sharecroppers all their lives. Many of them had never been outside the state of Mississippi before. But they were all about to shake this nation's two party system to its core, and the aftershocks of their bold and courageous action were felt for decades, as Andrew Young explains: "The legacy of the Mississippi Freedom Democratic Party is apparent at every Democratic National Convention, as democratically elected delegates of every hue, male and female, young and old gather to nominate the party's standard-bearer. Thirty years later, the state of Mississippi has more black elected officials than any state in the Union, many with roots in the gallant MFDP."[3] Civil rights activists, most notably members of the Student Nonviolent Coordinating Committee, helped to create the MFDP in 1964 in an effort to combat the ruthless repression and political exclusion suffered by black Mississippians.

When Lawrence Guyot, who was the chairman of the MFDP, thinks of the group's historic challenge to Mississippi's segregated Democratic Party in 1964, his eyes sparkle with zeal for the citizen involvement and the citizen empowerment that were the MFDP's lifeblood. He is convinced that the historic victory of Barack Obama is born of the same citizen involvement and citizen empowerment that he witnessed in the 1960s. Guyot has waited a long time to see this kind of enthusiasm for the political process again. When he was chairman of the Mississippi Freedom Democratic Party, many of the people he worked with were poor, dispossessed sharecroppers who had been denied the franchise. More recently, when Guyot worked with Barack Obama's campaign, he noticed that many of the Obama supporters he encountered had been lukewarm about politics at best, and totally apathetic at worst—until the junior senator from Illinois excited them. Guyot explains, "This campaign was bigger than us as individuals and bigger than Senator Obama. It was about creating a politics that brings people together. It was about creating an America that all of us can be proud of. It was about the triumph of hope and unity over fear and division. This was the sentiment at the heart of the civil rights movement that I was proud to join as a young man—and this is the sentiment that inspires the Obama campaign today."[4] This atmosphere of grassroots citizen empowerment that was such a pivotal part of the Mississippi Freedom Summer Project in 1964 is also a critical part of the atmosphere in which Barack Obama came of age. When he was a college freshman in the early 1980s, he witnessed important "bottom-up" movements in Eastern Europe, such as Poland's Solidarity organization. As a result, according to speechwriter Ben Rhodes, "Economically, he (Obama) believes in bottom-up growth and development. Similarly, in foreign policy, he believes security starts at the individual level."[5] So Obama's vision fits quite comfortably with the belief in citizen empowerment that Lawrence Guyot embraces to this day, and every time Guyot ponders the link between his civil-rights-movement past and this bright young twenty-first-century black leader of the future, he smiles broadly.

Rev. Samuel Billy Kyles, who was standing on the balcony of the Lorraine Motel with Dr. King when he was assassinated, is convinced that the movement actually provided the foundation on which Obama could base his candidacy and ultimately his victory: "We were the foundation, and foundations don't get much credit cause you don't see them. But you don't dare build a building without a foundation and the civil rights movement was the foundation that was laid for him [Obama] to build on; he and many others like him: mayors of cities and governors. They didn't even know personally about sitting on the back of the bus and all those kinds of things. But they know it as history, and they have an appreciation, a great appreciation for those who laid the foundation."[6]

Rev. Bernard Lafayette, a veteran of SNCC's Selma Project, recalls in vivid detail the sacrifices made by African Americans who were determined to register and vote, no matter what. When Lafayette looks at Obama's victory, he sees a direct connection with King's philosophy, because "he [Obama] studied Dr. King."[7] Another of King's close associates, Dr. Dorothy Cotton, insists that Obama's way of looking at the world is reminiscent of Martin Luther King's vision. She explains, "[Obama] puts forth a vision that I know is a vision that's going to help us. Not only in this country, but on the planet. . . . I don't think that's an exaggeration." Cotton adds, "I can tie it [Obama's vision] to the vision that Martin Luther King had when he said we must learn to live together on this planet, or we will perish together as fools." Although Cotton believes African Americans are facing a huge crisis in the new millennium, Barack Obama's vision has finally given her a reason to hope again, and she sometimes gets emotional when she listens to the young man speak. "The Obama presidential campaign means a whole lot to me. And I have even felt highly emotional about it. I remember listening to one of Obama's speeches and walking around my house in tears."[8]

Of course, Barack Obama was a very young child when the major legislative civil rights victories of the 1960s were won. Yet he is acutely aware of the connection between the civil rights movement and his historic candidacy. He is also aware of the importance of the civil rights movement as a cultural symbol that resonates with a broad cross section of Americans, young and old, black and white, rich and poor. Consequently, during his campaign, as he articulated his vision for "change we can believe in" to Americans in the twenty-first century, he routinely reached back into the twentieth century and drew on the symbols and language of the movement. For example, in a speech he delivered in Atlanta, Georgia, on January 20, 2008, Obama freely invoked the transcendent nature of King's message. The young candidate advised his audience that they would have to work hard to change society, because "that is how we will bring about the change we seek. That is how Dr. King led this country through the wilderness. He did it with words—words that he spoke not just to the children of slaves, but the children of slave owners. Words that inspired not just black but also white; not just the Christian but the Jew; not just the Southerner but also the Northerner." And although King's message was important, Obama insisted, the civil rights leader did much more than speak: "He led with words, but he also led with deeds. He also led by example." Furthermore, "He led by marching and going to jail and suffering threats and being away from his family. He led by taking a stand against the war, knowing full well that it would diminish his popularity. He led by challenging our economic structures, understanding that it would cause discomfort." Clearly, the civil rights symbols that Obama invokes resonate with many Americans.

Another powerful symbol of hope from our relatively recent past is embodied in the presidency of John F. Kennedy. Memories of the handsome young president, his stylish and beautiful wife, and the tragic circumstances surrounding his death reside in the national consciousness. It seemed that during that brief, magical time when John F. Kennedy was president, patriotism was at an all-time high, and Americans thought they had the power to change the world. It was the same era that is associated with important advances in civil rights for African Americans. That is why when Caroline Kennedy, President Kennedy's daughter, endorsed Barack Obama's candidacy, many Americans were deeply moved. Kennedy's op-ed piece in the *New York Times* on January 27, 2008, announcing her support for Obama, is entitled, "A President like My Father." Although Caroline Kennedy was just a little girl when her father was assassinated, she grew up in the midst of the mystique surrounding the martyred young president. Thus, when she wrote, "I have never had a president who inspired me the way people tell me that my father inspired them. But for the first time, I believe I have found the man who could be that president—not just for me, but for a new generation of Americans,"[9] people all over the country were deeply moved.

Along with the tantalizing possibilities for change represented by Barack Obama's victory come reminders that much remains to be done in order to bring about those changes. The president indicated in the speech he delivered in Atlanta on January 20, 2008, that he is fully aware of America's problems. He called them the country's deficits: "We have an empathy deficit when we're still sending our children down corridors of shame—schools in the forgotten corners of America where the color of your skin still affects the content of your education." In addition, he said, "we have a deficit when CEOs are making more in ten minutes than some workers make in ten months; when families lose their homes so that lenders make a profit; when mothers can't afford a doctor when their children get sick." Obama's voice gathered strength as he enumerated other deficits in American society. "We have a deficit when homeless veterans sleep on the streets of our cities; when innocents are slaughtered in the streets of Darfur; when young Americans serve tour after tour of duty in a war that should've never been authorized and never been waged." Finally, he concluded, "So we have a deficit to close. We have walls—barriers to justice and equality—that must come down. And to do this, we know that unity is the great need of this hour." The wildly enthusiastic audience, undaunted by this enumeration of the enormous problems they face, chanted in unison, "Yes we can; yes we can."

Barack Obama's victory is the latest piece of compelling evidence that black inclusion in the political process is an unqualified success four decades after the passage of the Voting Rights Act of 1965. Of course, before the Obama victory, African Americans had successfully run for a variety of local, state, and national political offices. But the Obama victory adds an exclamation point to the assertion that after all their struggles, African Americans have finally become an integral part of their nation's political process. The question of black inclusion in the American mainstream in other ways remains to be answered, however. Some social critics insist that despite African Americans' political success, black "social incorporation is half finished and may be regressing." Moreover, in an ironic twist, some argue, "in the private sphere, blacks remain almost completely apart from whites. Indeed, they are more separate now, in most areas of the country, than at the end of the '60s. *And segregation is worse in those parts of the country that have the highest levels of black participation in public life.* New York, the liberal heartland of America, in a state where a black man is governor, has among the worst levels of segregation in the nation. So does Chicago, the city that gave Massachusetts its current black governor"[10] and America its first black president.

Political success notwithstanding, African Americans' continued exclusion from the American mainstream has consigned them to the economic, social, and educational margins of American society. Depressing statistics leave virtually no room for doubt: "The black middle class has a fragile hold on its status. Its median household income declined to $30,945 between 2003 and 2005, a mere 63 percent of the white median." Furthermore, "In 2002 the median net worth of white Americans ($88,000) was 14.5 times that of blacks, whose net worth (the total value of all their assets, less all their debts and liabilities) was a paltry $6,000." Because the black middle class has such a limited net worth, it is not at all surprising that "half of all blacks born to middle class parents are downwardly mobile; more than half of them fall to the very bottom of the income ladder."[11] Such a grim reality contrasts starkly with the American dream of generational progress.

Some of the ghosts of America's racial past thus continue to haunt the American psyche. Rev. Samuel Billy Kyles is sure that this country has the opportunity to bury those racial ghosts once and for all. "It [Obama's candidacy] is an opportunity for America to put up or shut up," he claims. "It really is. . . . We are beating up on nations around the world with regard to democracy, and voting and voting rights. And America's opportunity now is—are we sincere—or are we not?" The wonder and awe in the minister's voice is unmistakable as he states, "I never thought it [a black presidential candidacy] would get this far in my lifetime. But, I'm blessed and honored to know that it has gotten this far." He frowns in concentration and says in a soft voice, "Time will tell."[12]

Barack Obama has the broadest constituency of any black leader in this country's history except Martin Luther King Jr. Many argue that Obama's inclusive twenty-first-century leadership has arisen from the roots planted by King's remarkable career. King demonstrated that it was possible for an African American leader to appeal to Americans of all racial, ethnic, religious, and regional categories. But even though a broad following is characteristic of both King and Obama, there is an essential difference: King was a moral leader who appealed to the conscience of the nation and the world, but Obama is a political leader who must be careful to juggle the interests of the different elements in his national constituency without appearing to favor any one group over the others. A miscalculation in any direction could neutralize Obama's effectiveness and compromise his prospects for reelection.

Meanwhile, African Americans view the miracle of Obama's victory with a mixture of awe, hope, and incredulity. After all, older African Americans reason, their ancestors were slaves not that long ago. Racial segregation was the law of the land not that long ago. African Americans were lynched not that long ago. The majority of African Americans could not even vote until 1965. Now, here is one of their own who has pierced the inner sanctum of white political power in America. Many shake their heads in disbelief because it seems too good to be true. Younger African Americans who celebrate Obama's victory do not feel the weight of America's segregated past as their elders do. However, when they look around them, they see a country that still does not treat African Americans fairly, where black people their age make up the lion's share of America's prison population, where affirmative action is in retreat, and where the industrial jobs that sustained their parents are not available for them. Now, here is a young black man who looks like them. He shoots hoops, he fist-bumps with his wife, and he listens to the music of rapper Jay-Z. These black young people want desperately to believe Obama when he says "Yes we can," because for so long, it seems that their country has told them "No you can't." His election has stirred hope like many have never experienced before. After all, he is a brother. He identifies with them.

Barack Obama's identity as an African American is all the more meaningful to many black youngsters because he made a conscious choice to identify himself that way. As a mixed-race child from an unusual background, he did not have to make that choice, but he did. It was not easy. When Obama entered college, he was still searching for his identity, and he was moved to ask himself, "Where do I belong?" The young man knew that he was a person of color; all he had to do was look in the mirror to confirm that. But he had never known his African father, and he was raised by his white mother's family in Kansas, one of the whitest states in the country. Obama concluded, "Whatever my father might say, I knew it was too late to ever truly claim Africa as my home."[13] It was sometime later that he decided he was African American. He explained his choice by invoking images of the civil rights movement of the 1960s: "In the sit-ins, the marches, the jailhouse songs, I saw the African-American community becoming more than just the place where you'd been born or the house where you'd been raised. Through organizing, through shared sacrifice, membership had been earned—because this community I imagined was still in the making, built on the promise that the larger American community, black, white, and brown, could somehow redefine itself—I believed that it might, over time, admit the uniqueness of my own life."[14]

Once the young Barack Obama chose to identify himself as an African American, he joyfully embraced his blackness. African Americans of all ages notice and appreciate that he walks like a "brother" and he makes the right gestures. For so many African Americans, he seems like a black everyman despite his Ivy League education. Thus, black people laughed during the campaign when some of Obama's white detractors tried to brand him as an elitist. Critics said he was an elitist because he could not bowl well. African Americans did not care about bowling, because Obama could shoot a respectable game of hoops. Other detractors charged that he was not comfortable having a beer with Joe Six Pack or Joe the Plumber, but black people laughed again, because they knew Obama was comfortable dancing to Motown tunes or listening to rapper Jay-Z. Finally, many black people felt, here was a black politician who could successfully navigate the corridors of power without surrendering his blackness. Was Barack Obama the one?, many asked themselves. Could he be the one who could finally show African Americans how to heal the century-old twoness defining the existence of black people in American society that W. E. B. Du Bois had so poignantly and passionately articulated at the beginning of the previous century? Whether Obama could help them heal their twoness or not, most African Americans deeply appreciated the way he had helped to elevate their culture and worldview to a point where it had never been before. Finally, it seemed that their culture and concerns were an integral part of the national narrative.

With so many black hopes and dreams riding on an Obama victory, there was a time during the latter part of the campaign when many African Americans became increasingly anxious. It was the first time since the civil rights movement of the 1960s that so many had real hope for change, and they would not relinquish it easily. It would have broken black hearts to lose this dream after they were finally so close to realizing it. Yet, as anxiety levels rose, some began to articulate the unthinkable. What if Obama loses? African Americans from all walks of life pondered the possibility as the end of the campaign drew near. For example, Rapper Snoop Dogg observed, "People that I know that have never cared about politics are registering to vote this time: gang members, ex-cons, you name it. . . . I hate to see a lot of that hope go down the drain, and if he loses, it will." Out on the West Coast, Daetwon Fisher, a twenty-one-year-old black construction worker, bluntly articulated his feelings. "I'm going to be mad, real mad if he loses. . . . Because for him to come this far and lose will be just shady, and a slap in black people's faces. I know there is already talk about protests and stuff if he loses, and I'm down for that." Jacon Richmond also worried about Obama's chances for victory, and he was amazed that he cared so much. Richmond, thirty-two, had been recently released from prison. He had never even thought about voting until Barack Obama became the Democratic candidate. After that, he became engaged and interested in his country's politics for the first time in his life. "I know it's crazy to go from not thinking a black man counts to thinking one should win the president of the United States for sure," he said, "but I'm not sure how I'll handle that if it doesn't happen."[15]

But of course, Obama did not lose. Instead, he won a convincing victory, and more Americans voted in that election than in any other election in forty years. By 11:00 P.M. on November 4, election analysts on television and on the Internet announced that Barack Obama had just been elected the forty-fourth president of the United States of America. Because Obama had managed to fire the hope and optimism of a majority of Americans of all races, people leaped for joy, they wept, they sang. Many African Americans waited in their churches on election night. It was eerily reminiscent of the night before President Lincoln's Emancipation Proclamation was scheduled to take effect. African Americans waited in their churches that night too, and when the word came down that the proclamation had gone into effect, they cheered, they cried, and they hoped that America would finally treat them like citizens instead of chattel. Some 145 years later, on November 4, 2008, when word came down that America had finally elected its first black president, African Americans cheered and cried again, and they hoped again that they would finally be treated like full participants in their country's political system.

In Obama's adopted hometown of Chicago, the evening of November 4 was unusually balmy, and people began streaming into Grant Park for a huge victory rally long before the polls closed. The atmosphere at the huge gathering crackled with excitement, and as dusk fell, tiny lights twinkled everywhere in the park. It seemed almost as though a swarm of fireflies had descended on the crowd and decided to stay awhile. But the lights were actually the flashes coming from thousands of cameras operated by people determined to memorialize this historic moment. They wanted to capture it, trap it for themselves so they could savor it later. By 11:00 P.M. eastern time, when word began to circulate that Barack Obama had been elected, a mighty roar went up from the thousands of throats of the assembled crowd. A short time later, the victorious young candidate ascended the podium, and a hush came over the crowd. As he spoke to those assembled in Grant Park, and those watching on their television sets in millions of homes all over the country, President-Elect Obama did not mince words. He said, "The road ahead will be long. The climb will be steep. We may not get there in one year, or even in one term."

One of those listening to the victory speech that night was Andrew Young, a former U.N. ambassador who had been a member of Dr. King's inner circle back during the civil rights movement. Like so many of those assembled in Grant Park, Young cried. He cried for joy because he had not thought he would live to see a black president. But he also wept because he worried about the bright young president-elect inheriting a country that is "trillions of dollars in debt with the whole world falling apart."[16] As Young listened to Obama's victory speech, he found his mind going back in time forty years, to a balmy April evening in 1968, when Dr. Martin Luther King Jr. delivered his Mountaintop Speech in Memphis, Tennessee. In that speech, King also talked about a difficult journey and a steep climb. He warned, "We've got some difficult days ahead." But he reassured his audience that God had allowed him to make the steep climb in advance. "I've been to the mountaintop. . . . I've looked over and I've seen the Promised Land. I may not get there with you. But I want you to know tonight that we as a people will get to the Promised Land."[17]

In 2008 Young was hearing another young black man warn about a difficult journey ahead and promise that we as a nation would "get there." Just as African Americans believed Dr. Martin Luther King Jr. forty years earlier when he told them that "we as a people will get to the Promised Land," many Americans of all colors today believe that Barack Obama can heal the rift between the red states and the blue states so that we can become the United States of America again. And many believe that this united America will finally be able to live up to its ideals of freedom, justice, and equality for all. Barack Obama is continuing the journey to the "Promised Land" that King led so many years ago; Obama just has more people who have signed up to go on the trip. So, in Grant Park on that magical evening of November 4, 2008, as Americans basked in the glow of the Obama victory, the young president-elect's supporters of all colors were laughing and crying as they roared, "Yes we can; Yes We Can; YES WE CAN." Ironically, in the midst of this sea of hope and promise, one young white man stood out that night. Like others, he had "tears in his eyes." But, as people all around him were leaping for joy and chanting "yes we can," he "stood quietly holding a torn piece of canvas on which he had fashioned letters out of duct tape: WE SHALL OVERCOME,"[18] freely mixing King's dream with Obama's promise.

Obama's words "yes we can, Yes We Can, YES WE CAN" have struck a chord with a broad cross section of Americans. But for African Americans in particular, Obama's affirmation "Yes we can" resonates in a deep place in their psyche that was created by the triumphs and tragedies that have defined the African American experience in America for centuries. To the east of the jubilant celebration in Grant Park, former Black Panther Maureen Taylor sat in her living room in Detroit, Michigan, listening intently to the young candidate's victory speech. Taylor is sure that this young black politician's "rise to the presidency is an historic time in America."[19] But at the same time, Taylor worries, because every day, as a community activist in Detroit, the beleaguered capital of the American auto industry, she sees employment rolls shrink while welfare rolls swell. Still, the combination of the inspiring sight of Obama's jubilant supporters and her old sixties optimism made her want to savor this historic night. She smiled broadly as the old Motown tune "Signed, Sealed, Delivered," by Motown icon Stevie Wonder, was played over the loudspeakers in Grant Park. It gave her a comfortable feeling of cultural inclusiveness and reminded her of her hometown's glory days, when the driving beat of Motown tunes was changing the face of American pop music, and when Detroit's big fins and big engines set the standard for the world's auto industry. But she shook her head to banish the pleasant memories, because regardless of who the president-elect is, the grim reality all around her would not let her dwell in the past or savor the present; she must work to create strategies for the future. Likewise, African American leaders all over the country must continue their work among their black constituents, and whether they are young or old, male or female, northern or southern, their efforts will undoubtedly be judged against the background of the successes of the civil rights movement and the iconic status of Dr. King on one hand, and the miracle of an Obama presidency on the other. But in the hopeful minutes, hours, and days in the wake of the Obama victory, the enthusiastic chant "Yes we can, Yes We Can, YES WE CAN" still rings in the ears of black leaders everywhere, including Maureen Taylor's. As this longtime community activist contemplates an uncertain future, she prays and sighs softly in concert with African American leaders all over the country, "I hope to God we can."[20]

Notes

Prologue

1. David Garrow, *Bearing the Cross, Martin Luther King, Jr., and the Southern Christian Leadership Conference* (New York: Vintage Books, 1988), 282.
2. Ibid., 283.
3. Ibid., 284.
4. Ibid.

1. Yes We Can

1. David Mendell, *Obama: From Promise to Power* (New York: HarperCollins, 2007), 277–78.
2. Ibid., 271.
3. Ibid., 281.
4. Ibid., 284.
5. Ibid., 303.
6. Alexander Jefferson, telephone interview by author, June 22, 2008.
7. Clayborne Carson and Kris Shepard, eds., *A Call to Conscience: The Landmark Speeches of Dr. Martin Luther King, Jr.* (New York: Warner Books, 2001), 223.
8. Samuel Billy Kyles, interview by author, November 11, 2002, Memphis, Tenn.
9. Ibid.
10. James Bevel, interview by author, June 24, 2003, Chicago, Ill.
11. Kyles interview.
12. Carson and Shepard, *A Call to Conscience,* 82–87.
13. Martin Luther King Jr., *Where Do We Go from Here? Chaos or Community* (Boston: Beacon Press, 1967), 7.
14. Allison Samuels, "At Arm's Length," *Newsweek,* July 21, 2008.
15. Ibid.
16. Clarence Lusane, *Race in the Global Era: African Americans at the Millennium* (Boston: South End Press, 1997), 9.
17. John Haller, *Outcasts from Evolution: Scientific Attitudes of Racial Inferiority, 1858–1900* (New York: McGraw-Hill, 1971), 48.

18. Harriet A. Washington, *Medical Apartheid: The Dark History of Medical Experimentation on Black Americans from Colonial Times to the Present* (New York: Doubleday, 2006), 20–21.

19. Lusane, *Race in the Global Era*, 11.

20. Todd Boyd, *The New H.N.I.C.: The Death of Civil Rights and the Reign of Hip Hop* (New York: New York Univ. Press, 2002), xxi.

21. Cynthia Griggs Fleming, *In the Shadow of Selma: The Continuing Struggle for Civil Rights in the Rural South* (Lanham, Md.: Rowman and Littlefield, 2004), 193.

22. Boyd, *The New H.N.I.C.*, 43.

2. Black Leadership in Historical Perspective

1. Booker T. Washington, *Up from Slavery*, in *Three Negro Classics*, edited by John Hope Franklin (New York: Avon, 1965), 148.

2. Ibid., 152–153.

3. Leon Litwack, *Trouble in Mind: Black Southerners in the Age of Jim Crow* (New York: Vintage Books, 1998), 7.

4. Ibid., 12.

5. Ibid.

6. Fleming, *In the Shadow of Selma*, 23.

7. Karl Evanzz, *The Messenger: The Rise and Fall of Elijah Muhammad* (New York: Pantheon Books, 1999), 23–24.

8. Fleming, *In the Shadow of Selma*, 92.

9. Benjamin Mays, *Born to Rebel* (New York: Scribner, 1971), 27–28.

10. John Hope Franklin, interview by author, August 27, 2005, Durham, N.C.

11. Ibid.

12. Joanne Bland, interview by author, March 22, 2008, Selma, Ala.

13. Ibid.

14. Ibid.

15. Haller, *Outcasts from Evolution*, 57.

16. Ibid., 55.

17. Beverly Guy-Sheftall, *Daughters of Sorrow: Attitudes toward Black Women, 1880–1920* (New York: Carlson, 1990), 44.

18. Ibid., emphasis added.

19. Ibid., 45, emphasis added.

20. Ibid., 49.

21. W. E. B. Du Bois, *The Souls of Black Folk*, in *Three Negro Classics*, edited by John Hope Franklin (New York: Avon, 1965), 215.

22. Deborah Gray White, *Too Heavy a Load: Black Women in Defense of Themselves, 1894–1994* (New York: Norton, 1999), 36.

23. Ibid.
24. Ibid., 37.
25. Ibid., 57.
26. V. P. Franklin, *Black Self-Determination: A Cultural History of the Faith of the | Fathers* (Westport, Conn.: Lawrence Hill, 1984), 146.
27. Franklin, *Black Self-Determination,* 15.
28. Ibid., 2.
29. Ibid., 3–4.
30. Eleanor Holmes Norton, interview by author, April 29, 2005, Washington, D.C.
31. Du Bois, *The Souls of Black Folk,* 242–243.
32. James Perkins, interview by author, July 22, 2003, Selma, Ala.
33. Charles Jones, interview by author, April 13, 2003, Charlotte, N.C.
34. John Lewis, interview by author, August 12, 2003, Atlanta, Ga.
35. Eddie Bernice Johnson, interview by author, May 20, 2003, Washington, D.C.
36. Bland interview.
37. Harold Middlebrook, interview by author, December 17, 2002, Knoxville, Tenn.
38. Kyles interview.
39. Richard Hatcher, interview by author, March 9, 2007, Chicago, Ill.
40. Andrew Young, interview by author, August 12, 2003, Atlanta, Ga.
41. Franklin interview.
42. Julian Bond, interview by author, May 19, 2003, Washington, D.C.
43. Ibid.
44. Frank Ballance, interview by author, April 14, 2003, Washington, D.C.
45. Litwack, *Trouble in Mind,* 16.
46. J. L. Chestnut Jr., interview by author, July 22, 2003, Selma, Ala.
47. J. L. Chestnut Jr. and Julia Cass, *Black in Selma: The Uncommon Life of J. L. Chestnut, Jr.* (New York: Farrar, Straus, and Giroux, 1990), 45.
48. Chestnut interview.
49. Ibid.
50. Chestnut and Cass, *Black in Selma,* 160.
51. Ibid., 166.
52. Ibid., 203.

3. After King, Where Do We Go from Here?

1. Michele Wallace, *Black Macho and the Myth of the Superwoman* (New York: Dial Press, 1978), 159.
2. Ibid., 72, emphasis added.
3. King, *Where Do We Go from Here?* 63.

4. Louis Lomax, *The Negro Revolt* (New York: Signet Books, 1962), 176.

5. *Life,* June 3, 1966, 88.

6. *Life,* March 26, 1965, 4.

7. *Life,* June 3, 1966, 90.

8. Ibid., 92.

9. Ibid., 94.

10. Ibid., 96.

11. Ibid., 90.

12. Bernard Lafayette, interview by author, May 3, 2003, Birmingham, Ala.

13. King, *Where Do We Go from Here?* 35.

14. Ibid., 43.

15. Ibid., 53.

16. Ibid., 36.

17. *Life,* June 10, 1966, 4.

18. Ibid., 100B.

19. Ibid.

20. Ibid., 104.

21. Ibid., 110.

22. *Life,* August 11, 1967, 56.

23. Ibid.

24. Ibid., 58.

25. Ibid., 60.

26. *Life,* June 10, 1966, 4.

27. *Life,* March 8, 1968, 100.

28. Written by Norman Whitfield and Barrett Strong, performed by the Temptations, and produced by Norman Whitfield; released by the Gordy record label, 1970.

29. Young interview.

30. Andrew Young, *An Easy Burden: The Civil Rights Movement and the Transformation of America* (New York: HarperCollins, 2004), 465.

31. Young interview.

32. Ibid.

33. Jones interview.

34. Lewis interview.

35. James Armstrong, interview by author, March 28, 2004, Birmingham, Ala.

36. Bond interview.

37. Bland interview.

38. Robert Booker, interview by author, December 14, 2006, Knoxville, Tenn.

39. Lafayette interview.

40. Al Sharpton, interview by author, October 25, 2005, Knoxville, Tenn.

41. Carol Moseley Braun, interview by author, September 13, 2004, Knoxville, Tenn.
42. Timuel Black, interview by author, November 23, 2002, Chicago, Ill.
43. Maureen Taylor, interview by author, August 14, 2005, Detroit, Mich.
44. Samuel F. Yette, *The Choice: The Issue of Black Survival in America* (New York: Putnam's, 1971), 27–28.
45. Jones interview.
46. Yette, *The Choice,* 27.
47. *Life,* April 19, 1968, 30.
48. Chestnut interview.
49. T. Randel Osburn and C. T. Vivian, interview by author, October 20, 2003, Atlanta, Ga.

4. The Media and the Message

1. August Meier, Elliott Rudwick, and John Bracey Jr., eds., *Black Protest in the Sixties: Articles from the New York Times* (New York: Marcus Wiener, 1991), 294.
2. Ibid., 295.
3. Young interview.
4. Julius Lester, *Look Out Whitey! Black Power's Gon' Get Your Mama!* (New York: Dial Press, 1968), 143.
5. Ibid., 23.
6. Yette, *The Choice,* 163–64.
7. Taylor interview.
8. Yette, *The Choice,* 167.
9. Ibid., 190.
10. Ibid., 171.
11. Ibid., 182–83.
12. Ibid., 190.
13. Ibid., 307, emphasis added.
14. Louis W. Liebovich, *Richard Nixon, Watergate, and the Press: An Historical Retrospective* (Westport, Conn.: Prager, 2003), 10.
15. Ibid., 50.
16. Ibid., 14.
17. Ibid., 104.
18. Lewis interview.
19. Norton interview.
20. Bond interview.
21. *Saturday Evening Post,* June 15, 1963, 15.
22. Ibid., 16.

23. *Life*, April 12, 1968, 4.
24. *Life*, March 5, 1965, 26–27.
25. Lewis interview.
26. Benjamin Hooks, interview by author, November 17, 2003, Knoxville, Tenn.
27. Hatcher interview.
28. Ibid.
29. Ibid.
30. Ibid.
31. Braun interview.
32. Chestnut interview.
33. Ibid.
34. Ibid.
35. Ibid.
36. Osburn-Vivian interview.
37. Bond interview.
38. Samuel Yette, interview by author, June 15, 2006, Knoxville, Tenn.
39. Lewis interview.
40. Dorothy Cotton, interview by author, April 4, 2008, Memphis, Tenn.
41. Cynthia McKinney, interview by author, July 23, 2005, Atlanta, Ga.
42. Kyles interview.
43. Haller, *Outcasts from Evolution*, 55.
44. Richard Kluger, *Simple Justice: The History of Brown v. Board of Education* (New York: Vintage Books, 1977), 306.
45. Ibid., 307.
46. Ibid., 311.
47. Ibid., 312.
48. Ibid., 313.
49. John Hope Franklin and Alfred A. Moss, *From Slavery to Freedom: A History of African Americans* (Boston: McGraw-Hill, 2000), 617.
50. Ellis Cose, *Color-Blind, Seeing beyond Race in a Race Obsessed World* (New York: HarperCollins, 1997), 27.
51. Ibid., 28.
52. James Forman, "Manifesto to the White Christian Churches and the Jewish Synagogues in the United States of America and All Other Racist Institutions," paper presented at the National Black Economic Development Conference, Detroit, Mich., April 26, 1969, 3–4.
53. Kyles interview.
54. Braun interview.
55. Henry Lewis Suggs, ed., *The Black Press in the South, 1865–1879* (Westport, Conn.: Greenwood Press, 1983), ix.

56. Ibid., x.
57. Ibid., ix.
58. Henry Lewis Suggs, ed., *The Black Press in the Middle West, 1865–1985* (West port, Conn.: Greenwood Press, 1996), 363.
59. George Curry, interview by author, January 26, 2008, Knoxville, Tenn.
60. Ibid.
61. *Life,* special issue, "The Dream—Then and Now," Spring 1988, 32.
62. Yette interview.
63. Curry interview.
64. Ibid.
65. Ibid.
66. Ibid.
67. Bond interview.
68. Franklin interview.
69. Ibid.
70. Ibid.
71. Ibid.
72. Norman Kelley, *The Head Negro in Charge Syndrome: The Dead End of Black Politics* (New York: Nation Books, 2004), 145–46.
73. Ibid., 148, emphasis added.
74. Ibid., 153.
75. Braun interview.

5. From Protest to Inclusion

1. Franklin and Moss, *From Slavery to Freedom,* 701, emphasis added.
2. Guy Carawan and Candie Carawan, eds., *Sing for Freedom: The Story of the Civil Rights Movement through Its Songs* (Bethlehem, Pa.: A Sing Out Publication, 1990), 264–65.
3. Carson and Shepard, *A Call to Conscience,* 131.
4. Franklin interview.
5. Bayard Rustin, *Down the Line: The Collected Writings of Bayard Rustin* (Chicago: Quadrangle Books, 1971), 120.
6. Ibid., 122.
7. Leonard N. Moore, *Carl B. Stokes and the Rise of Black Power* (Urbana: Univ. of Illinois Press, 2002), 4.
8. Fleming, *In the Shadow of Selma,* 246.
9. Ibid., 247.
10. Johnny Ford, interview by author, July 23, 2005, Atlanta, Ga.
11. Perkins interview.

12. Leslie H. Fishel Jr. and Benjamin Quarles, eds., *The Negro American: A Documentary History* (New York: Scott, Foresman, 1967), 275, emphasis added.
13. Franklin and Moss, *From Slavery to Freedom,* 423–24.
14. Ballance interview.
15. Hatcher interview.
16. Ibid.
17. Ibid.
18. Ibid.
19. Ibid.
20. Ibid.
21. Andrew Young, interview by author, May 6, 2008, Atlanta, Ga.
22. Lewis interview.
23. Norton interview.
24. Bond interview.
25. Ibid.
26. Booker interview.
27. Chestnut interview.
28. Joe Leonard, interview by author, April 29, 2005, Washington, D.C.
29. Hooks interview.
30. Braun interview. "Rope a dope" refers to a tactic used by boxer Muhammad Ali: he would fall back on the rope, pretending to be subdued by his opponent.
31. Ballance interview.
32. Perkins interview.
33. Ibid.
34. Kwame Brown, interview by author, April 28, 2005, Washington, D.C.
35. Artur Davis, interview by author, August 30, 2002, Birmingham, Ala.
36. Ibid.
37. Ballance interview.
38. Hooks interview.
39. Franklin and Moss, *From Slavery to Freedom,* 423.
40. Bond interview.
41. Chestnut interview.
42. J. C. Watts Jr., *What Color Is a Conservative? My Life and My Politics* (New York: HarperCollins, 2002), 34–35. J. C. Watts was interviewed by the author, May 20, 2003, Arlington, Va., but no quotations from the interview appear in this book.
43. Ibid., 35.
44. Ibid., 34–35.
45. Ibid., 152.

46. Ibid., 3.
47. Ibid., 2–3.
48. Ibid, 3.
49. Hooks interview.
50. Ford interview.
51. Ibid.
52. Ibid.
53. Braun interview.
54. Eugene Walker, interview by author, October 19, 2003, Atlanta, Ga.
55. *Newsweek,* January 3, 2005, 77.
56. Chestnut interview.
57. Ballance interview.
58. Bond interview.
59. Davis interview.
60. Ford interview.
61. Perkins interview.
62. Norton interview.
63. Braun interview.
64. Walker interview.
65. Leonard interview.
66. Ibid.
67. King, *Where Do We Go from Here?* 148.
68. Ibid., 149–50.
69. Fleming, *In the Shadow of Selma,* 274.
70. Abraham Woods, interview by author, March 27, 2004, Birmingham, Ala.
71. James Lawson and C. T. Vivian, interview by author, Birmingham, Ala.
72. Franklin interview.
73. Kelley, *The Head Negro in Charge Syndrome,* 48.
74. Written, performed, and produced by James Brown; recorded in 1968 and released by Polydor Records.
75. Fleming, *In the Shadow of Selma,* 274.
76. Ibid., 267.
77. Ibid., 268.
78. Braun interview.
79. *Newsweek,* September 30, 2002, 34.
80. *Newsweek,* January 28, 2002, 51.
81. Hooks interview.
82. Ford interview.
83. Walker interview.
84. Ibid.

85. Ibid.

86. *Newsweek,* December 16, 2002, cover.

87. Ibid., 34.

6. The Continuing Challenge of Black Economic Underdevelopment

1. Davis interview.

2. V. P. Franklin, *Black Self-Determination,* 105–6.

3. Ibid., 105.

4. Armstrong interview.

5. Ibid.

6. Black interview.

7. Taylor interview.

8. Cotton interview.

9. Woods interview.

10. Lawrence Guyot, interview by author, April 30, 2005, Washington, D.C.

11. King, *Where Do We Go From Here?* 17.

12. Ibid., 7.

13. Ibid., 139.

14. Stokely Carmichael and Charles V. Hamilton, *Black Power: The Politics of Liberation in America* (New York: Random House, 1967), 16–17.

15. Ibid., 17.

16. Forman, "Manifesto," 3, emphasis added.

17. King, *Where Do We Go from Here?* 130, emphasis added.

18. Bond interview.

19. King, *Where Do We Go from Here?* 132.

20. Bond interview.

21. Ibid.

22. Sheryll Cashin, *The Failures of Integration: How Race and Class Are Undermining the American Dream* (New York: Public Affairs, 2004), xii.

23. *Newsweek,* January 28, 2002, 44.

24. Sharpton interview.

25. Black interview.

26. Leonard interview.

27. Cashin, *The Failures of Integration,* xii.

28. *Knoxville Enlightener,* August 14, 2006.

29. Leonard interview.

30. Ballance interview.

31. Walker interview.

32. Jones interview.

33. Yette, *The Choice,* 17, emphasis added.
34. Ibid., 18.
35. Ibid.
36. Yette interview.
37. Norton interview.
38. Lusane, *Race in the Global Era,* xii.
39. Ibid., xvii.
40. Ibid., xii.
41. Manning Marable, *Black Liberation in Conservative America* (Boston: South End Press, 1997), 3.
42. Office of Minority Health, Data/Statistics, African American Profile, http://omhrc.gov/templates/browse.aspx?lvllD=51.
43. James S. Jackson, Research Center for Group Dynamics, Institute for Social Research, Univ. of Michigan, at www.blackcollegian.com/issues/30thAnn/demographic2001–30th.shtml (last accessed January 2007).
44. Office of Minority Health, Data/Statistics, African American Profile.
45. Charlie LeDuff, "Keiara Dreams of Escaping Poverty," in *Detroit News,* June 7, 2008.
46. Ibid.
47. Office of Minority Health, Data/Statistics, African American Profile.
48. *Detroit News,* June 7, 2008.
49. Forman, "Manifesto," 4.
50. McKinney interview.
51. Taylor interview.
52. Davis interview.
53. Ford interview.
54. Ibid.
55. Brown interview.
56. Lester, *Look Out Whitey!* 26, emphasis added.
57. *Savoy,* December 2002–January 2003, 56.
58. Brown interview.
59. Boyd, *The New H.N.I.C.,* 77.
60. Brown interview.
61. Boyd, *The New H.N.I.C.,* 77.

7. Black Culture Then and Now

1. Franklin, *Black Self-Determination,* 5.
2. Ibid., 6.
3. Ford interview.

4. Courtland Cox, interview by author, April 28, 2005, Washington, D.C.
5. Booker interview.
6. Jones interview.
7. Bond interview.
8. Bakari Kitwana, *The Hip Hop Generation: Young Blacks and the Crisis in African American Culture* (New York: Basic Books, 2002), 12.
9. Ibid., 13.
10. Ibid., 12.
11. Ibid., 13.
12. Ibid.
13. Fred Shuttlesworth, interview by author, May 24, 2003, Cincinnati, Ohio.
14. Braun interview.
15. McKinney interview.
16. Woods interview.
17. Armstrong interview.
18. Booker interview.
19. Hooks interview.
20. Bland interview.
21. Bond interview.
22. Booker interview.
23. Franklin interview.
24. Unita Blackwell, interview by the author, September 17, 2005, Mayersville, Miss.
25. Middlebrook interview.
26. Osburn-Vivian interview.
27. Ibid.
28. Lawson-Vivian interview.
29. Walker interview.
30. Booker interview.
31. Jones interview.
32. Leonard interview.
33. Ibid.
34. Boyd, *The New H.N.I.C.*, 77.
35. Lewis interview.
36. Brown interview.
37. Ibid.
38. Lawson-Vivian interview.
39. Guyot interview.
40. Lafayette interview, emphasis added.
41. Kyles interview.
42. Black interview.

43. Chestnut interview.

44. Walker interview.

45. Davis interview.

46. Kitwana, *The Hip Hop Generation*, 9.

47. Ibid., 10.

48. Ibid.

49. Ibid., 3–4.

50. Nelson George, *Hip Hop America* (New York: Penguin Books, 1999), 223.

51. Ibid., 186.

52. Ibid., 186–87.

53. Ford interview.

54. Leonard interview.

55. Norton interview.

56. Yette interview.

57. Guyot interview.

58. George, *Hip Hop America*, 178.

59. Ibid., 187.

60. Kitwana, *The Hip Hop Generation*, 93.

61. Cynthia Griggs Fleming, *Soon We Will Not Cry: The Liberation of Ruby Doris Smith Robinson* (Lanham, Md.: Rowman and Littlefield, 1998), 168.

62. Cotton interview.

63. Fleming, *Soon We Will Not Cry*, 167.

64. Guyot interview.

65. Cox interview.

66. Jeffrey O. G. Ogbar, *Black Power: Radical Politics and African American Identity* (Baltimore: Johns Hopkins Univ. Press, 2004), 25.

67. Ibid., 24.

68. Woods interview.

69. Kitwana, *The Hip Hop Generation*, 77.

70. Woods interview.

71. Kitwana, *The Hip Hop Generation*, 87.

72. McKinney interview. The ideology to which McKinney refers is based on the belief that loyalty to the race and race unity should be the predominant factor in African Americans' identity, politics, and so forth.

73. Sharpton interview.

74. Brown interview.

75. Ibid.

76. Leonard interview.

77. Kitwana, *The Hip Hop Generation*, 46.

78. Leonard interview.

79. Ibid.
80. Bond interview.

8. Black Community and Black Identity

1. Du Bois, *The Souls of Black Folk*, 215.
2. Ibid.
3. Randall Robinson, *The Debt: What America Owes to Blacks* (New York: Plume 2000), 28.
4. Franklin, *Black Self-Determination*, 3–4.
5. Norton interview.
6. Black interview.
7. Taylor interview.
8. Walker interview.
9. Bond interview.
10. Leonard interview.
11. Perkins interview.
12. Bland interview.
13. Middlebrook interview.
14. Blackwell interview.
15. Hooks interview.
16. Taylor interview.
17. Norton interview.
18. Walker interview.
19. Franklin interview.
20. Shuttlesworth interview.
21. Randall Robinson, *The Reckoning: What Blacks Owe to Each Other* (New York: Plume, 2002), 255.
22. Yette interview.
23. Braun interview.
24. Middlebrook interview.
25. Osburn-Vivian interview.
26. Black interview.
27. Blackwell interview.
28. Robinson, *The Reckoning,* 158.
29. Ford interview.
30. Davis interview.
31. Ibid.
32. Brown interview.
33. Ibid.

34. Ballance interview.
35. Guyot interview.
36. Chestnut interview.
37. Bevel interview.
38. Woods interview.
39. Ibid.
40. Walker interview.
41. Taylor interview.
42. Ibid.
43. McKinney interview.
44. *Newsweek,* September 11, 2006, 27.
45. Ibid.
46. Pete Seeger and Bob Reiser, *Everybody Say Freedom: A History of the Civil Rights Movement in Songs and Pictures* (New York: Norton, 1989), 65.

9. A Crisis of Victory

1. Robert C. Smith, *We Have No Leaders: African Americans in the Post-Civil Rights Era* (Albany: State Univ. of New York Press, 1996), 24.
2. Ibid., 133.
3. Ibid., 137, emphasis added.
4. Ibid., 122–23.
5. Gayle T. Tate and Lewis A. Randolph, eds., *Dimensions of Black Conservatism in the United States: Made in America* (New York: Palgrave, 2002), 149.
6. Thomas Frank, *What's the Matter With Kansas? How Conservatives Won the Heart of America* (New York: Henry Holt, 2004), 5.
7. Smith, *We Have No Leaders,* 225.
8. Lawson-Vivian interview.
9. Kelley, *The Head Negro in Charge Syndrome,* 183.
10. Boyd, *The New H.N.I.C.,* 13.
11. Harold Cruse, *The Crisis of the Negro Intellectual: A Historical Analysis of the Failure of Black Leadership* (New York: New York Review Books, 1967), 415.
12. Tate and Randolph, *Dimensions of Black Conservatism in the United States,* 170.
13. Chestnut interview.
14. Lewis interview.
15. Osburn-Vivian interview.
16. Kyles interview.
17. Booker interview.

18. Hooks interview.
19. Ibid.
20. Ballance interview.
21. Shuttlesworth interview.
22. Col. Stone Johnson, interview by author, March 27, 2004, Birmingham, Ala.
23. Lafayette interview.
24. Ibid.
25. Ford interview.
26. Sharpton interview.
27. Guyot interview.
28. Braun interview.
29. Norton interview.
30. Brown interview.
31. Ibid.
32. Walker interview.
33. Yette interview.
34. Marable, *Black Liberation in Conservative America,* 7.
35. Jones interview.
36. Hooks interview.
37. Marable, *Black Liberation in Conservative America,* 6, emphasis added.
38. Blackwell interview.
39. Chestnut interview.
40. Jones interview.
41. Woods interview.
42. Leonard interview.
43. Ibid.
44. "Too Little Too Late: President Clinton's Prison Legacy," press release, Center on Juvenile and Criminal Justice, 5, www.cjcj.org/pubs/clinton/clinton.html (last accessed January 2007).
45. Ibid., 2.
46. Ibid., 1.
47. Kitwana, *The Hip Hop Generation,* 76.
48. Office of Minority Health, Data/Statistics, African American Profile.
49. Black interview.

Epilogue

1. Joanne Bland, telephone interview by author, November 10, 2008.
2. *New York Times,* October 11, 2008, A12.

3. Young, *An Easy Burden,* 310.

4. Lawrence Guyot, telephone interview by author, November 5, 2008.

5. Michael Hirsh, "How They See the World," *Newsweek,* October 6, 2008.

6. Samuel Billy Kyles, interview by author, June 2, 2008, Memphis, Tenn.

7. Bernard Lafayette, interview by author, June 4, 2008, Nashville, Tenn.

8. Cotton interview.

9. *New York Times,* January 27, 2008.

10. Orlando Patterson, "The New Mainstream," *Newsweek,* November 10, 2008, emphasis added.

11. Ibid.

12. Kyles interview, June 2, 2008.

13. Barack Obama, *Dreams from My Father: A Story of Race and Inheritance* (New York: Three Rivers Press, 2004), 115.

14. Ibid., 134–35.

15. Allison Samuels, "What If Obama Loses?" *Newsweek,* October 6, 2008.

16. Andrew Young, interview by author, December 8, 2008, Atlanta, Ga.

17. Carson and Shepard, *A Call to Conscience,* 222–23.

18. Sandra Sobieraj Westfall and Bill Hewitt, "All Things Are Possible," *People Weekly,* November 17, 2008.

19. Maureen Taylor, telephone interview by author, November 5, 2008.

20. Ibid.

Bibliographic Essay

Because the literature on the subject of African American leadership in American society is voluminous, I include here only some of the more significant works. Deliberately omitted are the many biographies and autobiographies of specific African American leaders, in order to keep this essay of manageable length. In addition, because black leadership is complex and multifaceted, the literature on the subject appears in many forms; I have chosen only the most obvious categories of black leadership literature to note here: scholarly books and articles and newspaper articles. These works were produced, for the most part, in the late twentieth and early twenty-first centuries. However, some are included that were written at the dawn of the civil rights movement. Many of the works on black leadership that came out during that volatile era focus on the obstacles and issues that confronted black leaders as they made the transition from accommodation to the new reality of protest and agitation.

One of the best-known of the works from the early period is Harold Cruse, *The Crisis of the Negro Intellectual: A Historical Analysis of the Failure of Black Leadership* (New York: New York Review Books, 1967), published during the height of the Black Power movement. In addition to Cruse's seminal work, others, such as Julius Lester's *Look Out Whitey! Black Power's Gon' Get Your Mama!* (New York: Dial Press, 1968) and Louis Lomax's *The Negro Revolt* (New York: Signet Books, 1962), were widely read at the time. Other works from the civil rights era include H. M. Blalock, "Situational Factors and Negro Leadership Activity in a Medium-Sized Community," *Journal of Negro Education* 29, no. 1 (1960); Allyn Boston, "Leadership in American Society; A Case Study of Black Leadership," *Sociological Resources for the Social Studies* (1969); Howard Brotz, *The Black Jews of Harlem: Negro Nationalism and the Dilemmas of Negro Leadership* (New York: Free Press of Glencoe, 1964); Tilman Cothran and William Phillips, "Negro Leadership in a Crisis Situation," *Phylon* 21, no. 2 (1960–1961); Hugh Hawkins, ed., *Booker T. Washington and His Critics: Black Leadership in Crisis* (Lexington, Mass.: Heath, 1974); Lewis Killian and Charles Smith, "Negro Protest Leaders in a Southern Community," *Social Forces* 38, no. 3 (1960); Thomas Monahan and Elizabeth Monahan, "Some Characteristics of American Negro Leaders," *American Sociological Review* 21, no. 5 (1956); George Nesbitt, "The Negro Race Relations Expert and Negro Community Leadership," *Journal of Negro Education* 21, no.

2 (1952); Peter Paris, *Black Leaders in Conflict: Joseph H. Jackson, Martin Luther King, Jr., Malcolm X, Adam Clayton Powell, Jr.* (New York: Pilgrim Press, 1978); Wilson Record, "Negro Intellectual Leadership in the National Association for the Advancement of Colored People: 1910–1940," *Phylon* 17, no. 4 (1956); and Jack Walker, "The Functions of Disunity: Negro Leadership in a Southern City," *Journal of Negro Education* 32, no. 3 (1963).

In the aftermath of the civil rights movement, especially by the end of the 1970s, people were reassessing black leadership in light of significant developments. One of the most important of the developments was the election to the presidency of actor-turned-politician Ronald Reagan in 1980. Many black people were sure that Reagan was sending them a clear message when he held a campaign rally in Philadelphia, Mississippi; this was the town where civil rights workers Andrew Goodman, James Chaney, and Michael Schwerner had been murdered during Mississippi Freedom Summer, in 1964. The nation's sharp turn to the right prompted the release of a host of black leadership studies. This generation of black leaders was going to have to operate in a different political climate from their predecessors. The sympathy for the plight of African Americans that had seemed to be a prominent part of America's popular consciousness in the 1960s, and even in the 1970s, was a thing of the past by the 1980s. During Reagan conservatism, numerous works were produced that evaluated the impact and effectiveness of black leadership in this new and, many insisted, hostile environment. Among them were Milton Coleman, "Black Leaders Hear Plan for Key Role in Democratic Convention: Conference in Atlanta Provides First Analysis of 1984 Prospects," *Washington Post*, March 13, 1983; King Davis, "The Status of Black Leadership: Implications for Black Followers in the 1980s," *Journal of Applied Behavioral Science* 18, no. 3 (1982); Dorothy Gilliam, "Black Leadership Will Be Topic Here," *Washington Post*, July 20, 1981; "Inventing Black Leaders," *Washington Post*, December 21, 1983; Ivan Van Sertima, "Great Black Leaders: Ancient and Modern," *Journal of African Civilizations* (1988); Juan Williams, "Civil Rights Panel Head Attacks Black Leaders," *Washington Post*, November 20, 1984; and Bette Woody, *Managing Crisis Cities: The New Black Leadership and the Politics of Resource Allocation* (Westport, Conn.: Greenwood Press, 1982).

In 1992 African Americans rejoiced. With the exception of Democratic president Jimmy Carter's administration (1976–1980), they had suffered through policies that many considered opposed to black advancement as one Republican president after another occupied the Oval Office. But with the election of Democrat William Jefferson Clinton, there was hope that the civil rights revolution that had seemed to languish for so many years would finally come to fruition. Many African Americans took to heart the theme song of the Clinton campaign,

"Don't Stop Thinking about Tomorrow," by Fleetwood Mac, as they looked forward to what they hoped would be a sympathetic administration. Some of the analyses from the earliest part of this era have titles like Lawrence Harrison's "A Dream Not Really Deferred: America Is Quietly Getting Closer to Martin Luther King's Vision," *Washington Post,* January 17, 1993. However, many other works from the ensuing years assess the condition of black leadership at this critical time. These works include Joseph Conti and Brad Stetson, *Challenging the Civil Rights Establishment: Profiles of a New Black Vanguard* (Westport, Conn.: Praeger, 1993); Clarence Lusane, *African Americans at the Crossroads: The Restructuring of Black Leadership and the 1992 Elections* (Boston: South End Press, 1994); and *Dilemmas of Black Politics: Issues of Leadership and Strategy* (New York: HarperCollins, 1993).

Throughout the decade of the 1990s, other writers sought to reevaluate the challenges facing black leaders as they looked to the new millennium: "The New Black Powers: Younger Leaders Lining Up with Clinton Have Clout but No Consensus," *Washington Post,* November 2, 1992; Felton Best, ed., *Black Religious Leadership from the Slave Community to the Million Man March: Flames of Fire* (Lewiston, N.Y.: Edwin Mellon Press, 1998); Leroy Davis, *A Clashing of the Soul: John Hope and the Dilemma of African American Leadership and Black Higher Education in the Early Twentieth Century* (Athens: Univ. of Georgia Press, 1998); Lenora Fulani, "Black Empowerment: New Notes on Black Leadership," *Pittsburgh Courier,* March 13, 1999; Kevin Gaines, *Uplifting the Race: Black Leadership, Politics, and Culture in the Twentieth Century* (Chapel Hill: Univ. of North Carolina Press, 1996); Joy James, *Transcending the Talented Tenth: Black Leaders and American Intellectuals* (New York: Routledge, 1997); Manning Marable, *Black Leadership* (New York: Columbia Univ. Press, 1998); Christopher Reed, *The Chicago NAACP and the Rise of Black Professional Leadership* (Bloomington: Indiana Univ. Press, 1997); Ronald Walters and Robert Smith, *African American Leadership* (Albany: State Univ. of New York Press, 1999).

With the coming of the new millennium, African Americans once again faced a serious political crossroads. Another dramatic political shift occurred with the election of conservative Republican George W. Bush; for that matter, in the last weeks of the Clinton administration, as black people pondered an uncertain future, many reluctantly had to admit that their struggle for equal rights had not advanced nearly as much as they had hoped even when a Democratic president had been in office. In this pessimistic atmosphere, numerous black leadership studies were produced, exploring a variety of ways of assessing black leadership: John Barber, *The Black Digital Elite: African American Leaders of the Information Revolution* (Westport, Conn.: Praeger, 2006); Jacob Gordon, *Black Leadership for Social Change* (Westport, Conn.: Greenwood Press, 2000); Zoltan

Hajnal, *Changing White Attitudes toward Black Political Leadership* (New York: Cambridge Univ. Press, 2007); Tyson King-Meadows, *Devolution and Black State Legislators: Challenges and Choices in the Twenty-First Century* (Albany: State Univ. of New York Press, 2006); and Clarence Taylor, *Black Religious Intellectuals: The Fight for Equality from Jim Crow to the Twenty-First Century* (New York: Routledge, 2002).

Other recent black leadership studies, clearly reflecting the pessimism that so many African Americans feel, are sharply critical of black leadership: Norman Kelley, *The Head Negro in Charge Syndrome: The Dead End of Black Politics* (New York: Nation Books, 2004); H. Viscount Nelson, *The Rise and Fall of Modern Black Leadership: Chronicle of a Twentieth Century Tragedy* (Lanham, Md.: Univ. Press of America, 2003); and Juan Williams, *Enough: The Phony Leaders, Dead-End Movements, and Culture of Failure That Are Undermining Black America—And What We Can Do about It* (New York: Crown, 2006).

Finally, moving beyond the standard Du Bois–Washington analytical framework that tended to masculinize notions of black leadership for so long, a number of studies of black women's leadership have been published, including Juliana Mosley Anderson, *Their Perceptions of How Others Perceive Them: Black Women Administrators Internalize Others' Perceptions of Them as Leaders* (Oxford, Ohio: Miami Univ., 2001); Patricia Parker, *Race, Gender, and Leadership: Re-Envisioning Organizational Leadership from the Perspectives of African American Women Executives,* Lea Communication Series (Mahwah, N.J.: Lawrence Erlbaum, 2004); Sheila Radford-Hill, *Black Women and the Politics of Empowerment* (Minneapolis: Univ. of Minnesota Press, 2000); Barbara Ransby, *Ella Baker and the Black Freedom Movement—A Radical Democratic Vision: Gender and American Culture* (Chapel Hill: Univ. of North Carolina Press, 2003) (although Ella Baker is the subject of Ransby's study, this biography contains an extensive discussion of some of the issues facing black female leaders); Patricia Reid-Merritt, *Sister Power: How Phenomenal Black Women Are Rising to the Top* (New York: J. Wiley, 1996); and Belinda Robnett, *How Long? How Long? African American Women in the Struggle for Civil Rights* (New York: Oxford Univ. Press, 1997). The latter study is particularly useful because it provides an analytical framework for black women's leadership.

Index